The Earley Years
(Official Biography)
by
John Scally

BLACKWATER PRESS

Editors
Brenda McNally
John O'Connor

Design & Layout
Paula Byrne

© 1992 Blackwater Press, Airton Road,
Tallaght,
Dublin 24.

Produced in Ireland by Blackwater Press

ISBN 0 86121 401 3 (HBK)
ISBN 0 86121 485 4 (PBK)

Dedication

To All Who Cherish The Primrose And Blue.

Contents

Foreword

My father was the greatest book worm I ever knew. Seldom can I remember him not reading some volume or other. Books were always stacked on the table beside his bed and each morning on arriving downstairs for breakfast you would find him reading his latest acquisition.

His interests were unbounded. Novels, fiction, poetry, the Geneva Convention and the Constitution were devoured and I often checked to see what what language he was now reading – English, Irish or Latin.

On occasions when we discussed the material he had in hand I discovered that he had read this book before. His reply to my question: "Why was it necessary to re-read them?" was: "It's important to re-read as you will always find something new from good writings." His ability to complement his argument with apt quotations was tremendous and those in the Irish language were special. I regret not taking his advice when he would say: "Remember that one. It's good to enhance your argument or point of view with a quotation or a sean-fhocal or two."

When Dad was not reading he was writing. Letters for people who needed assistance in the community, reports on projects in which he was involved or speeches for the many meetings he attended. One day I asked him why wouldn't he write a book. He replied that this was something that he was going to do: "It will most likely be tré Gaeilge but I haven't time just now." Sadly that book was never written.

The question has been put to me many times: "Why don't you write a book?" or a comment passed like: "I hope you are keeping a diary for your book." This question was posed at the end of last year (1991) after good reaction to a radio documentary in which I took part, entitled *The Winner Takes All* presented by John Scally. As I contemplated the questions more seriously than ever before, John Scally had similar thoughts. We discussed the possibility briefly and as I sat one night with thoughts of layout, order and content on my mind I thought of my father's unfulfilled intention, to write a book.

As my mind wandered, I overheard the background sound from the television of an advertisement for a sports company which ended with the words: "Just do it." The decision was made and the work begun.

Brendan O'Heithir dedicated his book *Over the bar* to the GAA man who cycled twelve miles in the torrents of rain to a board meeting and when business was completed, cycled home again in a downpour. In recognition of the supporters without whom the games would be meaningless, I dedicate this book with John Scally to supporters in general but especially to those who support "the primrose and blue".

I am most grateful to John Scally for the patience and understanding he showed as we worked together and particularly for his enthusiasm which encouraged me to press ahead. He has done justice to my tale.

Nothing would have been achieved were it not for the support, encouragement and love that I constantly get from Mary, David, Conor, Dermot, Paula, Anne-Marie and Noelle. This story would not have been possible without them.

Dermot Earley
14 September 1992

Acknowledgements

I would like to thank everybody who contributed directly or indirectly to the writing and publication of this book.

My thanks are due primarily to Dermot Earley. It has been an enormous privilege for me to have been his choice of biographer. I only hope that I can justify his confidence in me. It requires an enormous act of faith to entrust somebody with one's thoughts, correspondences, and diaries. I am very grateful to Dermot for sharing these private collections with me and more fundamentally for baring his soul to me. I also deeply appreciate his generosity with his time in giving me endless hours of interviews.

In the last year more than anything else I have treasured his friendship.

I am also grateful to Mary for her co-operation and patience. She never complained when Dermot returned at all kinds of ungodly hours after our 'sessions'. (Honest we weren't spending the time down in Leeson Street!)

My apologies to David, Conor, Dermot, Paula, Anne-Marie, and Noelle for stealing their father from them so often.

Thanks also to Dermot's mother and his brother, Paul for their input and interest.

I am indebted to Michael Commins for his recollections and to Brendan Kennelly for use of his poem *A Religious Occasion*.

Thanks to *The Roscommon Herald, The Connacht Telegraph* and Patsy Glynn for photographs.

In the course of my research I contacted a number of former great players for their memories of Dermot. I am grateful to Matt Connor, Joe Connolly, Paddy Cullen, Tommy Doyle, Dermot Flanagan, Billy Joyce, Robbie Kelleher, Denis Ogie Moran, Billy Morgan, Brian McEniff, Frank McGuigan, Gerry O'Malley, Colm O'Rourke, and Jack O'Shea for their time.

Very special thanks to Packie Bonner and Tony McManus.

I am grateful to John O'Connor of Blackwater Press who backed the book enthusiastically from day one.

Finally my heartfelt thanks to the penetrating eye of Brenda McNally who fine tuned the text and Anna O'Donovan for her helpful suggestions.

John Scally
14 September 1992

Introduction

"We don't need another hero". This was the title of a Tina Turner song a few years back. But she is wrong. At no stage in one's life is the need for a hero more apparent than in the formative years of childhood. A role model offers standards to aspire to, feats to emulate, and personal qualities to imitate. Growing up in Roscommon in the 1970s one obvious hero presented himself.

It is impossible to rationally explain the intense, almost tribal, loyalty which genuine followers of the GAA give to their county. Words are sometimes inadequate vehicles to describe deep-rooted emotions. Their presentations are but vain attempts to do justice to the meaning of particularly deep feelings; their expressions can only point to a reality which they can not really illuminate.

How can you explain that people become so caught up with the fate of their team that they almost hurt? How can you make intelligible the fierce identification with fifteen players because of the colour of their jerseys? Somehow those players represented you. One's very identity was inexplicably entangled with those fifteen players. They were part of what and who you were.

Even at a very early age one becomes aware that people in the west of Ireland face disadvantages which are not shared by the population at large. Farms are generally small. Land is often poor. There is no significant industrial base. The shadow of emigration lurks like a vulture hovering over its prey. Economic bad news is as common as showers in April.

The ritual political promises before every election about the draining of the Shannon are a symptom of the way we are treated by the political establishment; lip-service rather than practical action. It's not that we are looking for a hand-out, but some of us need a hand-up. People struggle to eke out a reasonable living. Sometimes it seems like nobody cares.

Football provided an escape from our problems and anxieties. It allowed us to dream of better days to come. Success, albeit at a very modest level, such as winning the Connacht Championship in 1972 increased our self-esteem. We walked that little bit taller, we talked just a little more boldly, and we wore our primrose and blue paper caps with pride.

To my eyes, one man alone was responsible for the pride, and the surge of passion that made me want to win with an intensity that was almost frightening. As a child I always thought that he was six inches taller than everybody else, and that he was stronger than everybody else. His aim seemed as true as Robin Hood's. When I was asked what I wanted to be when I grew up, I always answered: 'Dermot Earley'. He was everything I wanted to be, the complete footballer, the perfect sportsman and an inspiration to others. It sounds clichéd but he seemed to be a nice man. Somehow that was important.

More than anything else it was his spirit which was an enduring fascination. His attitude always seemed to be: 'Never say die'. Even when faced with an uphill battle, and there were many such battles for Roscommon, I always felt he could pull something special out of the fire. There were many times when a miracle was called for and often he transformed the mundane into the miraculous. The clue to Dermot Earley was always his facial expression, its intensity, its determination, its appetite, and its total commitment. He played (always fairly) like a man possessed, as if consumed by an inner fire.

Dermot was the battery that drove my imaginative life and dared me to see Roscommon in a very different light. The hours spent watching him was time spent wondering at the wonderful. Everyday I became him for an hour after school. Homework was ignored as I went off on my own for an hour to play an imaginary match in 'Broke Park'. In our fields Roscommon won an All-Ireland everyday.

Every evening as I milked the cows I entertained myself (though not the cows!) with my abysmal impersonation of Micheal O'Hehir. I was always the youngest boy ever, to play in an All-Ireland final and in every match our opponents (usually Kerry) were confronted by a dynamic duo, Dermot Earley and I. We would interchange passes and set up scores for each other. The only issue at stake was the size of our win. The more milk the cows had, the bigger was the size of our win!

My enduring memory of Dermot Earley as a player goes back to a League game against Cork in 1973. It was a beautiful clear December day in Dr Hyde Park. Cork were reigning All-Ireland Champions. Inspired by a five-star performance by Earley, Roscommon had built up a commanding lead. However, Cork rallied and cut the deficit to one point with only minutes to go. The Roscommon defence were under siege. Time was almost up when Cork got a sideline ball about 40 yds from the Roscommon goal. The entire Cork team apart from their goalie, Billy Morgan, descended on the Roscommon square. The kick was taken. At least forty hands seem to go up for it as it flew like a jet towards the Roscommon goal. Although a marked chill had set in, my body temperature was so high I was afraid I would explode. Then Dermot Earley soared like an eagle and grabbed the ball authoritatively and under unbelievable pressure cleared the ball to safety. The Messiah had saved us once again.

What passed for a summer in 1980 was a disaster for the farming community. The hay rotted in the fields. The turf situation was no better and there was little joy with the spuds. As we soaked in the world's weary wash, a voice within, faintly but insistently, said: 'This is our year' and we were uplifted and found the strength to go on. In the chill of the bracing wind as we filled barn after barn with almost worthless musty hay, the talk was of nothing but football. Roscommon would win and Dermot Earley would get that elusive All-Ireland medal. Times were tough but that dream sustained us in those difficult months. Young children, girls and boys, kicked footballs in the creeping hedgerows anticipating Roscommon's victory.

As I stood in the Canal End, slowly suffocating in airless discomfort, I watched 'his' All-Ireland slipping away. Like seeds dreaming of spring beneath the snow, my heart dreamt that his day would come but the hope went into decline.

As a sports fanatic, I have read many sports biographies. In the vast majority of cases I have gone away disappointed. Although all the sporting careers were impressively documented I felt I came away knowing little about the stars as people, their thoughts, their philosophy of life, their feelings. For this reason I have not attempted to catalogue every point that Dermot scored, or sought out all the compliments that have been paid to him over the years. Instead I have tried to portray Dermot Earley the man, the footballer, and the army officer. Inevitably it is not possible to cover everything. In as far as is practicable I have attempted to present the story through his own eyes.

1. Champagne in the Dressing-Room

'The Champagne is on Ice' has always been a popular heading for articles in the sporting pages. It describes a situation when a team or an individual is on the threshold of a major sporting achievement but has to endure a tantalising delay before they can claim their ultimate prize. Champagne is synonymous with success and is instinctively associated with occasions of great joy and celebration.

In the course of Dermot Earley's long and distinguished inter-county career with Roscommon, there was only one occasion when he had champagne in the immediate aftermath of a big match. Ironically, the only time there was champagne in the dressing-room was on the day when he played his last match for Roscommon against Mayo (the county of his birth) in the Connacht final of 1985. The setting was more akin to a morgue than a party. In those traumatic moments nothing seemed more inappropriate than a glass of champagne. Yet less than three hours earlier it had all promised to be so different.

Champagne Stuff from Roscommon

Roscommon entered the game as hot favourites following their defeat of Galway in the Connacht semi-final. That circle of people, collectively known as the 'experts', had all tipped Galway to regain their provincial crown for a fourth consecutive year. The previous year Galway had inflicted a heavy defeat on Roscommon in the semi-final of the Connacht Championship. In 1985 Roscommon were fortunate to snatch a draw with Galway in Hyde Park, getting a late equalising point from a Dermot Earley free.

However, misfortune struck a cruel blow to Roscommon late in the game. As they clung on desperately to their slender lead, Dermot Earley found himself dragged deeper and deeper into his own defence.

"I was marking one of the Galway forwards and trying to turn him on to his weak foot but as he turned, his head accidentally clashed against my face, breaking my jaw. I felt the blow and went down on one knee knowing that I had been hit pretty hard, but the biggest pain was to see the delicate left foot kick the point. The ball went way up into the air and scraped over the crossbar. I left the field accompanied by Mick Mullen, who was an assistant to the team. Having to leave the field with ten minutes to go and Roscommon leading by just a point or two was very disappointing. One of the vivid memories I have of that day was the sustained applause I received as I made my way along the sideline to the dressing-room. It was like a wave rolling with me all the way until I exited the field. The team held out well and won the game.

The Final Curtain

Following the defeat of Galway, Roscommon's build-up to the match was hampered by the tag of favouritism, a mantle which Roscommon traditionally wore uncomfortably. As the senior statesman on the team, Earley's views on the match were the subject of particular interest in media circles. On the Friday before the Connacht final he recorded an interview for the sports feature *as Gaeilge* which used to follow the One-Thirty News on Radio One on Saturday afternoons. In the course of the interview he indicated that it was to be his last Connacht Championship match for Roscommon, unless the final ended in a draw.

"I was definite in my own mind that this was going to be my last year in inter-county football. In the back of my mind I felt that it would indeed be my last Connacht Championship match but that we would go on to the All-Ireland semi-final and perhaps even greater glory."

The following day saw the team convening for a final kick-around in Hyde Park. Although 1985 was a dreadful summer (the real summer did not arrive until September) it was a beautiful day. A pleasantly-relaxed atmosphere prevailed in the Roscommon camp. The team exuded a sense of quiet confidence.

"As I prepared to leave the ground and return home to Newbridge the One-Thirty News came on the radio. Some of the mentors heard the interview which I had recorded the day before. They smiled as they heard my intentions and said: 'Ah sure you might stay on for another year'."

Saint Bob

When he drove home that evening his family were all watching television. Like millions of people all over the world they were watching the most spectacular popular music event in history, the Live-Aid Concert. That day, 13 July was hailed as the day pop music 'grew up' and channelled its energies into the service of humankind. Thoughts of the Connacht final were temporarily put to one side.

The first act he saw was U2, who stole the show. The conviction and energy of their Wembley performance were infectious. The charisma of Bono as he strode self-confidently into the audience whilst singing the classic song 'Bad' left a deep impression. When he moved to America in 1987, Earley was to see at first hand just how big U2 had become. Their album 'The Joshua Tree' had just been released and they dominated rock music in America. The fact that four young men from Dublin had conquered the music world did wonders for the 'new Irelands' profile in America. They were ambassadors for an Ireland that shattered the typical American stereotype. U2 mania hit the Earley household, with 'I still haven't found what I'm looking for' becoming a firm favourite.

Although Earley was entertained by the music, he was also disturbed and moved by the harrowing images of thousands of people dying of starvation in Ethiopia. As the magnitude of the achievement of Live-Aid became clearer, his heart swelled with pride as an Irishman, Bob Geldof, succeeded in moving the conscience of the world.

His mind went back twenty-five years to a classroom on a miserable wet day in west Roscommon. As he looked up from his desk he could see his father with a piece of chalk in his hand. He was talking about the great famine. He spoke about the workhouses and the coffin ships with such feeling that they almost came alive before the pupils' eyes. His words painted pictures in their imagination. Now twenty-five years later he was seeing pictures of a famine even more horrific in its chain of destruction, all the more offensive because the means were there to alleviate the scale of suffering, with food mountains lying idly in storage depots. Now at least an Irishman was showing the way to the rest of the world. His father would have been proud of that.

On 25 November 1991, his mind went back to that concert. Apart from U2, the other stars of the day were the supergroup Queen. Now, six years later, Freddie Mercury had died from AIDS. In Wembley he held the crowd in the palm of his hand, he enraptured millions on television, his every gesture seemed to say 'I own you'. He looked indestructible. As the music world mourned one of its greatest stars, Dermot Earley thought about the things in life that really matter. The former Liverpool manager, Bill Shankley, once said: "Football is not just a matter of life and death. It's more important." In the heat of battle many footballers fall victim to the same illusion. Freddie Mercury's death was one of those moments which helped to put Dermot's sporting disappointments in perspective.

That night he kept an eye on the clock as he watched the concert. The following day he would play his biggest game in four years, since Roscommon played Galway in the League Final in 1981. It was important to get a good night's sleep. He was determined to finish his career in Connacht football on a high note.

The next morning he awoke with a spring in his step. The Sunday papers spoke almost with one voice – that Roscommon would emerge as provincial champions.

"I don't usually read the papers on the day of a game; I would certainly glance at the headlines, but that particular day all the papers indicated that Roscommon should win easily."

"As I left my home in Newbridge on that fateful day I was convinced it was going to be an ideal day for football. The weather was warm, dry and calm, but as I drove down I noticed that the wind was beginning to pick up."

Mission Impossible

"When I reached Hyde Park I got the usual friendly welcome from the stewards. As I drove into the ground I was distracted by one thing – the Tricolour. It was flying so strongly and stiffly, from the town goal to the graveyard goal. I can remember the flag so vividly. I was very disappointed."

Windy conditions are every footballer's nightmare because the flight of the ball is so unpredictable. High temperatures, rain, muddy conditions are all accepted as part and parcel of football. Meticulously laid plans are thrown into chaos. A match which had promised to be a classic can end up as a lottery. The skill factor is mitigated with boring predictability. Complex tactical moves dissolve into quicksand. Nothing is more frustrating than watching great players having to play second fiddle to the weather.

"I would normally go over and watch the minor match but on this occasion I was so disappointed by the strength of the wind that I decided to go into the Hyde Centre instead. I remember talking to Sean Young our manager and discussing the wind. My advice was to play with the breeze.

"There were two things that my father always said to me, that he considered to be certainties. He said: 'Never play into the breeze and never go for a goal from a fourteen yards free'. Now I know that there is no such thing as 'never'. There can be the expectation in a specific tactical situation where you might decide to play against the breeze for a specific reason, or you might decide to go for a goal from a fourteen yards free, but only in very exceptional circumstances. His intuition was correct. You should take your advantages when they come, and take your points as they present themselves.

"So, I have taken those two insights on board. I would always try and play with the breeze and kick the points from frees when the opportunity arose. Seamus Hayden who was captain on the day talked with me about the wind and it was decided once and for all that we would play with the breeze if we won the toss."

A Domestic Crisis

One of the casualties of the Galway match had been Earley's number ten jersey. He had gingerly taken off his jersey to avoid further pain to his jaw and cast it to one side. In the excitement of Roscommon's victory, which ensured that they were to play in the Connacht final for the first time in five years, the Roscommon players had swapped their jerseys with their counterparts from Galway. A new set of jerseys was necessary for the Connacht final. In the scenes of unbridled excitement which followed the Galway match in the Roscommon dressing-room, the spare number ten jersey mysteriously went absent without leave. Somebody's souvenir collection was augmented.

"In the week that followed, my oldest son David wanted a Roscommon jersey. His younger brothers, Conor and Dermot Jnr had two small Roscommon jerseys that fitted them, but David was getting a little bit bigger; he was now nearly 10 years old and he wanted a real jersey. He wanted the one that I had played in, in the Connacht semi-final against Galway. I knew I could not get that particular one but I also knew how much a 'real' jersey would transform David's spirits. I explained the situation to our county secretary, Paddy Francis Dwyer. I thought that he might have one from an old set at home that David could wear and support Roscommon with pride."

"I was the first into the dressing-room. As I sat there on my own I felt strong, I felt good. David was hovering around the dressing-room wondering if he would get a jersey. The one niggling worry at the back of my mind was the wind. Then Paddy Francis came in the door. As he came in he had something in his hand which he threw to me. It was a number ten jersey which he had obviously ordered specially for me, a gesture which I appreciated very much. David was delighted and after I handed him the jersey, he put it on, tucked it inside his shorts and was ready to head out. He was full of emotion that his request was acceded to, and overjoyed that I had come up trumps. With tears in his eyes he gave me a big hug and said: 'Good Luck. Win the game'. Then he was gone."

Omega Point

Any attempt to unlock the secrets of a player's mind before a match is fraught with pitfalls. Objectivity goes out the window. Dreams transcend the limitations of individual players or a team. In the mysterious depths of the human mind delusions are often fostered. Nowhere is the adage 'hope springs eternal' more evident than on a football field just before the throw-in. Yet, within minutes, reality reared its ugly head. Earley's dream of crowning his momentous career in Connacht football with a blaze of glory was to shatter abruptly.

"To my grave disappointment as we lined up, Seamus Hayden indicated that we were playing against the breeze. I discovered later that Seamus had won the toss and played against the wind on Sean Young's suggestion. I took my place at right-half forward and from the throw-in I can remember spending the next twenty minutes or so in the Roscommon half of the field, defending."

"Mayo got a whirlwind start, scoring a number of points and pegging us into our own half. Any time we worked the ball up towards the Mayo goal they would sweep up our attack and they had numerous players available to take a pass and set up a new attack. Dermot Flanagan was playing particularly well at left-corner back and so was John Finn immediately outside him, whom I was playing on. The Mayo team seemed to have an extra man all over the place and were able to find one another very accurately. Still they were only able to put six or seven points up when we conceded a goal, put away by Noel Durkin.

"We went in at half-time having scored only three points. Those three points were all scored from frees which were a poor return for thirty-five minutes of Connacht final football. Although we were trailing by eight or nine points we still felt that with a tremendous fight we could pull the game out of the fire. However, that was not to be.

"I think the main turning point in the game was when my brother Paul got the ball and took on the Mayo defence. He had burst his way through when his rasper of a shot crashed off the crossbar and came back to the ground. He managed to retrieve the ball, but running at speed and trying to hit the ball from a very acute angle meant that it went into the side netting. Had we got the goal we might have turned the game and won the day.

"A few moments from the end of the game, I picked up a ball and took on John Maughan, an army colleague of mine like Kevin McStay, who was centre-half back from Mayo and has now achieved great success as the Clare team manager. We had played together on the army football team. I knew his play well and he knew mine and as I dummied by him he put his arms gently around me and hauled me to the ground, perhaps fourteen or twenty yards out directly in front of the goal. As we lay there he said: 'I'm sorry to have to foul you but we don't want to let you in'. There were only seconds remaining as I placed the ball. The referee, Mickey Kearins, himself one of the greatest players Connacht has ever produced, said to me: 'If it was close you wouldn't have got it.' It was a peculiar comment from Mickey but that was what he said. Maybe he thought I invited the foul. I ran up to the ball and tapped it over the bar. It was my last touch of a Gaelic football with Roscommon and it was a point with my right foot."

The Pride and the Passion

The well-known comedian Frank Carson's catchphrase is: 'It's the way I tell them'. Listening to Earley talking about his last match for Roscommon it is not what he says, but the way he says it, that is so revealing. What strikes you most forcefully is not the words or even the story itself, but the emotion. Many times his voice breaks up. The words come fitfully and slowly. He appears to be almost choking with raw emotion. It is as if he is re-enacting every second of those moments, which remain firmly entrenched on his brain.

Such is the intensity of his memories that I feel as though I am in the psychiatrist's chair. We have long since passed the point of ordinary conversation. I have a powerful sense that I am seeing the soul of Dermot Earley. The room is something analogous to a confessional box in which no inner feeling can be concealed. Although our conversation is slow, almost tortuous, time seems suspended and it is much later when

I become conscious of the clock. The silences speak louder than the words.

He appeared a little self-conscious about getting so worked up by a football match seven years ago. "When I played I certainly wanted to put every drop of energy into the game. Sometimes that did not happen of course, but you would end up, when the game was over, feeling emotional about winning or losing, particularly in important games. You would have tremendous satisfaction, something spectacular had been achieved. You had great pride in what you did, and what your team mates did and you were happy for the supporters.

"Perhaps, I am an emotional person. I remember Micheal O Muircheartaigh interviewing me following our League quarter-final victory over Kerry in 1979. 'I believe', he said 'a tear was shed'. I had no hesitation in saying that I did in fact shed a tear of immense satisfaction because it was the first time ever in my playing career that Roscommon had beaten Kerry in a national knock-out competition. I felt that we had arrived. To a degree, we had arrived; because we had won the League that year, qualified for the All-Ireland final the following year and the League final in 1981. We were up there, if not at the very top, then pretty close to it.

"I never felt that I should be any other way but emotional when I won or lost. I never wanted to show frustration in losing. My father always said you had to win games just as you lost games. Nowadays, I see victories being won without any emotion and I feel that is wrong. You need to experience and show emotion. There's no crime in that.

"As I look back now I realise that the sense of enjoyment I got as a player was matched by the whole-heartedness of the supporter who came to you and hugged you when the game was over. Many of these men and women were shaking with excitement; they were people who might not be able to express their emotions to you, but who used a gesture instead, such as a hug or a slap on the back and that meant an awful lot to me.

"When Roscommon presented Pat Lindsay and myself with a trophy in February 1986 both of us had some words to say, people to thank and matches to be recounted. I think I said I had played in many jerseys in my time but I could never run as fast, or jump as high, or catch as cleanly, or kick as straight as when I wore the primrose and blue.

"It meant so much to me that even now when I talk about it, I get emotional. When I think of that jersey, I think of the honour it brings to the county and the pride that the supporters have in you when you go to play in a championship match, particularly in an All-Ireland final. Even when we lost people always said 'What harm', and that still happens when I go back down to Roscommon today. People approach me, often I have no idea who they are, and say: 'You gave me twenty years of extraordinary pleasure. Thank you very much'."

A Pleasant Embarrassment

There is a well established protocol which is observed almost ritually after every major provincial final. The victors and the vanquished embrace. Handshakes and words of congratulations or commiserations are exchanged in a gracious manner. The acute disappointment of defeat is concealed as manfully as possible while the courtesies are adhered to. The elation of victory is temporarily moderated as the winning team shows appropriate sensitivity to the feelings of the players who are still reeling from defeat. The pleasantries completed, the winning team are free to begin their celebrations in earnest. Invariably the winning captain or star of the day is hoisted high on his team mates' shoulders and led on a victory celebration. Dermot Earley recalls how this convention was disrupted in the aftermath of the 1985 Connacht final with a mixture of amusement and bemusement. The central character in the drama was Mayo's 'Ian Botham look-alike', Willie Joe Padden.

"I was in the middle of the field when the referee blew the whistle. One man, Willie Joe Padden, stood out more than anybody else, and as we walked towards one another to shake hands, I said 'Good Luck in the All-Ireland semi-final, I hope you win the All-Ireland final'. I went to turn away and as I turned Willie Joe held on to me, he shouted to a few of the Mayo players and they all gathered around and held me up on their shoulders. I was embarrassed and did not want it to happen but they held me up there for a short period. I can still hear the applause of the crowd ringing in my ears. As I dropped on the ground there were many claps on the back and further shaking of hands."

The Silence of the Speaker

Having received the adulation of the crowd in this unique tribute, Dermot Earley walked over to hear the Mayo captain Henry Gavin make his victory speech. As he walked, his two youngest sons Conor and Dermot Jnr joined him. He held both by the hand. As he waited for the presentation of the Nestor Cup, Tom Rooney of RTE Radio invited him to join Jimmy Magee for an interview on the *Sunday Sports Programme* after the ceremony was finished.

A winning captain's speech has a number of essential ingredients: a statement about the honour of captaining one's county to victory, words of thanks to all the players, mentors (who are mentioned by name) and supporters as well as the almost obligatory call for three cheers for the losing team. When Henry Gavin completed the traditional elements he superseded the bounds of conventional practice and made specific reference to Earley on the occasion of his retirement.

"As soon as he mentioned my name the microphone went dead. He continued to speak, not realising that the Public Address was dead. Nobody heard what he had to say. There were remarks of kindness and good wishes for my retirement. I couldn't help but see the irony; you lost a game that everybody expected you to win, it was your last game and then, at the precise moment when Henry was about to offer complimentary words, the microphone went dead."

The Mayor

As he smiled ruefully at the irony of the situation he looked around at Roscommon's long-serving full-back Pat Lindsay who was stoically watching the proceedings in a dignified silence. Their eyes met. No words passed between them even though they stood beside one another. Yet a few minutes later the Roscommon team was to be shocked by the announcement of retirement of the pillar of their Roscommon defence for so many years.

Known and cherished to all Roscommon fans simply as 'Lindsay', his popularity with the supporters was eclipsed only by Earley himself. Indeed their careers dovetailed closely for many years. Although army duties had sometimes taken Earley to foreign pastures, it seemed almost impossible to conceive of a Roscommon team without Lindsay.

When opposing forward lines came to plunder the Roscommon goal, their invading intentions were often thwarted by an almost invincible fortress in the shape of the massive frame of Pat Lindsay. A player who must be considered extremely unfortunate to have won only one All-Star award (in 1977) in the light of his trojan work in the Roscommon defence. Solid, consistent, unspectacular defence were the hallmarks of his play. Yet, because he did not play with the flair and panaché of a footballing stylist like Kevin Moran, he never got the national recognition he deserved. Having adorned the primrose and blue jersey for so long, he too had decided to call it a day. For Dermot Earley, Pat Lindsay's retirement added yet another layer of sadness to his ever-increasing gloom. A sudden smile appears on his face as he is reminded of a happier memory of Lindsay.

"As you left the football pitch spectators often passed remarks about you, particularly if you won. People would shout: 'Fair play to you', or 'Well done'. Of course, there would also be many derogatory comments when things did not go so well like: 'What the hell were ye at' – one of the mildest and most polite of such comments.

"One day in Hyde Park, Lindsay and I were leaving the pitch, it was a particularly mucky day, the ground was heavy and we were both plastered in mud. As we came towards the gate someone looked at the two of us as we walked by and said to his friend: 'Jaysus - would you look at the legs of them. I have bullocks at home on silage and I wish they had legs on them like that!' That was probably the most outrageous compliment I ever got in my playing days.

"Pat Lindsay had been the stalwart of the Roscommon defence for many years. The defence had been built around him and perhaps the team too. He had captained the team on a number of occasions and was respected and looked up to by every player. His speeches before matches when he was captain were short, well prepared and to the point but the most important thing about him was that he led by example. He was a big man but a fair player.

"He was known to us affectionately as 'the Mayor' because of his namesake Mayor Lindsay of New York. The Mayor would arrive into the dressing-room for training or for a match, fully prepared. His gear would be immaculate and his boots properly taken care of and polished. Everything was exactly right. He had a ritual of leaving everything beside him: the jersey, the togs, the gloves and his neatly folded towel. Everything that he had in his bag would be left on a line along his seat. He had always togged out at my right hand side."

"There were many times when I remember high balls falling in the Roscommon square when we were leading by a point or two, hanging on for dear life and then Lindsay would appear with the ball ably supported by Harry Keegan and Tom Heneghan or Gerry Connellan. I was very disappointed when I went back to the dressing-room to hear that he had retired. He was gone at that stage having made a rousing speech. I did not expect him to retire. I felt that he still had a number of years to give to the game. I never spoke to him afterwards about his decision that day.

The one regret I have, apart from the fact that he did not play on any longer, was that I was not in the dressing-room to hear his speech."

Baring a Soul to the Nation

Following the presentation and the victory speech Earley went up with Tom Rooney to do the interview with Jimmy Magee, who was operating from the RTE studies in Donnybrook. Dermot Flanagan and Liam O'Neill, the Mayo manager, followed behind. The interview covered the match itself, games from the past and the decision to retire.

"I cannot remember all the aspects of the interview, but I remember vividly looking out on Hyde Park from the highest position on the stand and thinking that the pitch never looked better or greener or as well marked, but that now it was all over and I would never play on it again.

"Jimmy Magee asked me: 'Now that is over what will you miss?' I thought for a moment; I knew there was a lump in my throat and that it was difficult to speak. As I looked across the pitch and saw the crowd outside the dressing-room, I said: 'Well, I will miss the training and the camaraderie, the run from the dressing-room and the roar from the crowd'. There was silence and Magee came back on from Dublin and said: 'The last five minutes have been pretty hard'. I can remember saying: 'Pretty tough Jimmy'. Then it was over.

"In the aftermath of the Connacht final, and particularly because of that interview, I received quite a lot of mail, comments and telephone calls from people around the country and outside the country indicating that they had sat and listened with a lot of emotion to my interview.

"I received a postcard from a referee and his wife, from Wicklow. They were on holidays, and were at the end of a quay in some part of Jersey trying to get the sports results from home. After they heard the interview, they dropped me a note to say how much they had enjoyed it, and indeed, seeing me play over the years. Everybody was complimentary of course. It was a nice way to go.

"Quite a number of people spoke to me afterwards about the interview and where they were, and what they were doing at the time. Some had cried a little. I know I was very emotional and as I tell it again I become emotional, because football meant so much to me, and Roscommon meant so much to me, and now it is finished. Regardless of how close you get to the team afterwards, whether you become County Chairman, Secretary or team manager, it's still not the same as being a player. All of the people who spoke to me about the interview said things like 'You had us in tears'. In one household everything stopped and when the interview was over there was a long lull before anybody spoke.

"The following Saturday morning I remember lying in bed as I listened to Treasa Davidson doing her playback programme. It never crossed my mind that I would be on the programme. All of a sudden she said: 'And then there was the Connacht final and Jimmy Magee's interview with Dermot Earley'. As far as I can remember almost all of the interview was replayed. At the end of the interview Treasa Davidson said: 'Jimmy Magee and a doleful Dermot Earley'."

18

The Player's Player

Dermot Flanagan, whose father Sean (a former T.D. and MEP) captained Mayo during their brace of All-Ireland victories in 1950 and 1951 and was chosen on the centenary 'Team of the Century' in 1984, remembers very little about the post-match celebrations.

"I got a belt in the head in the last few minutes of the game, in fact I had just broken my nose, so my mind was still in a blur and I don't remember the incident very well. It was a very sad day, not just for Roscommon but for football in general, when he retired. He was one of the major influences on my game as I grew up. I have always regarded him as one of the most complete footballers of all time because of his outstanding skill, athleticism and drive. I regard myself as very fortunate to have played with him for three years (1983-'85) when he was the player-manager of the Connacht team. In many ways he carried the team. For all the recognition he achieved it was an awful shame that he never won an All-Ireland medal. No player ever deserved the honour more than he did."

"After the interview people came by and shook hands with me and congratulated me. They wished me well and many said 'You will be back again next year'. Those little words of thanks and encouragement meant more to me than any eloquent speech. Little things do mean a lot.

"By the time I got back to the dressing-room about forty minutes had elapsed from the end of the presentation. There was a small group of people outside and they all applauded. By then, the dressing-room was almost empty. The team had already left."

Flat Spirits and Flat Champagne

"There were only three people left inside the dressing-room, Sean Young, Paddy Francis Dwyer and Cyril O'Neill. The jerseys had been packed and Dwyer told me to keep mine. Sean Young informed me that Pat Lindsay had retired and Cyril O'Neill handed me an almost empty bottle of champagne. It was a little flat. He said: 'We had champagne in the dressing-room, and we kept a little for you.' It was the first and only time I had ever had champagne in the dressing-room.

"When I went outside there were still a few people around; the old stalwarts who had waited to shake hands with me. Although the crowds had dispersed, there was still a traffic jam outside. It took us a long time to get back to the hotel. Not all the players had returned. Some had gone for a drink. The big effort was over. The team would not be the same again. Pat Lindsay was not going to play again, and neither was I. Roscommon would have to start afresh, later that year, for the League.

A Private Ceremony

"The drive home to Newbridge seemed to take longer than usual. Nobody was in the form for conversation. The car radio was on but the passengers were oblivious to it. Even the children appreciated the uniqueness of the situation. The strange atmosphere subdued their normal enthusiasm. The journey complete, Dermot Earley sought comfort in solitude.

"I went into the garage and took my boots out of my bag. I polished them and in a small little ceremony of my own, I put them up on the top shelf. I have never worn those boots since. In 1987, when I was going to America, I carefully wrapped up the boots and put them up in the attic. When I came home in 1991, I checked that they were still okay and they stayed there until March 1992. I took them down one day and gave them to my eldest son, David. He wore them the day he played his first inter-county hurling game for Kildare against Dublin in the Leinster Hurling Minor League Special. He wears them playing hurling because they are lighter than the ones he now has for football."

It's All Over

As he sat alone in his garage the atmosphere was conducive to sadness. Memories came flooding back of the twenty-three years wearing the primose and blue since he first played for Roscommon as a minor as a raw corner-back, when he was just fifteen. Sweet memories were recalled with affection. The 'might-have-beens' were discarded wistfully. A few sad moments were quickly brushed to one side.

"I suppose as I sat in the garage I felt lighter than I had felt for a long time. There was a weight off my shoulders. The pressure of other people's expectations had been taken away from me. One of the questions Jimmy Magee had asked me was: 'Is it all over?' I said 'It's all over. There's no going back now Jimmy'. The almost overwhelming sense of sadness gave away to relief, as I thought about the consequences of my decision – I took in some deep gulps of air."

In sports, stars come and go in fairly rapid succession. Dermot Earley had twenty years of inter-county football, not just lasting that length of time, but also managing to turn in consistently high standards – staying at the top for that period of time demands tough sacrifices. Family life suffers. Retirement was as much a beginning as it was an end.

The Babysitter

As he took a last loving look up at his football boots before returning inside for a much needed cup of tea, two memories came into his mind. Both concerned Mayo's Dermot Flanagan, but were separated by a gap of twenty years.

"Dermot had played exceptionally well that day. He had kept us under so much pressure with his frees, which penned us back into our own half for a long time. I couldn't help but think that here was a young man from Ballaghadreen, whom I had babysat on one occasion in 1965. I'd been going out with a girl from Ballaghadreen at the time, so one night I sat in babysitting Dermot with her. Now he was playing corner-back for Mayo, in the same position his father had played and putting me under immense pressure. Perhaps it was high time for me to call it a day."

2. Can You Kick With Your Left Foot?

When the first child of Mr and Mrs Peadar Earley was born in Castlebar on 24 February 1948, football fans in Roscommon could have not foreseen that this birth would have such significance for their football fortunes in years to come.

Peadar Earley was an only child. His father died when he was two and his mother when he was thirteen. From then on he was reared by family friends. He was a scholarship boy winning a scholarship to St Gerald's college for his secondary education and then to the De La Salle training college in Waterford where he qualified as a national teacher.

His first posting was in Limerick but he returned a year later to his native Mayo to take up a teaching post there. An important consideration in the move was that it allowed him to be close to his sweetheart, Catherine (Kitty) Byrne. Her family owned a pub in Main Street, Castlebar. They also had an egg exporting licence. One of Earley's most vivid childhood memories is of being surrounded by an ocean of eggs in a massive shed where they were packaged for export.

The family lived in a rented house in Cruck outside Balla. In 1953 they moved to Cloonbonniffe outside Castlerea where Peadar took up his appointment as principal. The attraction of the school was that there was a good chance that a house would become available which would serve as the teacher's house on a permanent basis.

It was here that Dermot Earley's football education began when his father taught him how to kick a football. It was only a small brown rubber ball but the rudiments of all of the skills of the game were learnt using that ball.

The school was steeped in history, being the school of the O'Connor Don and having been established by the descendants of the O'Connor family, former High Kings of Ireland. Peadar Earley became actively involved in the community. Almost immediately he established a football club which quickly folded after he left the area. In the event, the house did not materialise and the family moved to Gorthaganny where a teacher's job and house were available in November 1955.

The house is set back against a hill, almost nestling into it. Gorthaganny lake is nearby. On a windy day the industry of the lake is a marvel. Little wave after little wave spends itself before starting again. The sound of the waves crashing and swirling off the rocks is soothing, almost hypnotic. In the distance the horizon seems so calm at the edge of the world. The world is in season.

By this time the Earley family was expanding rapidly. A year and a day after Dermot was born came Denise (now living in Australia) and after that came Margaret (now living in London) and two sons Peter and Paul.

For a seven-year-old Dermot Earley the house had two main attractions. It was right beside a shop which meant that it was easy to buy lollipops and there was also a big garden attached which was ideal for playing football.

In 1956 Peadar Earley founded Gorthaganny GAA club. The club was called after Michael Glavey who was killed in an attack on Ballinlough RIC Barracks on 14 September 1920.

A Bedside Companion

The star of the Michael Glaveys side was John Lynch who played full-back on the Roscommon side. In the 1980s the word 'wannabe' entered popular parlance. It described the thousands of young girls who wanted to look like Madonna. Before Madonna was even born Dermot Earley was a 'wannabe'. He wanted to be like John Lynch.

A central character in all of this was Earley's neighbour and best friend Haulie McNulty. Every evening in the Earley's front garden they played their own Connacht final. Earley was always John Lynch, Haulie was Frank Stockwell, Gerry O' Malley or Sean Purcell. On special occasions they played All-Ireland finals. One of their epic games ended in a draw. The score was 9-35 to 10-32.

The matches were played with such intensity that hens, ducks, geese and even cattle were afraid to come near the immediate vicinity. However, it was the two aspiring footballers turn to be scared when they managed to send a ball crashing through the window of the shop one day during the summer holidays. There was glass everywhere and an unmerciful racket as the ball went crashing through the window. The culprits vanished into the fields. When they cautiously sneaked back hours later, they saw Peadar Earley returning from Ballyhaunis with a big pane of glass under his arm having made the journey on his bicycle as the family had no car. The window was restored and there was no retribution.

The Earley family had to pay a price for Dermot's football fanaticism. One day they were all gathering for the dinner. Denise was calling in her big brother for his meal but was being ignored as he continued to kick the football up against the wall as if his life depended on it. His mother had put all the food on the table and was not prepared to tolerate any more delay. She ran outside to tell her son emphatically, that he had to come in for his dinner. The response she got was: "Just one more kick." The kick shattered all the glass in the window beside the dinner table. Not a single scrap of food could be saved. It would be a bread and jam lunch instead of a hot meal.

Christmas was also dominated by thoughts of football. One of Earley's first letters to Santa Claus asked for a pair of football boots. Santa came up trumps. By contemporary standards the boots were ugly – they were a pair of very high ankle brown leather boots, but to their new owner aesthetic splendour was not paramount. They were the most beautiful sight that he had ever seen.

The following Christmas a 'real' football was asked for. Again Santa obliged. The white leather ball was discovered at 4 a.m. and although everybody in the house had agreed the night before to stay in bed until 6 a.m. nobody could get a wink of sleep because of the sound of the new ball being thrown against the wall and caught by its proud owner over and over again.

That year was a white Christmas so the new ball could not be tried out for a few days. Then the Earleys were visited by family friend and star of the Roscommon team, Gerry O'Malley. If John Lynch was superman then Gerry O'Malley was God. The new football was placed strategically beside the door. Dermot saw O'Malley eyeing the ball and his heart started thumping madly. Outside the snowflakes were falling like a scene from a picturesque Christmas card. It would be too much to hope for that he would get a few kicks with the great Gerry O'Malley in such weather. However, the child in O'Malley took over and he brought the boy outside. It was the highlight of the youngster's life up to then.

Gerry O'Malley remembers that day vividly: "We could hardly see the white ball with the snow but Dermot was in heaven. I could see from early on that he had something special. His father always knew that he was capable of great things."

From that day on the new football was brought to bed every night.

The Master

School life was also influenced by football. As the principal, Peadar Earley would sometimes extend lunchbreak if a particularly exciting match was taking place. For the Earley children there were advantages and disadvantages in having their father as a teacher. The advantages were that they could call their father whenever they needed assistance with their homework or required points of clarification. The disadvantages were that they could never skip on homework or use the classic excuse: "Please Sir, I forgot my copy." There was one time that Dermot Earley realised that his father often saw more than he let on at home.

"We were given particularly difficult sums involving addition, subtraction, multiplication and division. If you made a mistake in the beginning you got the whole thing wrong. My father was watching me that night but did not make any comment. The next day he was correcting the sums when he asked all those who got them right to put up their hands. I put up my hand. He walked down and said: 'Is that the answer on the board?' I said: 'No'. He said nothing more until later that evening. All the lads were gathering outside to play football. I was all set to go out to play with them but my father said: 'Come here you. Where are you going?', 'Out to play football'. 'No you are not. You told me a lie today. You are staying in all evening'.

"He never said anything else. I stood at the window watching the lads going to the match. It was the longest two hours that I ever spent. I will never forget it. It taught me a lesson. Never tell a lie. We often talked about it afterwards. When I had kids of my own and chastised them for telling lies he would say: 'Your Daddy will tell you all about telling lies'. It was the right way to do it. It extracted the maximum punishment and he never laid a finger on me."

Apart from his teaching duties and his football work Earley was actively involved in community life. As 'the master' he was the most educated person in the parish apart from the priest. In an era when most adults in rural Ireland, particularly elderly people, had very little education Peadar Earley's services were eagerly sought after by those who were applying for pensions or who had formal letters to write.

Even in the 1950s memories of the hungry 1930s were very strong. The local agricultural adviser was Gerry O'Malley. He remembers Peader Earley's efforts to extend agricultural knowledge in the community: "He was a marvellous community man. He used to organise all kinds of talks to spread education about farming matters. His wife is a great woman too."

Every Face Tells A Story

As Earley's every wakening moment seemed to go into football his mother became increasingly distressed that his exploits in sport were hampering his progress in school.

One night he was given an ultimatum: "More of the books less of the boots."

Before every match she gave her son the same advice: "Don't get hurt and don't hurt anybody." Invariably she would make the same response every time he came home with a sad face. She would ask: "Did ye win?"

The facial expression would say everything and she would give her standard answer to her own question: "No. What harm."

Even when her son's career was at its zenith she would not attend matches. She would travel but would spend her time in the Church.

"I could never bear watching either Dermot or Paul playing. I was terrified they would hurt themselves. If either of them got hurt I was never told. In 1985 somebody asked me: 'Was Dermot better.' It was only then that I discovered that Dermot had broken his jaw in a match a few weeks earlier."

Apart from safety her primary concern was that her son would look well on the pitch. This was a difficult task.

As a ten-year-old Earley asked his father if it would be possible to buy a pair of togs. They went to Castlerea and spent ten shillings, a small fortune, on a pair of togs. They were much too big for him, going down below his knees and almost up to his shoulders. All his friends had a great laugh at him but he did not mind. He had a pair of togs of his own. Now he was a real player.

As he played on his own in the garden he wore a Glaveys' jersey. The chairman of the club passed by at one stage and told him he was no good of a footballer unless he had his togs dirty. Immediately young Earley went into the neighbour's field and sat in a cow dung. Twenty minutes later the chairman passed by again. This time he shouted in that Earley was a great player because he had dirty togs. His mother was less than pleased at the dirt and the smell which ensued.

After getting his first pair of togs Earley was panic stricken when he saw his mother using a sewing needle on them. He was terrified that they might be torn. His anxiety abated when he discovered that she was just sewing a miraculous medal onto them. Up to the time of his marriage every pair of togs he wore had some kind of holy medal attached.

"Apart from being a religious woman my mother is also a superstitious woman. In our house on New Year's Eve we had the same ritual every year. My mother believes that if a man with a black head of hair is the first to knock at the door in the New Year it will bring luck for the rest of the year. Every year my father would slip out the back and then knock at the front door. My mother would always answer. When my father's hair started to go grey I took over.

"Another thing she would do was read to us every night. The sort of books she read were *Treasure Island* and *A Pilgrim's Progress*. She always encouraged us to read. Sometimes she told us stories of her own. I remember one was about the emergency. There was a black-out in Castlerea. All the lights were out apart from one old lady's. The soldiers went up to her and said: 'Margaret do you know there is a black-out tonight?' She replied immediately: 'If there is I'll friggin scald him'."

A recurring problem faced by Mrs Earley was to keep her son in shoes. He was always wearing out the soles of his shoes kicking ball. One day she bought him a new pair of sandals. That evening the sandals were a casualty of the ball. A piece of string concealed the evidence for two days until the crime was uncovered. For the next few hours Earley kept well out of his mother's way.

Another tense moment arose when Dermot decided to change his diet. He heard a story that the top English soccer players ate raw liver to give them additional strength. One day Earley sneaked into the kitchen and helped himself to half the liver. It was very difficult to digest and tasted ghastly but he figured it was a small price to pay for such a worthy cause. Some time later he evacuated his house with the speed of light when he heard his mother shouting: "What happened to my liver?"

Kitty Earley glows visibly as she talks about her eldest son. Her memories centre on Dermot's relationship with his father.

"Dermot never seemed to be at home. He was always either out in the fields kicking ball, farming with the neighbours or off with his dad. They were very close. Dermot has his father's temperament. Both of them got on very well with people, but I would say Dermot is more strict with his children than his father was.

"Dermot could do no wrong in his father's eyes. Now and again somebody would say Dermot had a terrible match. Peadar would always say: 'Ah no. He wasn't that bad'."

The Young Ones

Every opportunity to play football was gratefully accepted. A slight problem was that the Earley children had to return home for their lunch every day. A football match took place during lunch break. The lads in the school would begin eating their sandwiches in the classroom as soon as class ended and would have finished their lunch by the time they went out into the school yard. Earley would charge home from school and gobble down his lunch in one and a half minutes to be back on the pitch for the start of the game.

The teams were picked at the start of first break on Monday and the teams were the same for all breaks for the rest of that week. At the last break on Friday evening a cumulative score was reached, e.g. 15-135 to 12-143. Special rules applied in the games. A goalie could not score except immediately following a score against him. On one break both goalies found perfect form and everyone else was redundant as they traded point after point for ten minutes.

The most important thing every week was to ensure that both teams were properly balanced. This had almost nothing to do with skill. It was all about footwear. It was important to ensure that there was a proper mix of lads wearing wellingtons and those wearing hobnailed boots. Otherwise the side which had more lads wearing hobnailed boots had an unfair advantage.

As an enterprising teacher Peadar Earley capitalised on all the interest in football by using the football one day as a teaching aid. He was trying to explain about latitude and longitude and used a piece of chalk on a brown ball to draw lines from the North pole to the South pole. Thirty-five years on this lesson is still remembered by Dermot Earley.

"I am an expert on latitude and longitude because of that lesson. All our eyes were rivetted on the ball. If any of us had gone into meteorology or shipping we would have had a head start."

Scout's Honour

One recreational activity which his mother was happy to encourage was membership of a boy scout troop. A wide variety of skills were learned: from map-reading, to tying knots, to making a rosary beads from berries and how to bake a chicken in mud. Every Sunday morning they gathered in the woods to put their skills into practice.

Earley was indirectly responsible for precipitating a major debate in the troop. The group had been set five tasks. The one task he was unable to perform was to make a cross. He enlisted his mother's help. Each child was asked if they had got a helping hand. Earley was the only one who admitted he had. A major debate ensued. Was he to be penalised for telling the truth? Was there a message communicated to the group as a whole that honesty was not the best policy?

Yes. Yes. Yes.

In all of the matches they watched together, his father would always draw attention to facets of the game which he should pay particular attention to and learn from. The benefits of acting on his father's advice was dramatically highlighted one summer's evening.

"Glaveys were playing a big match and were losing by a big score. The game was being played in Loughlynn, in the field by the lake and John Gallagher was organising the team at half-time. He placed the goalie, backs and midfield and then looked around for forwards. I was closest to him, looking on in awe, and he caught me by the arm and said: 'Can you kick with your left foot?' My heart beat faster than ever before and I said: 'Yes'. Left half-forward he shouted, and pushed me into a position – I was on the team at the tender age of eight and a half. I got three kicks at the ball (one blocked down) but I did not care. My Dad was proud of me but not as proud as I was of myself. It was the beginning of a way of life. I am eternally grateful to John for grabbing me by the arm and also to my father who had encouraged me to practice with my left foot. 'In order to be good,' he said, 'you must kick with both feet'. Because of him I was able to play my first game with Glaveys."

Peadar Earley took every available opportunity to broaden his son's horizons. A big event in the Earley household was the purchase of their first radio. When Peadar brought the radio home on his bicycle the family wanted him to assemble it and try it out immediately. However, the operation had to be put on ice for three hours as Dermot was off playing football. His father would not hear of doing anything with the radio until he arrived back.

The radio brought a major change not just in the Earley family, but in the village as a whole because they were one of the first families to have a radio in the locality. A neighbour called around to visit the house the night they first got the radio but refused to come in because of all the strange voices. Every Sunday the GAA fans in the area would converge onto the Earley household to hear commentaries of matches on the radio.

All conversation amongst the family stopped for fifteen minutes at six-thirty while the main news was on, as Peadar listened attentively to every item. One evening he forgot about the time and made a dash for the radio at the precise moment the news was finishing. There was absolute silence as no one was sure as to how he would react to this disappointment. Then a small smile came on his lips which was the cue for everybody to laugh with gusto.

On another occasion he found himself minding the children on his own which was a very unusual occurrence as his wife was normally around. As he washed the dishes an unmerciful rumpus broke out when the children began a 'jumping off the chair competition'. Instead of getting angry that they were making so much noise his concern was that they were not jumping off the chair properly. He stood back to give them a demonstration but as the roof in the back-kitchen was very low he struck an unmerciful wallop on his head. Again the sequence of events were the same – shocked silence, apprehension, a small smile and riotous laughter.

Dermot Earley's own philosophy of life was shaped to a large extent by conversations with his father.

"I remember going to the bog with him one day. It was looking like rain and we were trying to save the turf. Our neighbours were making cocks of hay but were looking anxiously at the gathering clouds. My father said: 'Let's give them a hand. The turf can take the rain but the hay cannot. We will get the turf later but they might not get the hay'. His philosophy was: 'Always be prepared to give a helping hand'."

A Shattering Experience

As with every thing else in young Dermot Earley's life his choice of secondary school was determined by football considerations. He chose to become a boarder in St Nathy's College, Ballaghadreen in 1960 because they had won the Hogan Cup (the All-Ireland colleges senior final) in 1957 and were beaten finalists in 1959.

The regime in St Nathy's was very strict. Parents were not allowed on the school premises during term. On Earley's first Sunday in the college he ran outside the gates where his father was waiting to hear all the news. His father was in for a shock because Dermot told him that he was going to play in the juvenile trial but would talk to him when it was over. An hour and a half later Dermot returned panting. Study started in five minutes time. His father had made a round trip of 20 miles on his bicycle for less than ten minutes of conversation. Nonetheless he returned home a contented man. His son was settling down satisfactorily in his new school and had acquitted himself in the juvenile trial.

Earley's first appearance in the St Nathy's colours was memorable for the wrong reason. They lost by 7-7 to 0-0.

In Earley's five years in St Nathy's the biggest footballing thorn in their side was St Jarlath's College Tuam, in general and their star player Jimmy Duggan, in particular St Jarlath's regularly thwarted St Nathy's ambitions in the Connacht championship at all grades. The only exceptions were in 1963 when Earley captained the juvenile team to the Connacht title and 1965 when he captained the junior side to championship glory.

Earley also made a big impression on the college basketball scene though he missed out on selection on the International under-age sides because of his footballing commitments.

One of the biggest handicaps of boarding school life at the time was that pupils were deprived of access to newspapers and radio. This created a lot of problems for the sports fanatics. One night in 1964 the whole dorm engaged in illicit activity by listening to the classic Mohammed Ali – Sonny Liston fight.

However, Earley's most enduring memory of his time in college is the day he discovered that his father did not have the full truth on every issue.

"Before I went to Nathy's my father said to me: 'You and me are more like brothers than father and son'. I had total and unreserved respect for him. I felt he was totally infallible. It was a grave disappointment to me to discover for the first time that he was not totally right about everything. I was absolutely devastated.

"I expected everybody else to have the exact same respect for him as I did. I remember once a man coming to our house who asked me to give a message to my 'auld fella'. I refused because he had called my father an 'auld fella'. I was furious that he could have such little respect for such a great man."

A Passionate Priest

News of young Earley's performances reached the ears of the Roscommon minor selectors. He was picked for a challenge match against Westmeath minors in 1963 when he was just fifteen. His opponent ran rings around him and scored at will.

At one point in the game a high ball came into the Roscommon square. Earley lunged desperately for it and accidentally struck his tormentor in the solar plexus with his elbow. His opponent went down like a sack of potatoes and was knocked out cold.

The Roscommon minor selectors were happy with his performance. Even though he had been completely outclassed, at least he had the capacity to 'look after' the main threat to the Roscommon goal. Accordingly he was retained for the Connacht minor semi-final against Leitrim. After their final training session before the game the team congregated in a cafe in Roscommon. Fr Pat Brady, whose brother Aidan is rated as one of the greatest goalkeepers of all time, was the team coach and he gave a lengthy talk on the tactics for the game. He made extensive use of the blackboard to illustrate the main points of his instructions.

Fr Brady's final words took the team by surprise: "I am living up there on the Leitrim border and I am sick to death hearing what Leitrim are going to do to Roscommon next Sunday. When ye have beaten Leitrim by 5 goals and 65 points would ye ever kick the skiterin football up their skiterin arses."

There was stunned silence. This was very avant-garde language from a priest in 1963. After what seemed like an eternity somebody laughed. Within 30 seconds the whole team had collapsed with laughter. Somebody whispered: "By Gawd. He's an awful man."

Apart from his own father Earley credits Fr Pat as one of the formative influences on his career. Other important people were Dr Donal Keenan the chairman of the county board, Phil Gannon the county secretary, Michael O'Callaghan the chairman of the minor selection committee, Sean Brady the county treasurer, Gerry Finneran who was responsible for transporting the team around, and Fr Tom Lynch who did a lot of coaching in Nathy's: "They were all gentlemen and ensured that I was properly looked after."

Roscommon did beat Leitrim but not by the score Fr Brady specified, but only to lose to Mayo in the Connacht final. Apart from Earley, the other player on the team who would play a major role in Roscommon football in years to come was Tom Heneghan, who scored a goal from a penalty in the Connacht final.

The disappointment at losing the Connacht final was quickly forgotten as Michael Glaveys won the Roscommon juvenile final. Apart from county medals the prize for winning was a trip to Croke Park for the All-Ireland final courtesy of a cigarette company who took a juvenile side from a different county each year. The whole team headed off on a bus to see Dublin beat Galway in the final.

The One That Got Away

Two years later Earley was back in Croke Park again, only this time as a player. As Connacht minor champions Roscommon played Derry in the All-Ireland semi-final. It was a significant weekend for Earley because his Leaving Cert results were out the day before the game. Earley headed for Dublin with the rest of the team as the results were being made available. He was not going to jeopardise his preparations for the game by waiting around for a piece of paper. That night Michael O'Callaghan congratulated all the players on the panel who had done their Leaving Cert because they had all passed.

"Looking back now I doubt very much that he had contacted all the schools involved to see if we had all passed our exams. However, I was delighted he said those words because it helped me to relax."

Roscommon played well only to lose by 4-8 to 4-5. The turning point in the match was when Earley missed a penalty.

"I hit the ball as hard as I could. It rose high for the top right-hand corner but as it got closer to the goal it started to tail badly wide. I fell prostrate on the ground. I had never felt such devastation up to that moment."

The following day it was back to Gorthaganny. He was still in a slump of depression. Not even confirmation of his Leaving Cert results raised a ghost of a smile.

Kitty Earley remembers the night well.

"I have never seen Dermot so quiet as he was after that game. We could hardly get a word out of him. It took him days to get over it. I know he lost bigger games after that, but that's the one that stands out in my mind as his worst moment."

That night his father tried to give him a lift by pointing out that he was now part of an elite group of players who had missed a penalty in Croke Park. He rattled off a list of illustrious players who had suffered the same fate. Whatever about the company he had joined he still felt absolutely miserable.

3. An Officer and a Gentleman

"What are you going to be when you grow up?" was the standard question all parents asked their children as they grew older. It is probably a symptom of the changing times we are living in, that today the question has become: "What are you going to do when you leave school?" Childhood ends much earlier these days. Teenagers take umbrage at any suggestion that they require any further maturity.

In rural Ireland in the early 1960s career options were limited. Free education was not a reality until the late 1960s, which meant that many young people, particularly boys, left school after completing their primary education. The yellow school buses which became a familiar part of the rural landscape in the 1970s, as they transported teenagers from the country areas, did not exist. This excluded many children from the education system at a young age. The 'lucky' ones were sent to boarding schools, where the parents could afford to pay their fees. A small minority were 'encouraged' to cycle into school every day. Some had a sixteen mile cycle twice a day.

Those lucky enough to get to the Leaving Certificate stage were an elite group. The most coveted prize awaiting them was a permanent pensionable job. Security was all important. Anything which involved risk was at best frowned upon, at worst discarded. For this reason, the Civil Service, the bank and teaching were the most popular choices. Even today, many people are still deprived of the opportunity to receive a third level education. Thirty years ago, the numbers attending university were considerably smaller. There was a quiet (in some cases not so quiet) satisfaction for any family which produced a priest or a nun.

For an aspiring young footballer in west Roscommon a particularly energetic and adventurous career was necessary. No single factor prompted Earley's decision to enter the army cadet school, but a variety of factors came together like converging lines.

"In my mind the army was the number one choice. Had I not got the army, I would have gone to university in Galway, probably to study agricultural science, but I was so set on joining the army that I never really considered anything else. My uncle had joined the cadet school in the 1950s and had been commissioned as an officer. I knew that army life involved adventure, excitement, sporting activities and tremendous variety. You never did the same army exercise twice in the one week.

"The army's profile received an enormous boost in 1960 when the government decided to send peace-keeping forces to the United Nations for the first time. We sent battalions to the Congo, and this attracted massive publicity and media attention. There were parades in Dublin and the travelling officers were received in Aras an Uachtarain. I still recall a photograph of President de Valera sitting in front of the officers, and I also remember a picture of my uncle with his foot on the bumper of a Landrover, as he made preparations to go with his battalion to the Congo – all this excited me."

However, it was exposure to the FCA which turned this interest into something more substantial.

"There was a unit of the FCA in Castlerea and a sub-unit in my area. The young men in the locality met on Tuesday nights at the local hall, where they practised drill and weapon training. I liked the order, the discipline, the unity of the effort, and the fact that the people acted on the prompt of a command. These are all little things but they left their mark on me.

"Then there were the stories of these young men going to camp, usually to Finner, near Bundoran, and having a great time shooting, taking part in sporting competitions and being away from home. A lot of these lads got big red boots with their issue of uniform. To many young people in the locality, it was important that they would be well shod for the winter. I was initially interested in joining the FCA because there was the possibility of being involved in a good football team.

"I joined the FCA when I was fourteen, which was illegal of course, but quite a number of young people were involved in the organisation at that time. It is much more difficult now, you have to be seventeen and produce your birth certificate.

"My father thought it was a good idea because you learned discipline. I was sworn in at the gate of my house one Friday night, with my father watching, by the local training officer, Captain Jim Fives. He played hurling for Galway, Waterford and Roscommon and was regarded as being a fine sportsman. (In 1984 he was selected as right full-back on the centenary team of greatest players who had never won an All-Ireland senior championship medal). My father knew him well and when Jim asked him about my joining the FCA, my father had no hesitation."

Lethal Weapon

Initially new recruits were taught the basic training techniques such as marching and drilling with a weapon. For many, FCA life was a cultural shock, with very early morning risings, having to be spic and span and not having their mothers to shine their buttons. The food was also very different. For breakfast and tea each recruit got a quarter of a batch loaf with a lump of butter on top. The only redeeming aspect of this spartan routine was that wash-ups presented no problem, as no plates were used! The main meal was lunch, which offered more substantial fare and a varied menu each day. As a special treat, a fry was provided on Sunday mornings.

Responsibility for the new recruits lay on the shoulders of the NCOs (non-commissioned officers). Apart from looking after their welfare, the NCOs also faced the hazardous task of moulding an ungainly group of green recruits into a competent, tightly-knit group of young 'soldiers'. They also had to ensure that the recruits returned home without inflicting any damage on themselves or on their companions, not the easiest of assignments as training involved learning to throw grenades and target practice. In their second year they were taught to shoot mortars.

"Never at any stage did it enter my head that all of this training in weapons was with a view to educating us to be able to kill or maim other human beings. At that time we only thought of the fun and excitement of it and of enjoying the crack. We were very lucky that there were older people who were more mature in the FCA who kept an eye on us and made sure we got back to the camp on time. There was never any conflict or problems with any of the groups in my time there."

Visiting the Public House

To help prevent monotony and to keep morale at the optimum level, a feature of the time in Finner was regular excursions into Bundoran. These trips allowed the recruits to be a bit more relaxed and to let their hair down a little, though excesses were not allowed nor even contemplated, because there was always a supervising presence in the immediate vicinity. With a twinkle in his eye Earley recounts a particular trip to Bundoran which provided a uniquely FCA version of the *Tales of the Unexpected.*

"One of the senior lads came along and said: 'Be ready in five minutes, we are going into Bundoran to the public house'. We all jumped to the one conclusion, but he had something else in mind. I was not so sure about the public house, but I went along to see what would happen. There was no question of us drinking alcohol, all we really wanted was a spin. A journey in an old Anglia car in normal circumstances would not excite great enthusiasm but it was preferable to walking.

"I will never forget the shock we got when we found out that the public house he was talking about, was in fact the Catholic Church in Bundoran. I've pulled that trick many times since then, on groups I've taken on football trips, and once on my own family. No one has ever complained. They all laugh and have the same reaction as I did.

"The following year I was involved in another incident with the same man and the same Anglia car. A group of us were travelling home from Finner to Roscommon. On the way home we called into the Carlton cafe in Sligo. We ordered a 'super-mix grill' which was going to consist of steak, rashers, sausage and egg. Ravenous with hunger we sat and waited for our meal, savouring all the smells from the kitchen. As she set the table the waitress noticed that one of the group was wearing a pioneer pin and she asked us in an embarrassed way if we realised that it was a Friday. Of course it had totally slipped our minds. In 1963 the 'Friday fast' was still in operation. The meal which had been half prepared was hastily cancelled and we made a more appropriate order of scrambled eggs."

Pay As You Earn

The fourteen year old prospective army officer returned from his first two-week stint with the FCA as the proud possessor of £9, a relative fortune for a boy in 1962. However, the money was not intended for any personal indulgence.

"My father's parents died when he was very young, and he told me a story that always remained at the back of my mind. He told me that he had given the first wages that he earned as a teacher to the man who had brought him up. I never forgot that story, so when I came back from Finner I gave the £9 to my mother. She refused to take it.

"Three years later when I entered the cadet school I got a cheque for £4 for my first week in the army. I cashed the cheque and sent four crisp pound notes to my father. I can still see those pound notes. They were bigger and greener than those of the 1980s. Apparently he was very moved by the gesture and put the money in his wallet. It was still in his wallet when we went through his personal effects after he died in 1983."

A Non-Trivial Pursuit

Apart from the £9 another addition to the Earley household was a new rifle which was part of his legacy from his stay in Finner. The rifle was carefully placed on top of the dresser and was periodically taken down to be cleaned and fondled affectionately.

One day, Dermot, as oldest child was entrusted with the responsibility of 'minding the house' and looking after this brothers and sisters. Unfortunately this duty was discharged with excessive zeal. A small group of young travellers were loitering around the family home when the rifle was swiftly taken down from the dresser and was suddenly produced out in the garden to scare off the travellers. Not surprisingly they dispersed with the speed of light.

"It is something I regret very much and obviously as I got more sense I saw the folly of my action. That family of travellers have remained in the area. Every time I return home they approach me and ask: 'Do you remember the time you took down the rifle?' Although it was very serious at the time it is a great laugh now."

JFK

Another contributory factor to his career plans was the visit of John F Kennedy to Ireland in 1963. Although most people were enthralled by the charismatic figure of the President, his moving speech to the Oireachtas, and his return to his ancestral homeland, the aspect of the visit which was noticed most by Earley was the time the cadets formed a guard of honour in his presence. The glamour of the occasion appealed enormously to a young lad who was thirsty for adventure and excitement. This appeal was accentuated when the Irish government received a request from America to be present at President Kennedy's funeral in Arlington, which the government acceded to. The eyes of Ireland and the world were on that funeral, and there in the midst of all that attention were the Irish cadets. If any proof was needed that life in the cadets would produce drama and excitement, this was it. This was the incident which finally sealed his career choice.

However, family conditioning also pointed to the army as a very attractive career option.

"My father was very nationalistic. I felt that when I confirmed relatives' queries about my intentions to join the army, that he thought this was a good choice. He never actually said anything about it, but I detected that he was secretly very pleased. An important consideration was that I would be serving my country. This may sound funny and old-fashioned, and I'm aware that a lot of people would reject this thinking today, but to me it was an important factor."

The Road Not Taken

Although when Earley made his decision to become an army officer he did not consider any other career, in later life he developed a keen interest in another profession.

"As I increased my knowledge of physical education during my army career, the thing that began to interest me most was the medical side. If I was to win the Lotto, I would love to have the opportunity to study medicine. I feel there is a lot of potential, in this profession, for somebody to do so much good, by improving the quality of health of the people. I am always impressed by the medical profession and the way they conduct themselves, by their calmness and dedication. I've never regretted not having a formal third education *per se*. When I entered the cadet school that option was not there, but nowadays our cadets have the opportunity to receive a third level education. If I could do it all again I would think seriously about medicine."

Fixing a Puncture and Turkish Cypriots

Having completed his Leaving Certificate the previous June, in August 1965 Earley travelled expectantly to St Bricin's Hospital to do a medical examination, an oral Irish exam, and then an interview for the army, all in the one day. In recent years the system has been changed so that preliminary interviews are conducted on a regional basis and successful applicants are sent for final interviews to McKee Barracks or St Bricin's Hospital in Dublin.

No information was forthcoming about his progress in the three examinations. However, he knew that he would not have been allowed to sit for the other two had he failed the initial medical. The oral Irish went extremely well until he was afflicted by a temporary surge of panic when he was asked to explain how he would go about fixing a puncture on a bicycle, in the conditional tense!

Although there were a number of people on the interview panel, one officer asked most of the questions, in accordance with conventional practice at the time.

"I cannot remember any of the questions I was asked or any of my answers, except one. I said there were far more Turkish Cypriots than Greek Cypriots in Cyprus and of course it was the other way around. I am not sure if they were impressed by the way I stuck to my guns when I was invited to reconsider my answer and declined to do so. To my horror, I discovered that my answer was hopelessly incorrect when I checked it out that night and the *faux pas* bothered me a bit. Nonetheless I was still hopeful that I would be accepted. Perhaps my conviction outweighed my ignorance."

Seven weeks later the postman finally brought the long awaited news and 26 October was designated as the day when the aspiring Officer Earley would begin his military training.

"In retrospect the journey from Gorthaganny to the Curragh was a major expedition, taking almost the whole day to get there before the appointed time of 4 p.m. We made it with half an hour to spare."

One of the first issues which had to be resolved was how army life could be married with an inter-county football career for Roscommon.

"I had played in the All-Ireland minor semi-final against Derry in August. A month later I played my first senior match for Roscommon, in the Gael-Linn cup against Leitrim in Carrick-on-Shannon and a few weeks later I played my first National League match. My father consulted the deputy cadet master, the late Commandant Eddie Condon about my footballing situation. Commandant Condon had played football for both Kerry and Galway and told me that once he had worn the Roscommon jersey. Months later I finally plucked up the courage to ask him about this. He explained that he had also played for Connacht, and in that capacity had worn the primrose and blue.

"He understood the situation I was in, on the verge of becoming an established player with Roscommon but also starting my army career. His decision was that he would not allow me to play county football for three months because I needed to devote all my attention into settling into a new way of life. After Christmas, if everything was going well, he saw no difficulty in my playing for Roscommon. He also said I would be playing plenty of football in the Curragh. I thought that was fair."

Hair Today, Gone Tomorrow

1978 is remembered by many people as 'the year of three popes'. The final week in October 1965 is remembered by Dermot Earley as the week of the three haircuts. The morning of his departure to the Curragh he made an early visit to a barber in Castlerea to look the part for this debut in army life. The next day he was introduced to the routine and regulations of life in the cadet school. The cadets were marched to all their destinations. In the middle of all this activity Dermot got a gentle tap on his shoulder from an NCO, and was despatched to the block for a haircut. Three hours later he was pulled aside by another army officer and sent for a further haircut.

"All of this seems very funny when you look back on it now, but at the time it was very serious. One wondered what was going to happen next. In actual fact the hair was not cut very short. At that time the fashion was to have very long hair. I remember going back to St Nathy's a few years later to talk to a group of Leaving Certs about a career in the army. The two main questions were how often do you have to get a haircut and how long can you wear your hair. It was not a question of having very short hair like in the marines but of ensuring that it was short at the back and sides. My black crop probably did not show enough white spaces at the back after the first and second visits to the barber, but the third attempt did the trick and brought me up to the required standard of presentation. In the following months one visit per week sufficed."

The regime in which the cadets operated was a very demanding one. Discipline was very strict. Some of the duties were menial. The hours were long. The old approach to training, which has since been quietly shelved, still prevailed in the 1960s. This approach was typified by the practice in Westpoint (though not in the Curragh) the famous American military academy, where senior cadets stood millimetres before trainee officers and stared them in the eyes for a few minutes. A young officer cadet was expected not to flinch, blink or return the stare. The theory was that this exercise helped to build up tremendous character. Failure to measure up to these standards led to draconian punishments, such as a few hundred press-ups or ten laps around the park.

"Some of the things you were asked to do were very stupid, such as digging the grass off the tarmacadam with a spoon. I could not see much point in repolishing brass when it was impossible to get a shine on any better. However, I knew there was a system to be upheld, you were not there to question, you just did it. The tasks were designated to ascertain whether or not you would follow orders without question. I've noticed that many of the officer regimes which put junior people under intense pressure are now being dropped, and dropped very quickly. There is a much more enlightened approach to nurturing young leaders today."

Lieutenant Late

Another pleasing aspect of military life was the number of new sports to which the cadets were introduced, such as rugby.

"I had never seen a rugby ball until I went into the army. When I was growing up in Gorthaganny, my father and I always listened to Ireland's rugby matches on the radio. There was always intense interest in these matches in our house because an All-Ireland team was competing. I can remember all the names of the players from my childhood, Niall Henderson at full-back kicking the penalties and later Tom Kiernan came on the team, Gordon Wood, Cecil Pedlow and Tony O'Reilly. In a pre-television era, I knew very little about the way the game was played, apart from a few things my father had told me. I knew that it involved moving the ball from one end of the field to the other. The phrase from the commentaries that always rung in my ears was 'he dived across the line for a try'. With a Gaelic football under my arm I would go out into the back garden after the matches and start diving through the air and crashing across an imaginary line for yet another try for Ireland."

On entering the Curragh, Dermot's size and weight alone ensured that he got a place on the rugby team, initially as a prop forward. However, there were two major adjustments to be made in his game. Every time he got the ball he ran forward but when he was tackled instead of passing the ball to a team mate he retained possession and his Gaelic training, which led him to instinctively kick the ball upfield, thus handing possession to the opposing team. He also caused intense aggravation to opponents and referees by engaging in the 'third man tackle' which was then allowed in Gaelic football. This enabled a player to legitimately tackle an opponent who was not in possession of the ball under certain circumstances. However, this practice was an anathema to rugby referees and cadet Earley's first matches were characterised by much finger wagging. On one or two occasions opposing teams thought a verbal rebuke from an irate referee was grossly insufficient and they took the law into their own hands. The lesson was quickly learned.

After starting his rugby career as a prop forward Dermot progressed or regressed, depending on your point of view, to the second row, to wing forward until eventually he found his best position at full-back. Apart from the enjoyment of playing the game, the rugby games were useful because they helped to bond the new cadets together away from the strict discipline and tension of military life. They also provided an outlet for people to get to know each other in a more informal setting.

An annual event in the military college was a triangular competition between Clongowes College, the Dominican College, Newbridge and the cadet school. In his second year, as place-kicker for the cadet school, Earley exchanged penalties with Mick Quinn, (who would eventually play in the out-half position for Ireland), in a match against Dominican College. The previous year he lost out on the place-kicking duel to a future captain of the Irish team, Tom Grace.

With practice, Dermot became an accomplished rugby player which led to his elevation to the senior rugby team at the Curragh to play in the Leinster Provincial Towns Cup. However, this advancement brought its own problems because the ban was still in operation, which prevented Gaelic footballers or hurlers from playing 'foreign' games. Now that he was playing rugby to a high standard, he had to play in front of the national media.

"It would have been folly for me to be seen playing rugby from a GAA point of view. We could only have fourteen players in the team photograph. Sometimes the referee might stand in for me. This became a great joke in rugby circles. I remember on one occasion a referee walking on to the field and saying: 'Let's get the photograph over, because I know I have to stand in here for your man'."

In the light of the ban it was not possible for a prominent player like Dermot Earley, to have his name appearing in reports about rugby matches without serious consequences. So an assumed name was invented for him by the press officer of the rugby team – Lieutenant Earley became Lieutenant Late.

"At no time did anyone ever approach me and say you should not play rugby because of the ban. I did receive a friendly warning once, after I played in a provincial town's semi-final with the Curragh in Tullamore against Navan. Dr Donal Keenan approached me a few weeks later and said: 'I know you were playing in that rugby match in Tullamore. I have got a warning from John Dowling, who was the Offaly county secretary at the time (later to become President of the GAA) just to be careful because there might be a few people in Leinster who might press for action against you or Roscommon, for that matter'. It was a very friendly warning. Neither of them had any real intention of taking any action against me."

On one occasion, when the Curragh won an important match, the headline in the match report on the following day read: 'Lieutenant Late scores winning try for the Curragh'.

"The whole thing with the ban had become ridiculous. During one of my first free weekends in the cadet school I went to see Shamrock Rovers play for the first time. They had been my favourite team since I was a young boy. I really wanted to see stars like Bobby Gilbert who were great players and household names, but I was not able to enjoy the match because I kept thinking someone would see me there and report me and I would get banned."

It is difficult to believe that twenty-five years ago such a situation existed. In 1943 one of the GAA's most illustrious sons, former Taoiseach, Jack Lynch, was suspended for three months for attending a rugby match. The ban went out with a whimper. Dermot Earley was one of the prominent hurlers and footballers who was polled by Mick Dunne on their views of the ban. Not a single player supported it. However,

Dermot has little time for wallowing in the past. He is much more anxious to shape the future.

Two Voices

Listening to Dermot Earley talking about the most controversial issues in the GAA one can hear two voices: that of a passionate supporter of the GAA, and that of a man who is genuinely concerned that the organisation may need to make some fundamental changes if it is to command the same loyalty in the next century as it has in the last one hundred and eight years.

Irish people do not like criticism. It is a national weakness. When we say 'he criticised me', it is not the words themselves but the pained tone which is all important. The tone is one of wounded offence. Criticism is almost always seen as a pejorative term. To be criticised is comparable to being assaulted.

In recent years the GAA has been subject to extensive criticism from certain quarters. Some of this criticism has been misinformed and unfair. In some cases the GAA's enormous contribution to Irish life is ignored. Understandably the GAA is sensitive to criticism.

Dermot Earley needs the GAA like the rest of us need oxygen. Any criticism of the GAA is not in spite of his love for the organisation but because of it. His main concern is to raise the right sort of questions and to offer helpful distinctions. When he does criticise the GAA it is never a blanket condemnation, but focuses on precise points. Critical comments are never cynical, never global, but always hit a very definite point with a definite purpose. They are offered in a spirit of service, an effort to improve the organisation's communication with a rapidly changing Irish society, while at the same time remaining very deeply concerned for the authenticity and identity of the organisation. He is always constructive.

"I know at one particular stage that the ban served a purpose, but it took us a long time to replace it and I think we have been the better for it. Everybody was glad that it went.

"Another question which has come to the fore, is whether there is a hidden ban in operation today which compels us to prevent soccer or rugby from interfering with our games. This problem was highlighted in 1991 with the infamous 'RDS affair'.

"As a GAA person I feel the responsibility for that debacle falls on my shoulders as much as anybody else's. We certainly handled the situation very badly. We did not keep the public informed as they deserved to be informed. Moreover we certainly did not appear to keep the club informed. They were led to believe that the game was going ahead and had put massive preparations into it. Then all of a sudden they had the rug pulled from under them. To this day nobody knows why.

"I think that had the GAA said no from the very outset, there would have been disappointment and some criticism initially, but that would have been the end of it. However, there was an agreement to have it, providing certain conditions were met. Great efforts were made to meet those conditions and then out of the blue the decision was reversed. We certainly shot ourselves in the foot.

"The biggest complaint I have is that people did not know what was going on. The GAA have a duty to inform people about such matters because it is the people in Newbridge, and west Roscommon and all over Ireland who are paying their hard-earned money to keep the GAA going. If we do not have our supporters, we have nothing. We treated them with a form of arrogance which is simply unacceptable."

Sporting Ecumenism

Earley is very clear about his own attitude to the GAA's relationship with other sporting bodies. In principle he favours the use of GAA facilities for other sporting activities in certain circumstances.

"The GAA is under pressure to have its pitches used for other sports. Broadly speaking I think that this would be a healthy development. However, I have one reservation, they should only be allowed on certain occasions. Otherwise we would have problems accommodating our own games and there might be a risk of damage to our pitches.

"If Ireland were doing well in the forthcoming World Cup series, and let us say they were playing their final home match in the knowledge that they needed a win to qualify, then if the FAI were to approach the

GAA to stage the match in Croke Park, we should accede to that request automatically. The team would be guaranteed an additional twenty thousand vociferous supporters and this would help the boys in green enormously. However, I would be opposed to Ireland playing all their soccer matches in Croke Park.

"I am convinced that if the GAA was to make such a gesture, an enormous fund of goodwill would be generated which would be to the organisation's advantage, even if it was only once a year that a match was played. There are those who would be very strongly opposed to the idea, but in my view they are only a minority. Unfortunately, they are in a controlling position in the GAA. Within the organisation it is very difficult to get changes introduced. For example, if I want to have a motion passed to allow soccer to be played, I have to go to my club with the motion, have it passed by my club, then go on and hopefully get it passed by my County Board and finally get it passed by Congress. How many prominent players go on to become top officials? Most people cannot be bothered by all the red tape and bureaucracy. I have absolutely no doubt that the majority of Irish people, particularly young people would like to see a much more flexible system in operation."

Many people find it strange that the GAA is unwilling to allow soccer matches in Croke Park but has apparently no problem in allowing it to be used for rock concerts. Some of the bands which have 'graced' GAA headquarters, such as Simple Minds, have little in common with the ideals of the organisation in cultural terms. However, rock concerts are not seen as a threat to the playing of Gaelic games whereas soccer matches are.

Two main problems with the staging of rock concerts in GAA stadia have presented themselves. Apparently there has been more damage done to Croke Park following some concerts in the past, than there would have been if soccer matches had been played on the pitch. Following the 'Trip to Tipp' concert in 1991 there was considerable comment that such concerts contributed to the problem of under-age drinking.

"I think it is good to have concerts in GAA stadia if that is what young people want, provided there are proper controls. Apart from anything else, concerts and soccer matches in our grounds make excellent commercial sense. The profits could be used to promote the game and to fund coaching programmes."

Although Dermot Earley is particularly concerned with what he sees as a 'hidden ban' in the GAA at the present time, in terms of its dealings with other sporting organisations, he is also very troubled by the one formal ban that still remains in the GAA constitution, which prevents British army or RUC personnel becoming members of the GAA. In this context, it is worth noting, that when the Down team returned home with the Sam Maguire Cup in 1991 – the most popular extradition in recent times – that while they stopped at the Border checkpoint, they noticed a huge Red and Black flag hanging from the British Army post.

"I feel that we have reached a stage in our development where we have no need for bans. A ban for whatever reason is negative. It would be a further stage of our development were we to end bans which block people from becoming members of our organisation. If we want to be not only an Irish organisation, but a worldwide organisation too, then we should be big enough to allow anybody to enter.

"I know that there are certain sections of the community, particularly in the north of Ireland, that feel it is necessary to have a ban as a protest against certain alleged activities of the RUC or the British army. For historic reasons these feelings are understandable.

"However, the GAA has to think of the organisation as a whole. Personally, I feel very strongly that this ban can no longer be justified. Does the ban not amount to our equivalent of the 'No Surrender' mentality?"

The normal pleasant, easy-going Earley manner promptly disappears at the notion that is sometimes expressed, that the ban is but a symptom of a deeper underlying anti-English feeling within the GAA. A perceptible undercurrent of anger is evident in his voice as he responds to that accusation.

"I always resent the implication that the GAA is bigoted and anti-English because immediately, as a member, I am tarnished with that accusation. I do not want to be associated with that kind of mentality. We have our games in many parts of England and we want to promote our games in England. Irish teams play in Luton town and at Wembley stadium. I played in Wembley in 1973 with the All-Stars. I wish I had played in Wembley many other times. It was wonderful to play there.

"We expect the British government to support our games over there and to make facilities and grants available. We will take any grant that is available from the authorities in Northern Ireland. There are a small minority of people in the GAA who have anti-English feelings. It saddens, and troubles me, particularly as these people tend to be in positions of authority. You have to admire people who put in the effort to take responsibility in the organisation, because too many of us have not the patience for committee work. As a result, minority views in terms of the overall membership sometimes take centre stage. Perhaps it is time that something was done to change this situation, so that the voice of the silent majority may be heard in the future."

Dermot has strong opinions on the development of the national games. In particular he would like to see the GAA blazing a greater trail on the international stage.

"I feel we have not made the most of the possibilities in this area. The New Zealand All-Blacks went to Trinity College for their warm-up before they played Australia in the rugby World Cup semi-final in 1991. They played a light game of Gaelic football. All of those guys knew how to play. This incident got little media coverage, but it was very significant. We are international now and we have to run with that. It is possible that because of the rules of the organisation, which stipulate that international trips have to be self-financing, we have hesitated developing the international dimension. The best way to promote our games internationally, is to send teams abroad, but that costs money. To date, the GAA has been reticent in investing funds in this area. I would like to see resources allocated in such a way that there is a greater international dimension possible.

"I feel that to a certain extent we are hamstrung by a siege mentality. At the moment we have a large slice of the national cake in sporting terms. Our priority is to hold on to that share of the cake rather than trying to earn a larger slice or to go for a different cake. If, through the playing of our games, we pick up another few crumbs of the cake, fair enough. However, we are not going out there aggressively enough to win the cake."

Comic Relief

Sporting activity was an important outlet from life in the cadet school, providing a welcome break from the tension of a regimented environment. However, tension was also diffused by funny incidents and misadventures, which transformed very serious situations into comedy shows. On other occasions the humour was evident only after the event itself.

"One day there was a room inspection. I had gathered all the rubbish that I needed to dispose of, but I had forgotten to actually dump it. To my horror I discovered it just before my room was due for inspection. Thinking quickly, I put the dustbin into my duffel bag, which I used to carry my football gear. Then I put the bag out the back window which faced on to a public road. Seconds later the inspection began. Everything was going beautifully until a little lad came bursting in the door carrying the bag in his hands saying: 'Is this yours mister?' As you can imagine this caused a little bit of difficulty.

"Another day I was in my room getting ready for an inspection in the square. It was one of those formal events where everything had to be absolutely perfect. Before I went out for parade I checked myself in the mirror. With my shoulders square, my chest out and my rifle on my back, I must confess that I thought I looked pretty good. Unfortunately, as I turned around and put my gun on my shoulder, the rifle hit an almighty wallop on the lampshade, shattering both the shade and the bulb to pieces. Pressed for time, I brushed myself off and disposed of the evidence under the bed. As I stood stiffly waiting for inspection the Officer-in-Charge walked behind me only to return with a large piece of lampshade. He was curious to what piece of new equipment I was introducing to army life! As I was going redder than beetroot with embarrassment, my colleagues were trying vainly not to breach military etiquette by bursting into laughter during inspection time.

"During the times we were on parade, giggles would start for the most trivial of reasons and the giggling would become infectious. The harder we tried to suppress them, the louder they became. For example, years later I returned to the cadet school to record a piece on physical fitness for an advertisement we were making. There was a stunningly beautiful lady photographer taking shots of the event, and to get the best possible picture she had to take up very suggestive postures from unusual angles. As you can imagine, our lads had never seen anything like it before, and they found it incredibly difficult to keep straight faces.

"Another time, one of my fellow cadets was marched into the Cadet Master's office. The cadet was very nervous. The NCO who was accompanying him suddenly cried 'Halt' not realising that the floor had just been polished – well the cadet went sliding in under the Cadet Master's desk and crashed straight into his chair. It was a sight to behold."

In the 1960s, all army business in the cadet school was done through Irish, as was every other subject apart from English. To this day commands are given in Irish but all other business is conducted through English. At that time, when cadets had to speak to officers, or on a formal basis to each other, the conversation was through Irish. To encourage cadets to improve their Gaeilge, a three week visit to Ring in County Waterford was an integral part of their training.

On one excursion the cadets went down with the Cadet Master and set up camp in a big field. There were thirty or forty tents for accommodation and large marquees for dining-rooms. All of the army vehicles were parked in the same field, but the Cadet Master was appalled to discover that all the trucks had been parked with their noses facing into the ditches. He instructed the Sergeant Major, in Gaeilge, to ensure that all the trucks were turned around before he returned two hours later. Unfortunately the Sergeant Major's Irish was not what it might have been. When the Cadet master returned two hours later he was surprised to see that there was not an army vehicle in sight. He asked the Sergeant major where they were gone. The Sergeant Major looked at his watch and said: 'I'd say they are in Clonmel by now'. He had thought the instruction had meant to send the trucks back - and he did!

A Young Man on the Up

Although many cadets found the going tough in the Curragh, Dermot Earley found life in the army almost a picnic. The ease with which he adjusted to army life proved baffling for the Cadet Master. In the course of their first one-to-one interview Dermot explained the reasons for his complete happiness in the army.

"I did not find the army discipline a problem. Before I arrived at the Curragh I had spent five years in St Nathy's. We were not allowed newspapers, radio, television (except for educational programmes), visitors or food parcels. That was a difficult regime to live in. At the Curragh, I had the papers laid on for me every day, radio and television and I was being paid for it all."

The Barracks

Having completed his two-year stint in the cadet school Dermot hoped for an exciting new challenge in fresh pastures. However, there was initial disappointment when he discovered that he was commissioned to McDonagh barracks which was little more than the proverbial stone's throw away from the cadet's school. After a week's leave the disappointment quickly dissipated and he returned full of enthusiasm for his first post.

His task was to take full responsibility of a platoon of new recruits and to turn them into fully fledged soldiers in a sixteen-to eighteen-weeks period. To help him achieve this objective he had the assistance of three or four experienced NCOs who showed him the ropes and helped him to become a good young officer. The cadet school had provided good theory and some invaluable practice experience, but much of the cut and thrust of army life cannot be learnt in a classroom. For a young officer, experience is the best teacher, and within a short time Dermot found himself in charge of one hundred and twenty men.

Apart from the actual training of the recruits, an essential element of the officer's workload was to ensure that morale was sustained at the highest level. This meant that every recruit's welfare had to be monitored on an individual basis and that collectively the group of young men with boundless energy had to be entertained. Anything that might hold a group's attention, from intellectual pursuits such as question times, to more physical activities such as boxing tournaments were organised.

Although sport was an essential component of the kaleidoscope of life in McDonagh barracks, discipline cast an all-embracing shadow on the recruits' daily routine. The first lesson a new recruit learns is that every officer must be addressed as 'Sir'. One new recruit learned this lesson in a dramatic fashion.

"One day I was walking out to meet a new platoon. My eyes met a young man from my home place and as he recognised me he said: 'Howya Dermot'. The company Sergeant, who was unfortunately hovering nearby, immediately hauled this young man away and for the next ten minutes roared into his ear, from about an inch behind him, all the reasons why he should speak to officers properly. That meant calling them by their proper name, which was 'Sir' only. He then told him, in the most emphatic way possible, that never ever in the history of his life in the army, was he to call an officer by his first name again.

"It was very difficult for me to subsequently approach this young man and quietly welcome him to the army. In a quiet moment I said: 'When we are in here, let's keep at a little distance, but when we are at home, it's the same as normal – I am no different than when you said: 'Howya Dermot' a few hours earlier'.

"The other memory I have of McDonagh barracks was the amount of effort some young men would put into trying to get everything exactly right. I remember the NCOs trying to teach a particular group of recruits how to salute, in which one young chap was so intent on getting it absolutely right that every time he tried to salute, his tongue would come out and lodge in the side of his face in a grotesque way. This spectacle threw both the officers and fellow recruits into fits of laughter. These were the lighter moments which eased the tension and brought an air of humanity to army training, by making it more enjoyable."

During his term in McDonagh barracks a vacancy arose for a Physical Training Instructor in the Army School of Physical Culture which was also in the McDonagh barracks. The position seemed tailor-made for a young officer with a rapidly developing reputation as a Gaelic footballer, and a passionate interest in physical fitness. Before Dermot could take up his new appointment he had to undergo an intensive six-month training course to qualify as a PTI, which entailed detail study of all aspects of physical training.

Having qualified, Dermot got involved in his new post with a vengeance. Not only was he involved in the actual training exercises, he was also obliged to help design the curriculum for the other instructors.

Around this time the Department of Education was seriously contemplating the establishment of a college of Physical Education in Ireland. They were looking in England for suitable colleges where they could send their first potential physical education teachers. St Mary's College, Strawberry Hill in London was the obvious choice, a training ground for PE teachers of the future. The army decided to send one of their key personnel in this area there for a year, to get a flavour of an alternative approach to training. The obvious choice was Captain Harry Quirke, head of the Army School of Physical Culture. In his absence, the acting head of the college for the academic year 1968-69, was Dermot Earley.

"It was a most challenging and rewarding year; I was able to do anything I wanted in terms of training. I was calling all the shots in relation to the type of courses we would run."

Shaggy Calf Lane

A year after Harry Quirke came back from Strawberry Hill, Dermot was sent there for a year as a 'postgraduate student'. He joined a group of ten Irish post-primary teachers which included Galway's star goal-keeper Johnny Geraghty and another goalie who was to go on to even bigger things, Cork's Billy Morgan. Billy Morgan has a number of memories of his year in college with Dermot Earley.

"Dermot had already left a lasting impression on me after playing against him in a challenge match against an army side in 1967. Dermot got a spectacular goal against me. He hit a rocket of a shot from forty yards which flew into the net. I don't think any goalie in the world would have stopped it.

"I remember there was a lot of talk in college, about his abilities as a rugby player, particularly after one match. The college team got a penalty in their own half of the field. The captain was shaping up to take it when Dermot asked if he could have a shot at the goal. To everyone's amazement he slotted the ball between the posts. The talk among those in the know was that he was good enough to become a full international for Ireland, if he concentrated all his energies on rugby. He also played in goal for an army soccer team. I am told he was an excellent goalie and could have made it at soccer too. He was a great all-rounder.

"A significant part of our studies was the writing of a thesis. We had to present a summary of our argument to the class. I did mine on Gaelic football. My essential point was that our tactics were too stagnant and that some innovation would improve the game. I stressed particularly the benefits of introducing a third man mid-fielder into the game. One member of the group objected vehemently to my suggestions and the others rowed in with him. The only man who spoke out in favour of my proposals was Dermot. He saw a lot of merit in the ideas I advocated.

"I had a number of discussions with him on Gaelic football during our year in London. I was always impressed by his ideas. In the light of all of his ideas, his expertise in physical training, his professional background and his lengthy football career, I am very surprised that Roscommon haven't, to date, used his expertise in a managerial capacity. I have no doubt that he would make a good manager."

The year in Strawberry Hill was a sports enthusiast's dream. All sports were covered from rugby, soccer and rowing on the Thames to Gaelic football, where Earley was the instructor. There were also a number of field trips, including a visit to Highbury and the Arsenal football team. Apart from the manager, Bertie Mee, famous players from the double winning side of that period encountered included George Graham (now Arsenal manager), Bob Wilson (now a distinguished soccer analyst with the BBC), Charlie George and an up and coming star called Peter

Marianello, a player whose career was tragically cut short by injury, but at that time his face seemed to be on all the billboards in London urging people to drink milk.

An integral component of the college year was teaching practice. Earley made the trek for his teaching practice to a part of Slough with the memorable name of Shaggy Calf Lane.

All students in the college were asked to select a thesis topic on an area of personal interest. Having had a little involvement with a Kildare based organisation called KARE, which catered for the needs of mentally and physically challenged people, Dermot did his thesis on the physical education of people challenged in this way. He researched the possibilities for the education of physically and mentally challenged people and argued that those who are normally mislabelled as 'handicapped' had the right to be involved in all the activities of which a 'normal' child would partake.

At the end of his course in Strawberry Hill, Earley was awarded a distinction and got first place in his group.

"It was a great boost to my self confidence. I was particularly gratified not being a graduate myself. All my army training helped me enormously. I think my result was not only a major boost for me, but also for the army."

"A Man's Life"

His Strawberry Hill experience provided him with many insights which were to prove very beneficial in subsequent years in his PT work. Another new challenge presented itself a few years later, when he was one of a group of army personnel who were asked to do some work on devising an advertisement for television which would encourage young men to join the army.

A series of exercises were filmed which showed a number of soldiers in action, some absailing down a cliff, others climbing up ropes and a squad of soldiers running in formation. The four soldiers at the head of this group were carefully chosen. They were: Senen Downes, who played football for Clare and Munster, Terry Young from Cork, who played soccer for the Cork Hibernians (he went on to captain St Mary's College to a Leinster Cup and was an Irish trialist in rugby), Denis Parsons, a Kilkenny hurler and Dermot Earley.

The group 'sang': *We are rangers, mighty, mighty rangers / We can do it, We can make it.*

The advertisement closed with the phrase 'The army: it's a man's life for you.'

This advertisement won an award in a European competition for 'ad of the year', but did it promote an excessively macho image of army life?

"I think it is necessary to have an aggressive element in army life, but equally you have to balance the machoism with the other elements, such as the sophistication, the technology and the human element. Probably the advertisement achieved its objective at the time, but today I would prefer to project a less one-dimensional image of the army.

"That advertisement might have fed into the common misconception that the army is a place for hard men. The joke in the Curragh is that a young lad has not been in the army for more than a year when he goes home for the holidays. The next Sunday the junior team is to be picked for the first round of the championship. Somebody says that they saw the 'army lad' at Mass that morning and says 'Pick him midfield, he'll be fit'. That does not really apply, but it does show the attitude of the general public."

The fact that this misconception exists, is a symptom of a more worrying problem of the level of ignorance about the army among the population at large.

From the People of the People

The primary purpose of an army is to defend the State but it also has three other functions: to aid the civil power, peace-keeping missions abroad with the United Nations and fishery protection.

"People in Ireland know very little about the army because very little of our work is in the public view apart from cash-escorts. I know that where I come from people know I am in the army but apart from my UN activities they have no idea what I actually do. I think there is a great need for the Irish people to realise that the army is for the people of the country. Our job is to uphold the constitution and we swear an oath to that effect when we are commissioned, so that we are from the people and of the people.

"One of the things that people say to me is: 'Sure what do you need an army for? Who is going to fight us anyway? If somebody did try to invade us, what could we do to repel an invasion'? Although we would have the ability to organise the population in an emergency, or a catastrophe such as a national emergency, I think it is vital to have some body of people on hand to assist the public should such difficult circumstances arise."

Your Country Needs You

Radio phone-ins have become a familiar feature of Irish broadcasting. In discussions about the growth of crime levels one solution which is advocated is mandatory national service for young people. The theory is that an exposure to army discipline would promote greater responsibility and respect for authority.

"We have a changing world where that aggressiveness I spoke about earlier should be receding. All over Europe we are trying to get away from a conflict situation. Nobody knows more about the consequences of fighting than the soldier. They can see the destruction of what a small round of ammunition can do. After a day's shooting with your platoon you go back and stand on the mound of earth behind the targets. It is almost like a ploughed field. To think that all those little bullets can do that much destruction. Then you realise the amount of destruction an entire orchestra of weapons can create. I often wonder if it's right to expose everybody to that type of training? The effort should be to get away from the necessity of having to be involved in war. Although we train our soldiers to control their aggressiveness, people with guns have massive power at the tip of their fingers. Is it necessary to put everybody through this experience? I don't think I could support the idea of conscription.

"One very positive move forward though has been the entry of women to the army in 1980. It took a little bit of time for some people to get used to it. There are still some areas from which women are excluded at the moment. The females are annoyed about this and rightly so. But progress is being made, for example, this year cadetships to the air corps were open to girls for the first time. I have no doubt that every effort will be made to open up the army for them in due course, once all the preparations are complete, like suitable accommodation.

"In certain areas there is still some resentment, and in other areas there is over-protection, where women are treated by their superiors as if they were their daughters. Thankfully, attitudes are changing. One argument against the inclusion of women in the army goes back to the Israeli experience. When a male soldier heard a female soldier crying in the trenches he was more likely to return and help her out, whereas if he heard a male he would go on with the battle – this was interpreted as weakness. Yet during the Gulf War women were actively involved in combat, for example women were involved in helicopter conflict and I can think of one American lady soldier who was killed in combat.

"Nothing ever stands still. Change and development must be a constant feature of army life. I look forward to the day when women have equal opportunities to men in every respect in the army."

Almost No Regrets

Having spent all his working life in the army, Earley glows with contentment as he reflects on all the positive aspects to his army career. The most exciting element was the level of responsibility, for example, during the 1977-78 period, when he had eight hundred men under his charge. The amazing variety of tasks and the opportunities to travel abroad were also very positive features.

"The only time I had a regret about my career choice, when I had to really think about whether I should stay in the army or not, was in the latter months of 1991. I had moved from a very high-powered post, one that held a lot of responsibility and a high level of decision-making, where my point of view was listened to and acted upon at the highest level to a job that I now find very satisfying, but initially, was less exhilarating than what I had been used to. Of course, my job as an instructor in the Commanding Staff-School is very important, but the 'buzz' is different.

"The real problem was that there was a high degree of resentment to the fact that I had been away for four years and that I had possibly benefitted in career terms from my time in the UN. Begrudgery is as alive and well in Ireland as it always has been and it is there in the army too. Once or twice during those early months I asked myself was it worth the hassle?

"In recent years the army has undergone tremendous changes which I have not been involved in because of being away. I think a lot of these changes are very good, but you have to be careful and introduce new ideas gradually. Representative Associations have been established and I agree with them, but people's attitudes have changed considerably, going from the attitude of a team to that of an individual. Perhaps I resented this myself.

"I was more sorry about the resentment that was directed against me than affected by it. Weighing the little bit of negative against all the positive, there was no contest. In particular, there were many opportunities to serve the national interest through my work in the security of our prisons, cash escorts and border duty. My childhood desire to serve my country has been realised and that gives me enormous satisfaction."

4. Primrose and Blue

Life is full of promise. Even in the depths of winter the promise of spring brings new hope; dawn follows the darkest night; war will give way to peace and even from the most negative experience seeds of possibility sprout forth. Having suffered the dual disappointment of missing a penalty against Derry and losing the match in the All-Ireland minor semi-final, a week later Dermot Earley was already thinking about the next year's minor championship. Many of the 1965 side would still be eligible the following year.

Out of the blue a new twist of Roy of the Rovers dimensions was introduced to the 17-year-old's career. The Roscommon senior side to face Leitrim in the Gael Linn cup a few weeks later featured the name of Dermot Earley, at right half-back. Now he was a countyman! It was as if all his Christmasses had come in one. He never dared to dream that the prize he coveted so zealously, the senior county jersey, would be realised so quickly. The September evening he heard the news of his selection he was on cloud nine. When he woke up the next morning he felt like a king.

Happy Days

There is a huge gulf between minor and senior football. Some Roscommon fans questioned the wisdom of selecting a 17-year-old on the senior side. News of these reservations reached 'young Earley' himself. Any doubts he himself had were quickly dispelled by his father who informed him with total conviction that if he was good enough, he was old enough. The lingering fears he retained about his own ability at the top level evaporated with the encouragement he got from 'established' players, particularly Eamon Curley, before, during, and after the game. The transition was made smoothly with the debutant contributing three points. Two came from long-range frees, the other came from a massive kick from out the field which hopped seven yards from the goal and sailed over the bar. It was an auspicious beginning.

After the match it was difficult to decide who was the happiest in the Earley household, the father or the son. Further progress in the Roscommon senior jersey was delayed because of his new responsibilities with the cadet school.

Although 1965 was the year of Earley's breakthrough, 1966 was the year he firmly established himself on the national GAA scene. He made history by becoming the first player to play inter-county football at minor, under-21, junior, and senior levels in the one year. The next player to achieve this distinction was Tyrone's Frank McGuigan.

However, Earley's preparation for the Connacht championship got off to a bad start when he cracked his ankle in a hurling match with the cadet school. Consequently he missed a number of Connacht championship games at under-21 level. Although he was some way short of full fitness he played with a heavily bandaged ankle at full-back for the minor final in which Roscommon relinquished their Connacht crown to Mayo. The intense disappointment was offset to some extent with the opportunity to see the senior final close-up, on the sideline, as Galway took another step to their three-in-a-row.

The only fly in the ointment in relation to Dermot's enjoyment of the game was his concern about the time. The Connacht final was played in the middle of the cadets' residential course in Ring in Waterford. In order to play in the Connacht final, cadet Earley was given special permission to leave the army camp on Saturday afternoon on condition that he returned by twelve midnight the following day. Having communicated this fact to Donal Keenan, Earley was assured that he would be returned to the camp on time. This would mean leaving the senior match at half-time. The problem was, that when it came to the crunch, no one was willing to leave the match at the appointed time which meant that he had no hope of beating the deadline. As a green 18-year-old, the footballing cadet was apprehensive that there would be trouble when he returned to camp. He was pleasantly surprised to find that a blind eye was turned to his tardiness.

He was restored to centre-field for the Connacht junior championship match in Athleague when Roscommon lost narrowly to

Galway. The big test though was in the senior championship against Galway. Roscommon entered the game more in hope than in confidence. The final score Galway 1-11, Roscommon 0-5 was a fair reflection of Galway's supremacy. Earley had a solid if unspectacular match. His enduring memory of the day came after the match.

"I found myself marking Pat Donellan and we walked off the pitch together. He told me that what you needed was total dedication. I always remember that. Years after that I asked Johnny Geraghty, the Galway goalie, how he knew that the three-in-a-row side was crumbling. He replied: 'I remember coming into training one day and one player did not have his boots polished. I put that down as the beginning of the end'. The preparation that was required was total. When that did not happen the team went downhill."

Having lost in the minor, junior, and senior championships Roscommon's only hope of glory lay with the under-21 side. They duly obliged, winning the Connacht title without the services of the injured Dermot Earley. He was back for the All-Ireland semi-final against Donegal in Ballybofey but played poorly. The harder he tried the more frustrated he became. The Roscommon forwards forgot their kicking boots shooting a horrendous twenty-two wides. They managed a derisory total of 2-2 but incredibly, given the windy conditions of the day, it was enough for Roscommon to scrape through to the All-Ireland final. Neutrals would have considered Donegal extremely unlucky to have lost.

So disappointed was Earley with his own performance that it was much later before the magnitude of Roscommon's achievement sunk in. Another lifetime's ambition had been achieved. He would play in an All-Ireland final, Roscommon's first in that grade. Not unnaturally the county was in a fever of excitement.

Amongst Lilywhites

Roscommon's opponents in the final would be the reigning champions and hot favourites Kildare. This put Earley in an unusual position. He would play in an All-Ireland final against the county in which he lived and worked. One of the Kildare subs was his classmate Niall Daly. In the weeks coming up to the match half the class were due to do an intensive physical training course which would be an ideal preparation for playing in an All-Ireland final. The other half would attend a course on tactical maneouvres. Niall Daly volunteered to do the tactical course allowing Earley to do the physical training course. "Niall said that he could train with Kildare whereas I could not train with Roscommon. I will always be grateful for that. It was a lovely gesture on his part. I was flying for the final."

The Friday before the game saw a commissioning ceremony in the cadet school which meant a free week-end for all the cadets. There was no point in Dermot Earley returning home for the game only to have to return to Dublin on the following day. That evening he was unexpectedly joined by Sgt Martin Sharkey who had been on the periphery of the 1943-44 Roscommon All-Ireland winning side. One of the great sagas in the army was to prompt strangers to approach Sharkey and say: "You look familiar. Have I seen you before?" He would reply: "If you paid your half a crown to get into the All-Ireland final in 1944 you would have seen me between the posts." Although this was not literally true, it had a grain of truth in it. Now he was ensuring that the new Roscommon star was properly prepared. With the words: "You can't bate proper feedin'," he handed Dermot a soggy brown paper bag which contained two pounds of the finest steak which was gratefully accepted and devoured.

The day of destiny dawned. Kildare with great players like Pat Dunny and Pat Mangan were hot favourites. The Artane Boys Band led the teams around the hallowed sod, roared on by a great sea of faces and rival colours. Although Roscommon held Kildare well in the first half, the Lilywhites got their second wind at the start of the second half, and led by five points with ten minutes remaining. In a switch born out of desperation Earley was moved to mid-field. He set about his task with an iron resolve, jumping higher than everybody else, and set up goals for Jimmy Finnegan and Jim Keane. Roscommon snatched victory by the slenderest of margins. For an 18-year-old the celebrations afterwards brought a level of joy and exhilaration he had never even dreamed of. The return to Roscommon brought still further heights of elation.

Great Expectations

An infusion of new talent from the under-21 winning side was expected to breathe new life into the senior team. However, instead of introducing them gradually and ensuring that a proper balance between youth and experience was attained, too many players were introduced at the one time and the expected upturn in Roscommon's fortunes did not materialise. As the losing streak continued many of the young players became disillusioned and their potential was never fulfilled.

The high hopes of 1966 were quickly shattered in the first match of the championship when, surprisingly, Roscommon lost at home to Leitrim. The game ended in controversy. Roscommon were trailing by two points when in the last minute they were awarded a fourteen yards free. The entire crowd seemed to descend around the goal. As he stood up to take the free, Earley unleashed a piledriver. The green flag was raised. The crowd went wild. No one was exactly sure what had happened. It emerged that the referee had disallowed the goal, claiming that the ball had been saved on the line by a Leitrim defender, Fergus O'Rourke (whose brother Colm went onto greater heights with Meath). If the ball had not crossed the line then the rules of the game dictated that a penalty should have been awarded, as O'Rourke had handled the ball on the ground. However, it would have been a travesty of justice if Roscommon had won.

Among the attendance was ten-year-old Tony McManus: "It was my first time to see Dermot Earley play. Every time after that when I kicked the ball against the wall I was Dermot Earley. He was my role model."

The next year saw Roscommon play Galway in Ballinasloe for the Connacht championship. Most of the three-in-a-row side were still around although Galway's aura of invincibility, had been shattered the previous year. The Galway players were shown to have feet of clay and Roscommon were less inhibited than in previous years but they lost narrowly to a more skillful team in a high-scoring match. Playing at centre-back Earley scored the best point of his career from a sixty-five yards free, a kick comparable to Derek Duggan's monstrous kick in the Connacht final in 1991.

1969 was a bad year for the Roscommon senior side and they lost again to Galway in the championship by 0-8 to 0-1, Earley scoring Roscommon's only point. His preparation for the game was hampered by his participation in a new one-month intensive army ranger's course. As one of a gang of twelve (the self-styled 'dirty dozen') who were involved in vigorous physical activity almost twenty-four hours a day, Earley's fitness was exceptional but his speed and skills were poor. The day of the match was the first time he had touched the ball in two weeks.

Family Matters

Apart from the army training, Earley's preparations for the match were interrupted by a domestic crisis. His army ranger's course brought him to Castlebar. On his only evening off that month he joined some of his army colleagues for a meal in the town. In the course of the evening he bumped into a number of the Mayo team. Each of them in turn asked him about his father's health. After confidently answering that all was well he became suspicious and rang a neighbour at home, as his own family did not have a phone. He heard that his father had had a heart-attack a few days earlier but was now out of danger. Having secured permission from the army authorities he made haste to Gorthaganny.

"My mother knew I was on the course and didn't want to involve me because she felt it would be detrimental to my career if I was pulled off this specialist course. Despite his pain my father had given explicit instructions that I was not to be contacted. I was shocked when I saw him. He looked so weak. When he saw me he said: 'I knew you would come'. Apparently he was in no great danger. He had been almost a chain smoker and was forced to give up smoking. All the smoking contributed to his death, as a result of chest problems, fourteen years later."

The National Holiday

Although 1969 brought disappointment it was also the year that Earley won his second Railway Cup medal. In the 1960s the Railway Cup was still a glamour competition. The final on St Patrick's Day was an important national occasion. In a pre-All-Star and International Compromise Rules era, the competition offered weaker counties their sole opportunity to gain representative honours.

In the 1967 final against Ulster Earley started out as a sub. Galway midfielder Pat Donnellan took a knock in the first half. At half-time team manager Tull Dunne informed him that if he wanted to come off: 'We have young Earley to put on'. For a more serious injury, such as two broken legs, it would have been necessary for Donnellan to leave the field. However, in the last ten minutes Earley replaced Mayo's Joe Langan and was quickly involved in the game making a modest contribution to Connacht's victory. For a 19-year-old to play in such distinguished company was a great experience and a great education.

Two years later Earley formed Connacht's midfield partnership with Jimmy Duggan in their comfortable win over Munster. The prize for the Connacht team was a trip to the United States to play in the Cardinal Cushing games, an annual series of games to raise money for charity. That year, 1969, was the first year a team had travelled out to play in the games. Previously only individuals had travelled.

As a child Earley had always listened in wonder to Micheál O' Hehir's late night commentaries from Gaelic Park but his first impression of the ground was a little disappointing. He had expected something more spectacular. Nonetheless his first trip to America enabled him to see some new types of sporting activity. He saw the New York Mets play their first baseball match of the season. That year they went on to win the World Series. Apart from three competitive fixtures the Connacht side also played an exhibition game under lights.

"The floodlights created a marvellous atmosphere. I know it would be expensive but I would like to see lights at some of our pitches. This would allow us to have Friday night football which I think would be popular with the fans and help us to prevent fixture congestion. It is important to adjust to changing times."

The three game series produced very close matches. Connacht lost the series in the final match. As Earley ran up to take a 14 yards free late in the game some spectators threw cans at the ball. "After the game I was absolutely shattered. I had played the game with great intensity. As I was walking off the pitch a New York player dissatisfied with how hard I had played, punched me in the back. I turned around as he walked away. I felt disgust that this had happened. I was there just to play football."

In 1969 Roscommon also qualified for another under-21 All-Ireland final. Roscommon only emerged from Connacht after a replay against Galway. The matches were the start of a long series of great clashes between Billy Joyce and Dermot Earley. Joyce remembers their first clash: "I hadn't played much football up to that point. I knew I was going to be marking this big star Dermot Earley. Dermot had to be moved out of midfield in both matches. I had trained for 43 consecutive nights to play on him. Although we lost the replay, all the training I did got me really interested in football. I always enjoyed playing against Dermot. He was a great player and a great sportsman."

Upstairs Downstairs

In 1970 Roscommon qualified for a Connacht final. Galway were in a different class and Roscommon were completely outplayed. The match was significant for two reasons. It was the first Connacht final which was played over forty minute halves, and the first such final to be televised live. In the light of the high level of fitness today, Earley is disappointed by the demise of the forty minutes game. He would also like to see a standard duration for all matches and not different times for league and championship matches.

The Connacht championship had brought one happy memory for Dermot Earley. His towering performance against Mayo in the semi-final brought him the first of his *Irish Independent* sportstar of the week awards.

September 1970 saw Dermot moving to London to undertake a one-year course in physical education in Strawberry Hill. His accommodation was a lot more plush than that of the average student. He spent his first three months with his uncle and aunt-in-law who worked as domestic staff for a member of the aristocracy, Lady Hitchinbrook. They lived in a mansion.

During his sojourn in London he commuted home for all of Roscommon's League matches but they lost them all. With the wealth of footballing talent in the small Irish group of students which included former Kerry manager Mickey O'Sullivan, a football team was established and they went on to win the All-Ireland club seven-a-side.

These Miss You Nights

The most difficult part of Earley's time in London was to be separated from Mary, his girlfriend of three years, although he did manage to keep in touch with her when he travelled home to play football. On 17 December 1970, the evening he returned home from his Christmas holidays they got engaged. The following September they got married.

Away from the discipline of army life the one major change in Earley's life was that his visits to the barber became less frequent. It was not a conscious decision but a reaction to the more relaxed atmosphere of campus life. When he returned to score the winning goal for Connacht in the Railway Cup semi-final against Leinster, Donal Keenan greeted him afterwards with the words: "It's George Best." The next day he got his hair cut.

The Ecstacy and the Agony

The year 1971 brought the now familiar disappointment when Roscommon lost to Sligo in the first ever Connnacht championship match to be played in Hyde Park. Earley played the entire match with a 'dead leg'. After the game he wondered if he would ever win a Connacht senior medal.

These doubts were magnified the following year when Roscommon squandered a big lead in Hyde Park to allow Galway to snatch a replay. There was an ugly incident after the match when a section of the Roscommon crowd, furious at some questionable decisions, attacked the referee. As the players gathered to protect the referee, they were joined by Mayo star John Morley who was there on garda duty. Having shocked Galway in the replay, Earley was literally to tangle with Morley in the Connacht final when they both came crashing to the ground because a stud from Morley's boot got caught in the loop of Earley's lace. Although Mayo got off to a whirlwind start on a scorching hot day, the hottest conditions Earley had ever played in during his entire career, Roscommon won 5-8 to 3-10. After the game Earley got physically sick, as he did after the All-Ireland semi-final against Kerry the following month. He never got sick after a match again.

After the joy of beating Mayo the Kerry game was a huge disappointment. Master-minded by Mick O'Connell and Mick O'Dwyer, Kerry ran out facile winners 1-22 to 1-12. A late Dermot Earley goal was too little too late for Roscommon. The only consolation for Roscommon fans came much later when Mick Freyne, who had an inspirational game for Roscommon in the semi-final, became the county's first All-Star.

However, Earley's performances did not go unnoticed. Watching the game that day was a Kerry teenager who would go on to play against Earley in an All-Ireland final, Tommy Doyle.

"I remember seeing Dermot play that day and I was very impressed with him. At the time I was only 16 years old but I still remember the fantastic performance he gave that day and I have followed him ever since. He was and still is one of the best players that ever played football. He had everything, great hands, both feet, physique, and above all a fantastic attitude. Attitude is what it is all about. He worked hard at his game and was totally dedicated and his attitude towards physical fitness was an example to all. I met him when I joined the army in 1976 and must say that he was like a second father to me and helped and guided me no end and for that I will always be grateful. May I also say that he was the same to all the other lads, very helpful and generous. His discipline was exceptional. I was very fortunate to experience his attitude at an early age because that prepared me for the discipline that Mick O'Dwyer demanded from all the Kerry players. He was always a perfect sportsman and gentlemen and I must say he has influenced me to this day."

Sports journalists too, were impressed with Earley's displays. At home and heading for Mass in Gorthaganny on a winter's morning at the beginning of 1973, Earley's sister came charging out the door waving the Sunday paper. The names of the All-Star replacements were out and they included that of Dermot Earley.

Murder Most Foul

As members of the International Military Sports Organisation the Irish army were invited to send twelve of its officers who were engaged in sports and physical education on a professional basis, to attend the Munich Olympics in 1972. Earley was one of the group chosen to learn more about sophisticated training techniques. However, his excitement about the trip was abruptly curtailed when he arrived with Mary at Shannon airport to fly to Munich, only to discover that due to a mix-up in times the flight had already departed. He journeyed to Tipperary with Mary resigned to spend his three weeks holidays in Ireland. The next morning a phone call from Aer Lingus brought the good news that a flight to Munich had been arranged. He arrived a day and a half late but that was a minor irritation when he had the privilege of seeing at first hand great sport stars such as the 'Flying Finn' Lasse Viren who won the 5,000 and 10,000 metres finals, Valery Borzov who won the double in the sprints, Mary Peters who won the gold in the pentathlon and Mark Spitz who won a record seven gold medals.

The Olympics were held in Germany for the first time since 1936. The Germans bent over backwards to erase the many disdainful memories of those games which Hitler had tried to manipulate for Nazi propaganda purposes and which had snubbed Jessie Owens, the winner of four gold medals, because of his 'race'.

A marvellous atmosphere prevailed until the morning of 5 September. Having arrived very early in the morning Earley was puzzled at the huge number of security people who were buzzing around the place. The news was breaking of a terrible tragedy.

At 5.10 a.m. a band of 'Black September' Arab guerillas had broken into the Israeli building in the Olympic village where 10,000 athletes were staying. Two Israelis were killed and nine were taken hostage. Within hours the site was surrounded by 12,000 police. The guerillas demanded the release of 200 Palestinians held in Israeli jails and safe passage out of Germany. The West German Chancellor, Willy Brandt, took personal charge of the negotiations. The terrorists were to be flown with their hostages to an Arab country. Having been taken to the military airport the guerillas and their hostages began to walk across the tarmac to a waiting Boeing 727 aircraft. Suddenly the airport lights were turned out and German police sharpshooters opened fire. The rescue attempt was a disaster with all nine hostages killed, as well as four Arabs and a policeman. Three Arabs were captured and one escaped.

The following day was a special day of mourning. For the only time in its history the Olympic flag flew at half-mast. Sitting in the stand Earley was deeply moved by the emotion of the occasion but one of his strongest convictions was to be reinforced.

"I don't think sport and politics should mix. I know sporting sanctions have been applied in South Africa and I understand the need for them in that particular situation. However, I feel that sport is a unifying force in the world and that it is a good way of keeping people in contact. I bitterly resent it when sports people are used as pawns in a political chess game."

Apart from the Olympic events there was also the opportunity to do some sightseeing in other parts of Germany. The most inspirational visit was to the Bavarian village of Oberammergau. In 1632 the devastating plague, the 'Black death', reached this village. The following year a 'Passion Play' was staged to prevent further deaths from occurring and a solemn vow was given to stage the event every ten years.

In marked contrast the next visit was to Dachau, the site of one of the most infamous concentration camps during World War Two. It was a chilling experience, the aura of terror and horror about the place was still very real.

The Irish contingent gathered every night in the canteen where military personnel from many countries converged, to relax. Earley has two specific memories from those social gatherings. One night a big

French man rushed from his table in very dramatic style. With one movement of his hand he managed to grab a snake which had mysteriously found its way into the canteen and twisted its head off. The whole thing happened so quickly that nobody knew what was going on. Everybody gaped in amazement as the French man coolly disposed of the snake in the waste paper basket and sat back in his chair.

Another night an animated conversation took place between a group of German soldiers which was so loud that everyone in the room could hear. They were reviewing German history and one member was espousing some very pro-Hitler views and doing everything bar making the Nazi salute. His views were emphatically rejected by his colleagues. On their final night the Irish delegation noted that the German soldier in question had never been seen in the camp since that discussion.

All in the Game

1973 saw Roscommon surrendering their Connacht title tamely to Galway in Hyde Park. However, that year was an incredible adventure for Earley who played three football trips abroad. Although he was delighted to be selected as an All-Star replacement, he felt it would be impossible for him to attend because he was completing a six months intensive army training course in the Curragh. Under duress from colleagues he reluctantly applied for permission to travel with the All-Stars. To his great surprise permission was granted. It was a very enjoyable trip particularly as Mary travelled with him.

Arriving back bleary-eyed, he had to face three days of 'final exams'. Thanks to the co-operation of students and tutors, he was able to catch up on lost ground. On his first day back an exercise was arranged which would keep everybody up half the night. Out of sympathy for his 'jet-lag', the tutors assigned him the least taxing task. At 2.30 a.m. he was tidying up the loose ends when he heard footsteps approaching in the darkness. A deep voice boomed out: "Who's there?" The polite reply was: "Lt Earley, Sir". Then came the disturbing words: "Oh you are back. Was it worth failing the course for?" As the person who made this remark was the Comdt of the school, Col Bill Carroll, it was a bit distressing to hear him speak in those terms, particularly as his voice betrayed not the slightest hint that he might be joking.

Accompanying Col Carroll that night was another officer, Lt Col Dermot Hurley. It was not the first time that the two Dermots' paths had crossed. The previous year Dermot Earley had returned from a match one night to discover a simple message under the door which stated: 'You are going to Cyprus'. Having done a medical at HQ he was really excited about doing his first tour of overseas duty. The excitement evaporated when a further message arrived three days later informing him that a clerical error had taken place. The officer going to Cyprus was Lt Col Dermot Hurley not Lt Dermot Earley.

A few weeks later it was off to Wembley to play with the All-Stars against Kerry.

"It was a dry day but the pitch was heavier than I anticipated. It took more out of my legs than I expected. I regretted not getting the opportunity to play there again. I especially remember the magnificent dressing-rooms and the big bath with hot water, which was something that I was not used to."

The disappointment at losing to Galway in the championship modified with the news that Roscommon had been invited to play Kerry in the Cardinal Cushing games. The three game programme provided a great boost to Roscommon football as they won the series.

The difficulties with the tour were off the field. Both teams were to be accommodated in Manhattan College. As there was no air-conditioning, the rooms were like a sauna at night time. After two nights the players moved out and found their own accommodation. The second problem related to the payment of allowances. Cheques were paid on a Friday night but it was not possible to cash them until Monday. Some players were running short of money and needed the cash immediately. The combination of accommodation and financial difficulties provided disquiet in both camps.

News of these complaints got back to John Kerry O'Donnell. He was so annoyed with them that he announced that he was not going to allow the match to go ahead. At the suggestion of the then president of the

GAA, Donal Keenan, Earley went out to plead with John Kerry O'Donnell. Earley began by thanking John Kerry for his hospitality and said how happy the players had been with the accommodation and arrangements and how much they looked forward to playing the game. O'Donnell likes players who always play as if their life depended upon it and had admired this trait in Earley both in 1969 and in the All-Star tour earlier that year. He said: "Only because it is yourself." A handshake signified that the match would go ahead. After the discussion Michael O'Callaghan said to Earley: "Sometimes you have to go with your cap in hand."

In the Hot Seat

The 1973-74 league series began with a new departure for the Roscommon team. Sean Young, a bank manager from Boyle, was appointed team manager. This was a new trend at the time, following Kevin Heffernan's appointment as team manager of Dublin. Young brought a new professionalism to the Roscommon team. The problem for these managers was that they had no precedent to refer to. They had to learn by trial and error. Inevitably there were teething problems. Just before a big match Young made a rousing speech and whipped the team into a frenzy. Then he caught them by surprise when he knelt down on one knee and asked all the players to join him in a prayer.

"There was no resentment or anti-religious feeling. We all said the Hail Mary. It didn't bother me. As far as I know nobody said anything but it seemed strange to whip us up and then quieten us down. It never happened again."

The league programme went well for Roscommon, the highlight had been a one point victory over All-Ireland champions, Cork in Hyde Park. However, Roscommon had not done enough to earn automatic qualification for a semi-final place. Roscommon's fate lay in a Kerry-Galway postponed match, a draw was necessary to ensure that Roscommon got through. Earley was stunned to hear the result of the match on the radio while serving as security officer in Portlaoise prison. In an unusual pairing, Roscommon would face Sligo in the semi-final at Croke Park.

An Eye for an Eye

Earley had a scare some days before the match when he was accidentally knocked-out cold by Sligo player, Robert Lipsett, in an army championship game. When he came to in the hospital he thought he had been involved in a car crash. This clash resulted in two magnificent black eyes on Earley's face.

The league semi-final resulted in a draw. At one point in the game Earley was struggling to retrieve the ball when his elbow made contact with a Sligo player behind him. He had not time to check who it was because he was chasing after Barnes Murphy. The following day Earley's army duties took him to Dundalk where he had a meeting with Robert Lipsett about a forthcoming army display. The first thing Earley noticed was that Lipsett's eye was decorated with a shiner. In that split second Earley realised who he had made contact with the day before. Earley jokes: "I still owe him one."

The replay was held in Castlebar. An outstanding display by Mickey Kearins ensured that Sligo were in the ascendancy in the first half. In what he regards as the finest display of his career Earley took control of the second half and carried Roscommon to victory.

In an interview after the game Mickey Kearins said: "Nobody could have lived with Earley today." Subsequently, Earley won his first GAA 'Personality of the Month' award for his starring role in Roscommon's victory. After the game the Roscommon team was mobbed. They were not so much carried off the field as carried around the pitch.

In the final against Kerry, Roscommon were in control of the game and led by three points with a minute to go when John Egan scored a late goal. A few minutes earlier Roscommon goalie Padraig Whyte had taken a heavy knock. Many Roscommon fans felt if he had been replaced by the sub goalie John McDermott, Roscommon would have held out. Earley disagrees with this opinion.

"It would have taken a great save to stop John Egan that day and would have been very hard on Padraig Whyte to have left the field with only minutes to go. To this day when Roscommon people talk about the league final, they always say John Egan robbed us of victory. I remember lying against the dressing-room wall unable to tog in because I was so disappointed. Mick Dunne interviewed me in the dressing-room. When he asked me what I felt, having got so close to winning our first league final, I could only say: 'Complete devastation'."

Black Friday

The replay was scheduled for 26 May. The game was preceded by a first round match in the Leinster championship between Dublin and Wexford. Few of the Kerry and Roscommon fans who arrived early for the game could have realised that 'Heffo's army' would go all the way that year.

Many fans were apprehensive about travelling up from the country because on Friday 17 May, three bombs had gone off in Dublin killing twenty-three people and a further five people were killed by a bomb in Monaghan, another shocking case in the court of human suffering. The tragedy of violent death on such a large scale cast a shadow over all aspects of Irish society. It was difficult to muster up enthusiasm for football in such difficult circumstances.

Kerry were never under any threat in the replay and ran out easy winners by six points. The game was a personal triumph for a player who had not kicked a ball in either match, Kerry's Mick O'Dwyer who won a record eighth league medal for his contribution to Kerry's success earlier in the competition.

The Connacht championship saw Roscommon paired against Sligo in the Connacht semi-final. An opportunist Earley goal helped Roscommon snatch a lucky draw. As he came off the field Earley was approached by a garda. He knew immediately it was bad news. The garda handed him a piece of paper and told him to ring immediately. It was Mary's home number in Tipperary.

Mary's mother had gone on the Cashel and Emily diocesan pilgrimage to Lourdes. She had left in perfect health with her sister. A phone call revealed that she had died in Lourdes. She had been to the grotto and the tranquillity of the place had prompted her to remark:

"Wouldn't this be a lovely place to die?" She died a short time later. Although there is a lot of unkind things said about mother-in-laws Earley felt her loss badly.

"She was the calmest lady that ever lived. She reared nine children. She was a lovely creature. We got on famously. When Mary and I announced our engagement she was almost childlike in her excitement."

After accounting for Sligo in the replay, Roscommon returned to the city of the tribes but once again lost badly in the Connacht final to Galway. Liam Salmon was Galway's inspiration. The point of no return for Roscommon came when Earley was fouled in the square and Mickey Freyne blasted the ball over the bar.

Defeat in the Connacht final, following so quickly after defeat in the league final, was a bitter pill for Earley to swallow. Not for the first or last time he was left to reflect on the gulf between being 'there' and 'nearly there'.

The Offaly Rover

The only silver lining in the cloud of gloom came when Earley received news of his selection for the first of his two All-Star awards. The second one came in 1979.

Earlier in 1974 he had travelled to America as a replacement All-Star. As always, many friendships were formed with players from different counties – Paddy Cullen of Dublin, Frank McGuigan of Tyrone, and Donegal's Brian McEniff all speak of Earley's dedication to his craft on these trips.

Frank McGuigan recalls: "Dermot would stay out and practise frees on his own when training was over. The flight of the ball was a bit different out there because we were higher above sea level. He would keep practising until he got it right."

On that particular trip Earley formed a special friendship with the late Offaly hurler Pat Carroll. Earley was the only Roscommon footballer on the trip. Carroll was the only Offaly hurler. They became very close. In June 1992, the memories of that trip came flooding back as Earley watched an edition of *The Sunday Game* which previewed the Leinster hurling semi-final between Offaly and Kilkenny. The programme showed jubilant Offaly players after their All-Ireland victory in 1981. In the middle of all this was Pat Carroll dancing with joy. The scene immediately brought back memories of Earley's attendance at Pat Carroll's funeral.

"The funeral was an unbelievable occasion. He was one of the most likeable people I ever met. The death created extraordinary grief, as it should have. The service was dignified and proper but the offertory procession will live forever in my memory. A lady played the 'Offaly Rover' on the violin. It was a very poignant moment. You could hear the sobs around the Church. As the crowd moved outside Pat Delaney sang the 'Offaly Rover' over the public address. Afterwards those who had travelled a long distance were brought back to the local hall for a meal. I always think of the magnificence of the GAA on these occasions, the crowds, the appropriate colour draped over the coffin, the parades and the hospitality. Whenever I hear the 'Offaly Rover' today I always think of Pat Carroll."

1974 also saw Earley topping the national scoring charts. He scored 126 points (10-96) in 25 games, averaging 5.04 points a game. Connacht footballers monopolised the top three positions with Micky Kearins second, 26 points behind, and Galway's John Tobin third.

Leaving on a Jet Plane

Roscommon's 1974-75 league campaign was undistinguished.

A new feature of Roscommon's tactics in the league series was the positioning of Earley at full-forward. The theory was that Roscommon should put their most lethal weapon where he could do the most damage in a scoring sense. If Earley did not pick up points from play himself he would at least set up scores for others and be fouled often enough to win scorable frees. The only flaw in the logic was that if this strategy was to work Earley needed good ball fed into him. Without their star in midfield who was going to supply the quality ball? It was robbing Peter to pay Paul. Roscommon did not make the play-off stages.

A few weeks before the 1975 Connacht championship Earley sustained a serious knee injury in a club match with Michael Glaveys against Boyle. His father charged out on to the pitch, in his anxiety he was blind to everything except his son's injury. The obvious pain on Dermot's face robbed him of his normal objectivity and he made a torrent of improper accusations about the Boyle team. This prompted Dermot to make a unique outburst against his father: "For God's sake would you ever shut up." The tone of his voice caught his father very much by surprise and achieved the desired result.

Dermot informed Sean Young, who was at the game, that he would be unable to play in the challenge match against Meath later that evening. At Young's request he agreed to travel to the match as a spectator. It was a decision he regretted. Sweat broke out on him during the game on a number of occasions because of the pain in his knee.

Three weeks later he returned to training with Roscommon but broke down almost immediately. He was due to go to the Middle East on a two year peace-keeping mission that July and he did not want to have to go for an operation because the period of hospitalisation would have ruled him out of the trip.

He played in the championship match against Mayo with a big bandage on his knee.The knee held up but he was not fit and was taken off late in the game. Mayo won by three points only to lose the Connacht final to Sligo after a replay. The great Mickey Kearins had an Indian summer, finally winning a Connacht medal with Sligo.

Earley left Ireland in July with two ambitions: to be a good peace-keeper and to return fit enough to resume his inter-county career with Roscommon.

5. Glory Days

Position Vacant. Experienced top class footballer wanted by ambitious team with designs on the Connacht championship. R.S.V.P.

This could have been the message sent by the Roscommon county board to Dermot Earley at Christmas 1976, weeks before he was due back from his peace-keeping duties in the Middle East. Instead he got a less dramatic message from the county board secretary, Phil Gannon, informing him that Roscommon were due to play a challenge match at the end of January. In the long history of the GAA it is difficult to imagine that a player was notified about a game at such a distance, particularly for a challenge match! For someone who had not worn the primrose and blue for a year and a half it was very gratifying to know that he was still as highly thought of as ever. He may have been gone but he was certainly not forgotten.

The knee problem which had plagued him in 1975 had not fully healed so he was unable to play in the challenge match when he returned in January. Nonetheless a vigorous training schedule with special weight training to build up the knee had been put into place and ensured that the prodigal son returned in good shape, if not yet ready to return to the high standards of old.

To the delight of all Roscommon fans, Earley's name featured in the list of substitutes for a league play-off fixture against Mayo in February. The match was played in atrocious conditions in Tuam. Mayo took control from the start. The small contingent of Roscommon supporters eyed the sidelines anxiously to see when their old favourite would enter the fray, Mayo's supremacy was tearing away their patience. As soon as Earley began his warm-up there was a great cheer and the applause reached a crescendo as he strode purposefully onto the pitch. However, after a short space of time it was obvious to everybody that he was rusty and not fit for the match. A cumbersome precautionary bandage on his suspect knee was quickly discarded, being more a hindrance than a help.

Many of the Roscommon side were familiar faces, such as Pat Lindsay, Harry Keegan, Tom Heneghan, Tom Donlon, and Eamon McManus among others, but some new blood had been brought into the side. Although Roscommon were well beaten, a ghost of a smile came on Earley's face as he saw one of the new forwards on the team, Tony McManus, in action. Here was a real treasure.

SuperMac

One test of fame is when the multitudes know you simply by your first name. Garret, Gay, Bono, and Jack, need no further introductions. When Tony McManus first joined the Roscommon team he was referred to as 'Tony McManus, Eamon's brother'. After quickly establishing himself as a player of exceptional class he graduated from 'Tony McManus' to 'Tony Mc'. Today all of Roscommon knows him simply as Tony. At the top of his list of admirers is Dermot Earley.

"I had heard a lot about Tony before I went to the Middle East. He was a teenage star with Clann na nGael but I never saw him play until the play-off match against Mayo in 1977. He has contributed magnificently to Roscommon football. I loved playing with him because he could read the game so well. We played well together and things happened between the two of us.

"I remember a goal he scored against Wexford when we were struggling. I sent him a pass from midfield when we were two points down. He gathered the ball on the fourteen yards line and with his left foot, placed it like a bullet in the right-hand corner of the net. He turned and smiled with satisfaction at the score and in appreciation of the pass. We had done it together and that was important.

"He could be a bit aggressive towards his own players and towards the referee. He did not suffer mediocrity easily. If you were not pulling your weight Tony would let you know about it. There was a lot of criticism about Clann na nGael's involvement in Roscommon football. From time to time you would hear critical comments on the sideline that there was too much passing from one Clann na nGael footballer to another. In one of our games the referee was getting annoyed with all the complaints he was getting from Tony and Eamon. He shouted back: 'Roscommon football is nothing but Eamon to Tony, Tony to Eamon, Eamon to Tony, Tony to Eamon.' That incensed both of them and it took some diplomacy on my part to keep things calm.

"I don't think it was ever a fair criticism. When you are a good player it is inevitable that you will have a special bond with your clubmates. This does not stop you from linking up with other players on the team. The same criticism was made when Eamon Jnr came on to the team. He became part of the trio. I always thought they were great players and what was good for Roscommon was all that was on their minds.

"I remember passing a ball to Eamon Snr during a league match in Hyde Park against Dublin where we were struggling to get a narrow victory. Eamon was running away from the goal. If I had passed to him directly he would have had to continue running away from the goal and then turn, wasting valuable time. So, I passed the ball inside to him. I am sure that he thought that it was a bad pass, not realising that there was no Dublin player near. As he turned, the ball bounced before him and all he had to do was catch it and tap it over the bar. He acknowledged the pass and the game went on. At the end of the game Tony was the man who complimented me. He had seen what was involved and knew that it was a great pass.

"When he came onto the scene back in 1977, I was certain that here was an extraordinary find for Roscommon. I was proved right."

Jigger

Although defeat by Mayo was Roscommon's lot in the league play-off, the first round of the championship provided an opportunity to extract revenge. On a glorious May day, Roscommon fans descended in their thousands on McHale Park. Their faith was soon put to the test as Mayo rattled off five points without reply. Ger Feeney was scoring with radar-like precision. Inspiration was required as the Roscommon side struggled to impose their will on the game. It came from a familiar source.

At the end of a protracted period of Mayo dominance Earley, playing at right half-forward, raised Roscommon's first flag with a well taken point from play. This was the signal for the rest of the team to step up a gear or two and another Earley point quickly followed.

At this stage Earley was struggling to cope both with the Mayo defence and one of his own players, John O'Connor. Carried away on a tide of memories Earley laughs loudly as he recalls one of his earliest encounters with the infamous 'Jigger'.

"Jigger was in at top of the right. I remember him coming out and asking me how he could deal with the problems the corner-back was causing him. I can still hear him saying: 'The fella marking me is quite mad.' I didn't know whether to laugh at him or to take him seriously. If he was serious, such questions should have been answered by himself, particularly in a Connacht championship game. When he asked a second time, I felt the problem needed attention. I told him to run the legs off his opponent. It seemed to work as John settled down and played well after that.

"Jigger had immense skill. He seemed to be able to do almost anything with the ball. He was a good winner of the ball and had a great shot."

Having resolved Jigger's problems Earley was free to concentrate on his own game. He went on to give a performance which will live forever in the collective memory of the Roscommon army of footballing fans, his experience and guile causing havoc in the Mayo defence. Although Roscommon had their noses in front, mid-way through the second half the game was still in Mayo's reach. Action was needed on the Roscommon sideline to safeguard their lead. A bold move was made. A very young, untried, inexperienced footballer was thrown into the cauldron of championship football. Amazingly, he had played with Roscommon's minor team immediately beforehand, in their one goal defeat by Mayo. Although his class had shone like a beacon in that match, he had missed a penalty. How could he be right, physically or mentally as he came on to play his first championship match? This was the question Roscommon fans were asking as Mick Finneran casually strolled on to the pitch as if he was playing in a club challenge match.

Speedie

"We were awarded a free almost fifty yards out from the Mayo goal and out towards the sideline. I was debating in my own mind whether I should go for a point or not. As I placed the ball, Mick Finneran came on as a sub on the Roscommon team and ran past me. Without even looking at me he said: 'Give it to me and I will give it back to you.' He took his position and as I ran forward to take the kick he darted towards me and I chipped the ball to him. I ran on and he passed it back. I was twenty yards nearer the goal and I tapped it over the bar. I thought here was a fella of immense confidence. He was prepared as a minor to speak his mind and do exactly as he said he would. He saw the opportunity to get the point, knowing that the Mayo team would not expect a sub to get involved immediately, as he had done. I thought it was a sign of great maturity and of course he also showed this in games he played afterwards.

"I always felt he was a lazy footballer. He had so much that he could give but he did not always give. He needed a lot of training but he did not like to train. My idea of training him would be to give him a hundred footballs and let him tire himself out kicking frees and points from play. He did not like lapping the field or sprinting up and down. I suppose the fact that we nicknamed him 'Speedie' indicated in a light-hearted way what we thought of him. When he was playing well he was a joy to watch and a great man to take a score."

Roscommon emerged victorious and Earley's performance earned him the 'B & I Personality of the Month' award.

The Shamrock

Less than a month later Roscommon faced Sligo in the Connacht semi-final in a confident mood. A Sunday newspaper carried a quote from Earley in one of its sporting headlines, 'This is our year'. In a conversation with a friend he jocosely remarked that he would not have to worry about getting All-Ireland final tickets as he would be playing in the final himself.

In the event Roscommon made heavy weather about beating Sligo, even though Sligo were without the services of the man who had so often inspired them, Mickey Kearins, who had retired the previous year only to make an ill-fated return in 1978. The sparkle which had been evident in the Mayo match was not much in evidence. However, the game itself was completely overshadowed by the tragedy which followed it.

"The next morning I was listening to the news on the radio. I was absolutely devastated when I heard the first item. Three young men had been killed on their way home from the match when their car was crushed by a train at a railway crossing. They were named and they all came from the Gorthaganny area. I had gone to school with them. I had played football and fished with them. The shock was almost overwhelming. I will never forget the grief at their funeral services."

To this day the cause of their accident has not been established. The sun shone brilliantly as they drove home. There was speculation that they may have been unable to see the railway gates as a result. Another theory was that the railway gates had not functioned properly.

Today a tombstone in the shape of a shamrock in the graveyard in Gorthaganny provides a permanent reminder of the tragedy. In the leaves of the shamrock is a photograph of the three victims Tom Flanagan, Joe Gorman, and Michael Mahon. An inscription underneath gives their names and ages and the date of their death 19 June, 1977.

The End of the Beginning

The reigning champions Galway were Roscommon's opponents in the Connacht final on a glorious July day in Hyde Park. Within minutes the home side were reeling from two goals by Brian Talty. Roscommon's tale of woe continued when Earley was involved in an accidental clash with Galway's Johnny Hughes, severing the middle finger of his right hand.

With the panic about Roscommon's problems on the pitch Earley did not get the normal level of attention. The problem was exacerbated when another Roscommon player Tom Heneghan sustained a serious injury. After a cursory examination of the finger from Donal Keenan the situation was diagnosed as a very minor injury and a bandage was hastily put on the finger. Accompanying Donal Keenan in the medical examination was Dr Mick Loftus. Earley took some crumbs of comfort from Loftus' comment: "The way ye are playing ye will win."

Within minutes Earley was back on the sideline as his bandage had slipped off. This time the atmosphere was more tranquil, as Roscommon were showing signs of recovery and a more thorough repair job was done on the finger. On the pitch Roscommon's cause was not helped when team captain Mick Freyne blasted a penalty wide.

The pin-point accuracy of Earley's frees clawed back the deficit and Freyne atoned for his miss with a late goal which helped Roscommon to victory by 1-12 to 2-8.

After the match, as the Roscommon players and fans basked in the glory of winning the Connacht final, Earley was immediately whisked away to Roscommon hospital. When the bandage was removed the injury was quite severe. Apart from a Connacht medal, Earley's enduring legacy of the game is a line across his middle finger with five little strokes which mark the points of his five stitches.

Here we Go. Here we Go.

The All-Ireland semi-final on 15 August was to be a repeat of the 1953 semi-final when Armagh beat Roscommon by 0-8 to 0-7. This time Roscommon were the favourites. The game was to initiate a close relationship between the both counties which culminated in a joint trip to America in autumn 1982.

The Armagh fans brought great colour to the proceedings with the Roscommon supporters giving them a good run for their money. Dublin's breakthrough in 1974 had not only revolutionised the game, it also transformed the ways teams were supported at big matches. Heffo's army brought vociferous support, banners, flags, and very strong identification of team and fans. None of those elements in isolation were new but the mix was. There was a perceptibly different atmosphere between that game in 1977 and that during the last time Roscommon played in a semi-final in 1972.

Eyebrows were raised before the match when the Roscommon selectors omitted John O'Connor from the team. By now Jigger was a cult figure among the county's footballing fraternity. It strained credulity to think that Roscommon had such a reservoir of talent that they could afford to shaft their most gifted player.

In the first half of the game Roscommon were in complete control. At half-time the only question for the Roscommon fans was what would be the extent of their winning margin? Roscommon began the second half as they had finished the first but although they were playing great football their finishing was not of the same standard.

Early in the second half Earley had missed a close in free. Although he scored 1-3 Earley squandered two further chances from frees. Those wides were to prove costly. By now Armagh had turned the tide, led by a sterling performance from their captain Jimmy Smyth. He was giving the Roscommon centre-back Richie O'Beirne a torrid time. To the amazement of the Roscommon fans already aggrieved by the failure to select John O'Connor, no changes were made to combat Smyth's dominance. The failure to make any change still puzzles Earley.

"First of all I remember being surprised Jigger was not selected. However, a bigger problem that day was that when corrective action was required it was not forthcoming. One of the things I have noticed about teams who are successful is that there is no room for sentimentality when it comes to making substitutions. Certainly we should have made changes that day, to respond to the way the game was slipping from our grasp. One of the problems at that stage was that we had a five man selector system. It was hard to reach a consensus in those circumstances."

A Paddy Moriarty penalty helped Armagh to draw level. With the score tied at Armagh 3-9 Roscommon 2-12, a controversial incident occurred before the last kick of the game. As Earley faced up to take a long distance placed ball to try and score the point that would put Roscommon into the All-Ireland final the Armagh trainer, Gerry O'Neill, ran across the field in front of him and shouted something at him. The kick sailed high and wide. As they left Croke Park Armagh fans were celebrating as if they had won the match.

There was much press comment on the 'O'Neill-Earley' incident in the following days. There were question marks about O'Neill's 'sportsmanship'. In his column in the *Evening Press,* Con Houlihan offered two All-Ireland tickets to the person who could tell him what O'Neill said to Earley.

"I don't know what Gerry O'Neill said to me. I didn't even know that he was talking to me until the very end. It did not put me off. The problem was that I tried not just to put the ball over the bar, but twenty yards over the bar. Technically I should have come at the kick from an angle. I approached it in a straight line. In the replay I put much more time into my free kicks. The first free was on the 14 yards line. I took an inordinate amount of time to be sure. This time I made no mistake. I have never been so careful with my free taking as I was on that day."

The replay took place on 29 August. The previous Sunday had seen Dublin beat Kerry by 3-12 to 1-13 in a classic semi-final, perhaps the greatest game in modern times.

Sadly the Armagh-Roscommon replay did not emulate the lofty heights of the previous Sunday or even of the first match. The replay was a much tighter game than its prequel. Roscommon made a succession of basic mistakes spurning many point scoring chances. They tried so hard to be careful and not waste opportunities that they over elaborated. The word used by more disgruntled Roscommon fans was 'dilly-dallying'.

Among the catalogue of errors made by Roscommon, Earley blames himself for giving the Armagh side a psychological boost as Roscommon rallied in the second half.

"I was bearing down on goal when the referee Paddy Collins penalised me for over-carrying the ball. The whistle had gone when I let go with a bullet of a shot which Brian McAlinden saved brilliantly. It didn't count but it gave a lift to McAlinden and the entire Armagh team. As soon as the ball left my foot I knew I had made a mistake. Brian and I spoke about this incident much later and he had the same thought."

In fact later that year McAlinden won the 'Save of the Year' competition and was runner up with two saves he made from John O'Gara in the clashes with Roscommon. Having beaten Roscommon

0-15 to 0-14, Armagh went under to Dublin 5-12 to 3-6 in the All-Ireland final.

Earley's championship total of 1-30 points in five games made him the joint top scorer in the national championship. He shared the honour with Dublin's sharpshooting ace Jimmy Keaveney.

The Second Coming

Roscommon opened their 1978 Connacht championship campaign with the benefit of a new acquisition to the team, Sean Kilbride, who had so often tormented Roscommon teams of the past in the Mayo colours. The other significant changes from the 1977 side were the selection of Gay Sheerin in goal, the switch of Eamon McManus from the forwards to the right half-back position and the switch of Dermot Earley from half-forward to his best position, midfield.

Roscommon comfortably disposed of Mayo in the semi-final. Earley was the tuning-fork, skilfully controlling the Roscommon orchestra. Ironically, the three players who did most to thwart Mayo that day Pat Lindsay, Sean Kilbride and Dermot Earley were all born in Mayo. Tony McManus recalls the match as yet another occasion when Earley steered Roscommon to victory.

"Dermot was great that day, as he was on so many other days. He was the one player who would always take responsibility at the end of a tight match. He would always be looking for the ball and the one man you would always want to have the ball. He dictated the pace of the game for us. He always knew when to slow it down and when to pick it up. I suppose I only realised just how important he was to the team when he retired. He has never been replaced."

Getting Your Priorities.....?

The Connacht final against Galway was scheduled for 9 July. The normal intensity of Earley's preparation for a big game was interrupted two days before the match. His smile is a mixture of pleasure and embarrassment as he recalls the incident.

"Our third son Dermot Jnr was born on 7 July. I was trying to spend the right amount of time with my family and the correct amount of time with Roscommon. That would have worked out at about 70 per cent Roscommon and 30 per cent family! Mary and I had decided that if it was a boy we would call him Dermot. Many people said to me that it was a mistake to inflict the name on him because he would always be the butt of questions about whether he would be as good as his father or not. Although he has been asked these questions, we have never regretted our decision and Dermot is very happy with his name."

Earley was driven down to the Connacht final by his army colleague and Cork senior player, John Courtney, the morning of the match with two ambitions, to win the Nestor Cup and to bring it back to Dublin to have Dermot Jnr photographed in it. Roscommon had suffered heavy defeats in Connacht finals against Galway in 1970 and 1974. This weighed heavy on the minds of the legions of Roscommon fans as they drove to their neighbouring county on a dull, almost foggy, day.

In the dressing-room, two of the Roscommon team, Mick Freyne and Sean Kilbride, were particularly fired up and exhorted their colleagues to give their last drop of blood to regain the Connacht title. Dermot Earley's input was to highlight the fact that there is an exceptionally large distance between the sideline and the crowd in Pearse Stadium which can be off-putting.

As the teams waited for the throw in, the bishop of Galway, Dr Eamon Casey came on to shake hands with the captains and start the game. He greeted the midfielders with the words: "Well lads, are ye nervous?"

Advance Warning

Roscommon took the game by the scruff of the neck and got off to a whirlwind start with two quick goals from Mickey Freyne. A third clear cut chance for Freyne came thundering back off the crossbar. Earley's abiding memory of the game comes from an incident in the second half.

"Galway got a kick out. A sub had come on their team unknown to me. After he placed the ball and turned around I saw a bright number 16 on his back. I recognised the player immediately as Stephen

Kinneavey, a garda recently transferred to Newbridge. A few days before the match I had gone out with Mick Walsh, a Galway man and an ex-Galway footballer, who now played for Sarsfields, for a few kicks of the ball. This new garda came with us. The thing I remembered about Steve that evening was that every ball he kicked went 40 yards further than anybody else's. Immediately, as I saw him lining up to take the kick out, I ran back twenty yards leaving Billy Joyce out on his own. The kick out went straight into my arms."

Both Kinneavey and Earley went on to play for Sarsfields and Connacht together. Their paths crossed unexpectedly on 16 March 1984 after Earley's house was burgled. Mary's jewellery and some of Earley's Connacht medals were stolen while they were at Mass. Kinneavey was the garda who came to investigate and test for fingerprints.

Roscommon beat Galway by 2-7 to 0-9. Both the 1952 and 1962 Connacht finals are referred to in Roscommon as "the Gerry O'Malley Connacht finals". 1978 is referred to as the "Earley final". His performance eclipsed even that of his vintage display the previous year.

After the game it was down to Castlerea to celebrate. In John Courtney's new capacity as Earley's chauffeur he too attended the celebrations. Much to his surprise he was greeted by a number of Roscommon fans who were as full of the celebratory spirit as the Roscommon players. One young lady assured him that he had played a magnificent game in the primrose and blue. The more vigorously he denied playing in the game the more he was congratulated and the more forcefully his hand was shaken!

In the midst of the celebrations Earley rang Mary in the hospital and went home that evening with the Nestor cup on his knee, having arranged to borrow it for a day or two, from team captain Pat Lindsay.

The following day the cup was smuggled into Mount Carmel hospital. As the pictures were being taken a nurse entered to check on Mary. The nurse turned out to be a sister of former Roscommon footballer, Willie Feeley. She was still rejoicing at Roscommon's triumph the day before.

Wet Wet Wet

In the build up to the All-Ireland semi-final between Kerry and Roscommon, a headline in one paper stated: 'Midfield to swing it for Roscommon'. Although Kerry were odds-on favourites to win the game there was a lot of speculation that the Connacht side would have the edge in midfield, in the wake of Earley's towering performance against Galway. For his immediate opponent, Jack O'Shea, the contest with Earley was a daunting prospect.

"As I lined up against Dermot Earley I felt a little bit intimidated. I only really appreciated the physique of the man at that stage. He is powerfully built. Of course he had a great reputation and was a player that everybody looked up to. I was really just a beginner by comparison."

The match was played in a torrential downpour. The Artane Boys band were forced to give their half-time recital from the sanctuary of the Nally Stand. Roscommon were comprehensively beaten 3-11 to 0-8. The result was was a fair reflection of Kerry's total dominance. One of Kerry's goals came from a dreadful kickout from Gay Sheerin which fell into the hands of Pat Spillane who dispatched the ball into the back of the net.

The only Westerner to emerge with an enhanced reputation was John O'Connor who capped a sparkling performance with four great points. O'Connor was now known to the Roscommon fans as 'Kempes' because of his physical similarity to Mario Kempes, star of Argentina's World cup winning side and because they both wore the number ten shirt and were both flamboyant characters on and off the field. It remains a mystery to Roscommon fans how O'Connor was overlooked for All-Star selection, particularly in 1978.

Twin Peaks

Following Kerry's demolition of Dublin in the All-Ireland final Roscommon got the opportunity to reverse their losing streak against Kerry in the Ceannarus final in Hyde Park. The match was a double header with the All-Ireland under-21 final between the same teams also taking place. As a result of a request from the Roscommon county board, their counterparts in Kerry had agreed to concede home advantage to the Connacht side. This magnificent gesture was greatly appreciated by all the football fans in Roscommon.

The disappointment of the All-Ireland semi-final defeat was quickly forgotten as Roscommon played great football to capture the Ceannarus. Again, John O'Connor was the side's star performer.

Then it was the turn of the under-21 sides to take centre stage. On their way back to the dressing-room the Roscommon side met the under-21 team. Earley remembers those moments vividly.

"We applauded them as they left the dressing-room. As the last player left I put my hand on my clubmate Gerry Fitzmaurice's shoulder. He turned around, and shook hands and I wished him well. Years later Gerry recalled that incident to me and said that it had inspired him."

Fitzmaurice went on to score what became the decisive goal in the second half. Roscommon won by one point. Late in the game as Roscommon clung onto a slender lead their fans were stunned to see Mick Finneran turning up two yards from his own goal and defending like a demon to ensure the under-21 title returned to the banks of the Shannon for the first time since 1966.

Commenting on what was described as 'the physical nature of the game, the wholesale fouling and reckless tackling that became par for the course' in the 1980 All-Ireland final, Owen McCrohan in his authorised biography of Mick O'Dwyer attributes much of what happened in the final to the Ceannarus match in 1978. He claims: "What is not generally known was the bitter rivalry that existed between several players on both sides." He cites the treatment of Eoin Liston and Ogie Moran by Roscommon fans who at various stages in the game chanted 'Ogie is a moron' and 'Liston is a monkey' during the Ceannarus final.

Ogie Moran does not recall the specific incident: "We would have liked to have won the Ceannarus final but Roscommon were hungry to win it. I was not aware of any bad feeling between our lads and the Roscommon team. Certainly both Eoin Liston and I had very good friendships with some of the Roscommon players."

Former Kerry great, Jimmy Deenihan TD, remembers the Ceannarus final but is puzzled by the suggestions that there was hostilities between Kerry and Roscommon: "Both the Roscommon players and people made us exceptionally welcome that weekend. If anything they treated us too well. Some of us were up drinking with them the night before the match and went on the field the next day with very sick heads! To my knowledge there was nothing but mutual respect between the teams and I know some very close friendships were formed. I am very surprised at the suggestion that the Ceannarus final, or any other league game, caused bad blood between Kerry and Roscommon."

The match was played on a lovely October Sunday. A carnival atmosphere prevailed as the fans made their way to Hyde Park. For a whole generation of Roscommon fans it was their first time to see their county play in an All-Ireland final at any grade. The fact that the game was on home soil added to the occasion.

Another factor in the equation was that the opposition in both games was Kerry. Since the glory days of Roscommon football when they won their only senior finals in 1943-44 and narrowly lost the 1946 final to Kerry, success against Kerry was the yardstick by which Roscommon teams are measured. Kerry came to Roscommon not only as reigning All-Ireland champions but with a star-studded side featuring Jack O'Shea, Sean Walsh and Eoin Liston (who had scored three goals in the All-Ireland final a few weeks before) which had won the three previous under-21 finals. The adrenalin levels were running high.

As they journeyed to the ground those who were listening on the car radio heard Larry Gogan counting down the Irish music charts on Radio One. It was a year before Radio 2 was born and eleven years before legal local stations were established. A song (using the word loosely!) called 'Jilted John' from a quickly forgotten artist also called 'Jilted John' was riding high in the charts. The song described the sad predicament of a young man called John who had been jilted by his girlfriend for a succession of boyfriends. Each of the boyfriends was named and with their name was the appendage '...is a moron'. A small but very vociferous minority of young supporters took it upon themselves to apply this phrase to Ogie Moran on that day.

It was childish behaviour that embarrassed the majority of Roscommon fans but was born out of immaturity rather than malice. Although Earley was fully committed to the action on the pitch he was distracted by this distasteful incident.

"For a group to single out any player and chant at him is totally wrong. The last person who deserved that kind of thing was Ogie Moran. I don't think the youngsters involved knew what they were doing or meant any harm. I can remember thinking at the time that this should not have happened."

In the joy of winning, many Roscommon fans were disappointed that the chanting had occurred, even though everybody recognised it was the fruit of misguided youthful enthusiasm. One of the clearest memories of this writer's five years in post-primary school, in Roscommon CBS, was of some of the players bringing in the under-21 trophy to the school the next day. Later that evening our religion teacher, normally the gentlest and most inoffensive of men launched into a tirade on the immorality of spectators abusing players from the sideline. The intensity of his conviction evoked a startled response, but typified the genuine Roscommon followers' respect for Kerry and discomfort with the antics of a minority of vocal fans.

Now is the Winter of our Content

Still on a high from the success against Kerry, Roscommon opened their league campaign with a win over Cavan. Defeat against Tyrone followed, despite a brilliant display by Danny Murray. Another vintage John O'Connor performance was not enough to prevent a loss to Down. The tide turned back in Roscommon's favour with a victory over Antrim in Kiltoom.

The final match of 1978 was played against Mayo in Ballinrobe. There was some debate as to whether the match would have to be cancelled or not due to the monsoon-like conditions. The match is recalled in Sean Og O'Ceallachain's autobiography. Sean Og was commentating on the game as a segment was being recorded for the *Sunday Sport* television programme later that night. The difficulties posed so much frustration that he used less than polite language at one stage and the offending item had to be extricated from the piece eventually broadcast.

The game is remembered for the brilliance of Earley's frees despite the howling gale and downpour, and Roscommon emerged with a narrow win.

Victory over Cavan in a play-off brought Roscommon face to face again with Kerry in the National league quarter-final. In a tense robust game the scores were tied at 1-11 to 1-11 with a minute to go when a great run by Danny Murray brought a free to Roscommon. Earley's free-taking had been immaculate during the game and he duly kicked the winner.

It was the only time in Earley's career that Roscommon beat Kerry in the knock-out stages of a National competition. He shed tears in the dressing-room afterwards.

A few days after, Dermot was invited to attend a charity auction for GOAL. The jersey he wore against Kerry was purchased for £100 by Terry Rodgers. In conversation afterwards Rodgers told him the reason for this purchase: "My father was from Roscommon but thanks be to God he got out of there early." Earley was unsure if he should feel complimented with the price, or insulted about the joke!

The star of the auction was Moss Keane. Ireland had lost narrowly to Wales in Cardiff Arms Park earlier in the year despite a breath-taking performance by Tony Ward. In his own distinctive style Moss held up a black plastic bag and recalled how he had gone into the Welsh dressing-room after the game to swop jerseys with Alan Martin the Welsh forward. On his way out big Moss remembered that Martin had not been a good man to buy a round of drinks on the Lions tour the previous year, so he went back inside and 'borrowed' Martin's tracksuit while he was in the shower, to compensate for all the drinks Keane had bought him the previous year.

Easter Sunday, 15 April saw Roscommon beat Offaly by 1-14 to 0-13 in the league semi-final. The highlight of the game was a penalty save by Roscommon goalie John McDermott, from a thunderbolt of a shot from Mick Wright.

Catch of the Day

The league final between Cork and Roscommon was played the day after the FA Cup final between Manchester United and Arsenal. There was a link between the two games. Man Utd lined up in red jerseys and white togs (the same colour as Cork) and Arsenal lined up in the Roscommon colours of yellow and blue. Arsenal were coasting to a 2-0 win with minutes to go when Manchester United scored two late goals. Then in the 89th minute Liam Brady set up Alan Sunderland for Arsenal's winner. Roscommon fans hoped it would be an omen of things to come.

In the build up to the game Earley trained in the Curragh with Sean Kilbride, his army colleague and Roscommon team-mate. Occasionally they were joined by Cork's John Courtney. A pact was made between Courtney and Earley, that the winner and his wife would take the loser and his wife out to dinner the week after the league final.

A serious problem for Roscommon was the late withdrawal of Harry Keegan, the only Roscommon player to win an All-Star award the previous year and the rock on which so many opposing attacks had perished. He was replaced by Seamus Tighe who had an auspicious debut in the big time, playing the game of his life.

Roscommon took control of the game from the outset. Two features of the game were the long range points scored by the Roscommon attack and a dazzling display at midfield by Earley. His high fielding gave Roscommon total dominance in the centre of the field and he scored 7 of the side's 15 points.

After the final whistle the first person to congratulate Earley was John Courtney who also took the opportunity to remind him about their dinner date. The long wait was over. The elusive National honour at senior level was finally attained.

In the scenes of unbridled joy that followed there was one notable absentee. The new player-manager Tom Heneghan, who had masterminded Roscommon's victory, had soared like an eagle in the match to make an unbelievable catch but had come crashing down on the ground and was badly concussed. He lay on the bench in the dressing-room as the team received the adulation of the crowd.

As the Earley family made their way to the Roscommon victory celebration in a Lucan hotel they were stopped at a traffic lights. Another car pulled up alongside. The driver was John Courtney. He and his wife Nuala were heading home – the difference between victory and defeat.

After a meal it was down to Roscommon where the excitement was at fever pitch. The following Friday the 'Sportstar of the Week' award was shared between Liam Brady and Dermot Earley.

As league champions, Roscommon were invited to play Dublin in a charity match for GOAL. Dublin won by 1-7 to 0-8. Although the match was for a good cause Earley felt the game was a mistake from a footballing perspective. A Dublin Roscommon All-Ireland semi-final later that year was a definite possibility. Earley did not want to present Dublin with a psychological advantage.

The Late Late Show

Roscommon began the defence of their Connacht title with a 3-11 to 1-11 victory over Galway in Hyde Park. Roscommon's star on the day was Eamon McManus who set up a series of scores with his penetrating runs down the left wing.

The Connacht final against Mayo was played in McHale Park. Roscommon made a sluggish start but Mayo were firing on all cylinders with top of the left Joe McGrath scoring 2-5 in a performance which earned him an All-Star award later that year. The accuracy of Earley's frees ensured that Roscommon never drifted too far behind. An inspirational second half performance from Sean Kilbride and a late scoring spree by Roscommon which featured a brilliant goal by Mick Finneran helped Roscommon to a 2-15 to 2-10 win.

A few weeks later Roscommon accounted for Louth in a challenge with a score of 6-11 to 0-7. It was an impressive scoreline but an unimpressive performance with superior fitness the decisive factor in the match. Among the attendance was a number of Dublin players and mentors, Roscommon's opponents in the semi-final.

Dub-le Trouble

There was considerable controversy in Roscommon when the semi-final team was announced. There was no place for Mick Finneran. A lot of rumours were circulating about the fitness of Mick Freyne. The anxieties were justified. Freyne was completely out of the game but astonishingly Finneran was left languishing on the subs bench until late in the second half. The Roscommon forwards were profligate in their shooting.

Paddy Cullen remembers the number of chances spurned: "There were so many balls kicked in from out the field that were either falling into my arms or bouncing in front of me. It was a game Roscommon had the winning of but did not take their chances."

Dublin's scoring machine, Jimmy Keaveney, missed the match through suspension, having been sent off in the Leinster final against Offaly. However, his replacement Mick Hickey kicked frees with the precision of the master at his best.

As the match entered its final stages Mick Finneran was finally introduced. Roscommon trailed by two points. Almost immediately Finneran scored a marvellous goal. Subsequently the goal was chosen as 'the goal of the year'. This goal should have been the signal for Roscommon to put the game out of Dublin's reach. For all Roscommon's possession it was the Dubs who came out on top 0-14 to 1-10.

An incident occurred when the sides were tied at 0-13 to 1-10 that is still remembered in Roscommon. The Western side were attacking and the ball was played to Sean Kilbride. As he waited for the ball to come into his hands Tommy Drumm came from nowhere, stuck out his hand and cleared the ball. The clearance yielded the winning point. Earley is distressed by the way the incident has been reported down through the years.

"Anyone in Roscommon who talks about the game refers to that incident. It happens at some stage to every single player. Players don't want to gamble about going back to retrieve the ball because it gives more time to their opponents to catch them. I always felt it was unfair to blame Sean Kilbride for Roscommon's loss. The blame should be put on every one of us. We did not play as well as we could and we gave away too many frees. Perhaps we did not pick the right team from the start. There was intense disappointment afterwards. We should have been in an All-Ireland final but we lost. It would have been an invaluable experience to have played in an All-Ireland final when we made our serious assault on the title in 1980."

Knock, Knock, Knocking on Heaven's Door

Apart from his disappointment with losing the match Earley's other regret about the match was that his old friend Jimmy Keaveney had not played. In 1978 Earley captained the Rest-of-Ireland team in a charity match against Dublin. In his after dinner speech he told the following story about Keaveney.

A famous Kerry full-back died and went to heaven. St Peter met him at the Golden Gates and apologised for striking him down in his prime. He informed him that he needed a full-back for the All-Heaven final. On the following Sunday St Peter showed the Kerry player the stadium he would play in. It was out of this world! When the game began the Kerry player had an exceptional game, clearing everything in sight. With ten minutes left, his side was leading by seven points. He was licking his lips at the prospect of adding an All-Heaven medal to his All-Ireland collection when he was rocked to the core by the sight of the sub coming on the other side. The sub was wearing a Dublin number 14 jersey. He was a bit heavy in the front and did not run very quickly. The first ball that came his way he caught, turned and scored a goal. The next two balls in his direction produced two delightful points. In the last minute he got the ball again and buried it into the net. The final whistle blew almost immediately. St Peter rushed onto the pitch to console the Kerry player and let him know he had played a blinder. The Kerry player only wanted to know what caused Jimmy's death. St Peter said: "Oh that was not Jimmy Keaveney. It was God. He only thinks he is Jimmy Keaveney!"

When the trophies were being presented Robbie Kelleher was heard to say as Keaveney strolled up to receive his prize: "He looks like he is walking on water!"

With his tongue in his cheek Earley professes to being a little bit annoyed about that evening. "The only complaint I have, is that I know Paddy Cullen has used that story a few times since. I put Paddy's success in the pub business down to the fact that he stole that joke from me."

Superstar

Roscommon's league campaign brought mixed results. They surrendered their title when defeated at the quarter final stage by Kerry in Limerick. Kerry won by 1-8 to 1-5. The highlight of Roscommon's performance was an outstanding goal from a John O'Connor fly-kick.

January 1980 saw Earley participating in the popular 'Superstars' series. The only problem was that he was scheduled for security-duty in Portlaoise prison in the preceding months. For the one and only time in his career he requested to be given a different set of duties to allow him to train for the competition. Unfortunately the army was not in a position to accede to his request which meant that he often went five or six days without training during those months.

In the light of the many disciplines he was competing in, he went into the competition without the level of preparation he would have liked. His fitness levels were satisfactory but his skill levels at some of the disciplines was not up to the standard he would have aspired to. Although he qualified for the final he finished last.

Despite the disappointment with his preparation it was a great opportunity to mingle with up-and-coming sportstars like Barry McGuigan and Stephen Roche. Bernard Brogan won the competition and continued the high standard of Irish performance in the international final which Pat Spillane had set in the previous year.

On the N17

Roscommon began their quest for their fourth consecutive Connacht final (which would have been a record for the county) with a total mismatch against London winning by 9-19 to 1-10.

On 15 June a much sterner test awaited them in the Connacht semifinal in Galway. It was a very difficult match for Roscommon. Before the game the Roscommon management and senior players tried to guess Galway's tactics. Their feeling was that Galway would try and drag Pat Lindsay all around the pitch. A new player had come onto the Roscommon team at left full-back, Gerry Connellan. Connellan would go on to win an All-Star award that year in his first year in championship football (in 1991 Roscommon's Enon Gavin emulated this feat playing in the exact same position). Connellan's instructions were to follow the roving forward and to leave Lindsay free in the centre. The guess proved correct. Galway's tactical ploy backfired when Connellan grabbed two loose balls and slotted them expertly over the bar.

A poor kick out from Pat Comer fell into the hands of Tony McManus and he coolly lobbed the ball into the net for the game's only goal. Roscommon won by 1-14 to 0-10.

Despite brilliant weather in an exceptionally bad summer the Connacht final on 13 July was overshadowed by the tragic death of former Mayo great, John Morley. There was a lot of speculation about the effect the death would have on the game.

Tony McManus recalls Tom Heneghan's instructions before the game: "Tom told us that we had as much respect for John Morley as anybody but once the game started we had to put all thoughts of him aside and remember that we had a match to win."

Roscommon took control of the game from the outset with Mick Finneran and Tony McManus forming a lethal combination. The final score, Roscommon 3-13 Mayo 0-8 was a fair reflection of their dominance on the day.

Controversy

The All-Ireland semi-final pairing of Armagh and Roscommon revived memories of 1977. Armagh had beaten Tyrone by 4-10 to 4-7 in the Ulster final.

As the Roscommon team left their Dublin hotel four and a half year old David Earley was togged out in his Roscommon outfit and by his father's side. David had become part of the furniture during the side's preparation and regarded himself as an unofficial sub on the Roscommon team. It had been patiently and painstakenly explained to David that he would accompany the team to the hotel but would then travel separately with his mother to the match. When the point of separation came David went into hysterics. After all efforts at placating him had failed his father reluctantly allowed him to travel with the team.

David was watching the teams getting ready for the parade from the dug-out when Roscommon mentor Danny Burke urged him to join his father on the pitch. This turn of events caught Dermot Earley completely by surprise but there was nothing he could do but take David's hand and parade with him.

As Roscommon already had a mascot there was controversy after the match about the incident. A press report referred to the 'immaturity' of Roscommon for allowing the situation to arise. GAA headquarters issued a directive before the All-Ireland final saying that no mascots would be allowed for the big game.

The semi-final itself was played on a very warm sunny day. Roscommon were doing well in the secondhalf until their goalie Gay Sheerin took his eye off the ball and let it slip through his fingers for a soft Armagh goal and the impetus was temporarily lost. However, two late goals saw Roscommon through on a scoreline 2-20 to 3-11. The last goal saw Earley gathering the ball from his own goal-line carrying it up the field and sending it on to Mick Finneran who, as cool as an iceberg put the ball into the Armagh net for the insurance score.

The high scoring semi-final was surpassed the following Sunday when Kerry beat Offaly 4-15 to 4-10. An interested spectator at the game was

Dermot Earley. At one stage the television cameras focused on him. Micheál O'Hehir commented: "He looks a worried man."

After the Armagh match the Roscommon fans were so ecstatic that young David Earley became frightened as he was engulfed by a sea of blue and yellow when Roscommon fans invaded the pitch. Having successfully retrieved and consoled him, his father was able to savour the joy of winning. He smiled as he noticed a banner which said: "Earley to rise."

His eyes sparkled as the magnitude of Roscommon's achievement became apparent. In all his childhood games in the garden in Gorthaganny he had played in make-believe All-Irelands. This one would be for real.

6. The Winner Takes It All

For the Roscommon fans the defeat of Armagh had a dual significance. It finally laid the ghost of the 1977 All-Ireland semi-final, 'the one that got away', to rest. Revenge had been achieved in the sweetest possible manner.

More importantly Roscommon had arrived on the big stage. The supporters were hungry for success. Many fans could not remember the glorious days of the side captained by Jimmy Murray that won the 1943 and 1944 finals and narrowly lost the 1946 final to Kerry. Younger fans could not even remember the 1962 All-Ireland final when Roscommon lost again to Kerry.

Hopes were high that should Kerry beat Offaly the following Sunday, in the other semi-final, then Roscommon would get the opportunity to make it third time lucky and prevent the Kerry team from making it three in a row.

Players and supporters mingled on the pitch united in their elation. No words were necessary. The joy on the faces told their own story.

It took a long time for the victorious team to leave their dressing-room. Although the 'old' dressing-rooms were by now a familiar sight to the Roscommon players there was a qualitative difference about this visit. Those dressing-rooms were steeped in tradition and home to a thousand happy memories. All the greats had celebrated there after All-Ireland victories, now the Roscommon team was about to take its place in that magical history. No player was anxious to leave this unique atmosphere. Everybody wanted to savour the experience to the fullest.

When the Roscommon team finally emerged from the dressing-room they were joined by the Armagh team. Congratulations and commiserations were exchanged. Earley exchanged jerseys with Jimmy Smyth.

"We had worn our alternative colours that day, a blue jersey with a gold hoop, something like the Tipperary colours but they were immensely heavy, far heavier than any jersey I had ever worn before. It was a very hot day and they were not very suitable. When I gave my jersey to Jimmy, he said in his best Armagh accent: 'God ye were wearing bloody anoraks out there today'."

A special victory celebration was held that night in a Dublin hotel, organised by the Roscommon Association in Dublin. A big screen was set up so that everyone could re-live the golden moments that brought Roscommon on the threshold of greatness.

The players were transmitting joy like electricity. They were like young children on Christmas morning. The wild reaction of the fans was both contributing to and feeding their delight. It was a virtuous circle of joy.

"Every schoolboy's dream is to win an All-Ireland medal. It is on a par with winning an Olympic gold medal. One of my clearest childhood memories is listening to the radio commentary of Ronnie Delany's gold medal performance in Melbourne, in 1956. To win a gold medal was the greatest thing that could happen to Ireland in our eyes as kids, but to win an All-Ireland medal would have been the greatest thing that could happen to any individual."

The team's victory gave a great lift to everyone in the county. Even 'non-football fans' basked in the team's success. Since 1977 Roscommon had been on a very successful run. The 1979 League victory had sparked-off great celebrations but the prospect of All-Ireland success provided a welcome release from people's worries. Nobody was immune from the tidal wave of enthusiasm which swept through the county.

However, if Roscommon were to win the ultimate prize a lot of hard work would be necessary.

Put Them Under Pressure

The first Sunday in September saw Galway beat Limerick to claim their second All-Ireland hurling title. That evening thoughts of a unique western double were uppermost in the Roscommon players minds as they assembled for their first training session in September.

For all of them it was a novel experience to be training intensively in September. Accordingly a new adjustment had to be made to training schedules.

"As I ran out for our first training session in September, the sun was lower in the sky than we were used to for training, even for an All-Ireland semi-final. I remember saying to Danny Murray: 'This is the first time we have ever trained in September.' It was different but it was great. I can still see the sun shining into our eyes from the Roscommon town goal as we got onto the pitch."

A plan was formulated to ensure that the Roscommon players took the field against Kerry in a state of peak physical fitness. To supplement the five training sessions per week, all the players agreed to take a week's holidays two weeks before the final itself to sharpen fitness, skills and team play. The training sessions for that week were conducted in St Coman's Park because the ground in Hyde Park was very hard despite the wet summer and took more out of the players. A training session was conducted each morning and afternoon. Lunch was followed by the screening of a video of either a Kerry or Roscommon match.

Tom Heneghan, Tom Donlon and Dermot Earley were the triumvirate responsible for the training sessions. As team manager, Tom Heneghan had overall responsibility. In the light of his professional expertise as a PE teacher, Tom Donlon took charge of the fitness element of training. Earley's focus was on the skills.

He was also asked to speak to the players about diet. Having outlined the benefits of a high protein diet, he also preached a fiery sermon on the evils of junk food such as hamburgers, chips and ice cream. This dissertation provoked great laughter from some of the players particularly those with a sweet tooth! Some of his prohibitions were received less than rapturously. Discomforting though this ascetic discipline was, everybody recognised that nothing could or should be left to chance in the effort to be 'lean and mean'.

Stepping down from this heightened plain of preparation to more conventional training methods, speed was identified as a high priority. Countless sprints did not produce any world records but players shaped by the rhythms of a rigorous training schedule did record significantly better times. Some players who normally took 14 seconds to do the 100 metres now did so in 12 seconds.

Nothing was left to chance. Tom Heneghan wrote what was expected of every player in their particular position on an index card.

Competitiveness was encouraged in practice games.

"There were great physical contests in training. Some unbelievable block downs were made. The man who was blocked down in the first place might regain the ball only to be blocked down a second and perhaps a third time, with the blocker throwing himself full length to prevent the kick. This would lift others and inspire us all to give every last ounce of energy."

Although the training regime pushed weary limbs to their limits, there were lighter moments which sustained morale and the enthusiasm to give of their very best.

"There were always good comments. Tom Heneghan would tell Tom Donlon to take us for a few slow laps around the pitch to start us off. Donlon was very precise and did everything by the book. His idea of slow laps differed radically from that of the players, especially Mick Finneran who was always bringing up the rear. One night as we were shuffling into first gear, groaning off the effects of the day before, Finneran was heard to say: 'Now Tom. Just slow, just slow'. It was a very small remark but it brought giggles of laughter. It broke the tension and got everybody going.

"Pat Lindsay always led by example. He would do everything perfectly. His laps would never be cut short. All his push-ups were done and maybe a few extra. Everyone could see this and took great heart from it.

"In the matches we would play between backs and forwards, Pat would be marking Tony McManus. There were great contests and great slagging afterwards. Tony would score a point. Pat would say he was trying to give Tony as much confidence as possible. Lindsay would come out and clear a ball and Tony would say something like that it was the first ball cleared out of the Roscommon defence since 1962. This type of banter was going on all the time and it kept our spirits up."

Not Quite Chariots of Fire

An Olympic final atmosphere took over during the sprints. Everybody wanted to be the first to the line. Seamus Hayden, Aidan Dooley and John O'Connor invariably featured prominently. One evening Earley actually won a sprint.

"If it had been the Olympics it certainly would have been classed as a 'break' and we would have to start again. There were many good humoured protests with calls of 'Stewarts Inquiry' and 'Disqualification'. These light moments broke the monotony but then it was back to the line and the serious business started again."

The most flamboyant character on the team was John O'Connor, the Ruud Gullit of Roscommon football. The supreme stylist, he electrified Roscommon fans with his skill and cheek. He had class stamped all over him and overwhelmed opponents by the sheer beauty of his play. He was the consummate footballing artist. His charismatic play was matched only by his impish personality. In the final days of training before the final John O'Connor became a central topic of conversation with his colleagues.

"He gave an interview with Mick Dunne 10 days before the match. John spoke very well, as he always did. He stressed the need for teamwork and the need for everyone to be decisive. For the next few days in training every time somebody got the ball people would shout: 'Be decisive'."

Roscommon fans were stunned when the team took the field for the All-Ireland final. There appeared to be no sign of John O'Connor as the team did its warm-up. Second or third glances established that the player wearing the number 10 jersey was in fact John O'Connor. The distinctive long flowing hair and headband reminiscent of a laid-back seventies hippy was no more. The 'new Jigger' looked like a candidate for the priesthood!

The Roscommon players who had been as shocked by the haircut a few days earlier took great delight in readjusting their team tactics to mark the occasion. A consensus was almost reached that everybody should play the ball so that the television cameras would always get

Jigger's 'good side'. The only dissenting voices were those who argued that their number 10 did not in fact have any 'good side'!

In the build-up to the match Tom Heneghan's concern was to get the best out of every single player. This meant that although everyone was asked to suffer the same pain barrier, not all players did the exact same in training. Individual players' problems were catered for. Harry Keegan was prone to hamstring injuries. This would be considered in sprint routines. The heavier players on the team such as Pat Lindsay and Dermot Earley were subjected to additional physical torture.

Mind Over Matter

A different psychological approach was also taken with each individual player.

"Gerry Connellan had a great Connacht championship in 1980, but did not play so well against Armagh in the semi-final. He was a player that you would talk quietly to. He would take a thump in the game and the next thing he was in the game with fire in his belly and determination in his eyes. After that every ball that came his way was his.

"John O'Connor was also a player who required quiet encouragement. You would tell him he was a great footballer and when he believed that, he could do anything on a football field without breaking into a sweat.

"On the other hand, Mick Finneran needed to be shouted at from time to time and his performance improved accordingly. If you did that to John O'Connor he would not play at all.

"Little psychological ploys can have a big impact on a match. I remember playing against Galway one day when Paul Hickey was marking Barry Brennan. At one stage Brennan was taking a shot in a dangerous position but Hickey put him under pressure and he shot wide. I went up to Hickey and told him that he was giving the greatest performance I had ever seen on that pitch and that his commitment was necessary to win matches. This had a two-fold effect. It lifted Paul and made Barry feel that he was up against it. Both players reminded me of that incident a few times afterwards for those different reasons.

"Sometimes you can be a victim of this ploy. In my later playing days when I was beaten for a catch, my opponents often told the player marking me that I was: 'only an auld man'. There were a few times when I thought to myself that maybe I was only an old man.

"A bit of unexpected verbal aggression can have a positive effect on a player. I remember winning a ball against Offaly, in the League semi-final in 1979, under Hill 16 and seeing the field open up in front of me. I passed the ball to Eamon McManus who was just in front of me and shouted at him 'to get up the f . . . . . . field'. He took off like a rocket. He told me afterwards that he was scared out of his wits."

Straight Talking

One of Earley's main reasons for wanting to have a book written about his life was to get the opportunity to set the record straight about the 1980 All-Ireland final. Specifically, he wanted to answer the repeated allegations made by Mick O'Dwyer, in particular, that Roscommon had used underhand tactics to take on Kerry.

"In all our discussions and practice sessions there was never once any mention of stopping, tripping, holding, or kicking an opponent. When they got the ball our job was to be as close as possible, to be absolutely committed to harass, to chase and to contest but always to play within the rules. When we got the ball our job was to be as elusive and creative as possible. At no stage was there even a hint that we should go out and be physical."

Although in recent years it has become fashionable for large crowds to attend training sessions before an All-Ireland final, the Roscommon team conducted their preparations in virtual isolation.

"In 1991 I was down in Tipperary to visit Mary's relatives. We went to Templemore one night to watch the hurling team in training, shortly before their All-Ireland final. There were more people watching the training than would have watched many of the club matches I ever played in.

"However, although we never had crowds like that, there was an excitement about Roscommon during the weeks before our All-Ireland final that I had never seen before or since. There was so much colour so much expectation."

The Hurlers on the Ditch

Speculation was rife in Roscommon about the composition of the team for the final. There were three main talking points.

A turning point in the semi-final victory over Armagh had been the replacement of Seamus Hayden by Marty McDermott in the Roscommon midfield. Although there were some who felt that McDermott's high-fielding exploits against Armagh would give him the edge for the second midfield position, the prevailing wisdom was that Hayden would get the nod.

The goalkeeping position attracted considerable comment both from Roscommon fans and the media. Gay Sheerin had conceded a soft goal in the semi-final and faced new competition with the recall of John McDermott to the Roscommon panel. McDermott had been one of the stars in the League final triumph in 1979. Speculation was intensified when McDermott was selected for a challenge match against Dublin. McDermott, like all his team-mates had a great match, with the Roscommon forwards scoring nine goals against John O'Leary. When the team was announced Tom Heneghan's thinking became clear. McDermott's recall was a shrewd tactical ploy to ensure that Sheerin was kept on his toes.

The other talking point was the selection of Aidan Dooley who was seen by some Roscommon fans as the team's Achilles heel. Whereas Gerry Connellan, the other newcomer to the county side in 1980, had stolen the hearts of Roscommon fans with his swashbuckling style, they were more reticent about Dooley. Although the Roscommon forward line had chalked up a phenomenal scoring tally on the way to the final, Aidan Dooley had only contributed two points. There was some dismay in the Armagh match when his "marker" Joey Donnelly scored two points.

"Aidan was the least known player on the team. He had tremendous skill and great speed. I always felt comfortable with him on the team. It was certainly not his fault that we lost the All-Ireland. There was disappointment for those players who did not make it. I thought the best team available was selected.

"I always felt that you needed 18 or 19 top class players to win an All-Ireland. Without being disrespectful to any of our panel we did not have enough great players. The great Kerry or Dublin teams always had a few players on the subs bench who were as good as the 15 on the field. We simply did not have that luxury. As it turned out what we had was nearly enough."

Roscommon fans were to learn the harsh lesson that 'nearly never does it'.

Within the management team there was a debate as to the most appropriate time to wind down before the final. The views of the team's most senior members were sought out.

"The former Tipperary star, now Adjutant General of the army, Tony Wall gave me an invaluable piece of advice: 'Always give yourself more rest than you think you need'.

"Ossie Bennet, the famous masseur, was working with us that year. He always wanted us to break training much earlier in the week before a game than we would want to. He felt that we should not look at a ball on the Friday or Saturday before a game.

"I remember going to a lecture in Trinity College one night on training methods in sports. The lecturer spoke about his own personal experiences as coach to the American Olympic swimming team. Three weeks before their Olympic trials one of their star swimmers got injured. Although he was unable to train, he took six seconds off his best time. The coach began to experiment with the amount of rest he allowed his swimmers and found that increased rest led to enhanced performance.

"Although I see the value of rest, it's very hard to take a break early. You always want to be at your peak and you get worried about losing an inch."

What It Said In The Papers

Roscommon's fitness level for the match could not have been higher and the preparations in general were very satisfactory. The only disappointment for Earley was the treatment of the press.

"The press are there and do a great job. They are more than part and parcel of the whole thing. My philosophy is that it is pointless to go out and beat the press. I always found it better to co-operate. I have found that if you make a request to journalists they will comply as regards confidentiality.

"We were a bit concerned about the massive build-up and wanted a low profile for Roscommon. We did have a press night which was beginning to be the trend at the time for All-Ireland finals. I disagree with that. I think it is a bit staged. The press want to see what is really going on and report it to their readers. I felt that the press should have been allowed to come in whenever they wanted.

"One evening John O'Shea came. He was ignored and not co-operated with. I felt that this detracted a bit from our preparations and said so at the time, but it was Tom Heneghan's decision and I understood the reasons for it. We were treated very fairly by the press but that incident was to be regretted."

There was one occasion when the hand of friendship was reached out to a member of the press.

"One night after a training session Eugene McGee came into our dressing-room. I didn't even know he was there until Michael O'Callaghan called for silence. He gave a short stirring speech to the effect that we should believe in our ability and that we had a fifty-fifty chance. There was no such thing as a certainty. If we went out and played with determination, heart and commitment we had every chance. He wished us well and left. A reporter from *The Kerryman* was also in the dressing-room. I saw him taking notes. I will always remember and be grateful to Eugene McGee for those encouraging comments."

Do I Remember? Will I Ever Forget?

A final light training session was arranged for the Saturday before the match. The previous day saw Dermot Earley taking a break from football by acting as best man at his brother Peter's wedding to Ena Courtney in Castlepollard. The day was memorable for a number of reasons.

"We had a lady photographer who took hours, after the ceremony, to ensure that the photos were right. At one stage she stood on the roof of a car to get the perfect shot. The wind blew her dress high in the air to the amusement of everybody as people were getting bored with all the waiting around.

"At the reception, as I was making my speech and thanking everybody, my mother was prompting me with names of people that I should not forget. Finally she reminded me of the photographer. I said: 'My mother is shouting at me not to forget the photographer'. To great applause I continued by saying: 'Will I ever forget the photographer?'"

"Various telegrams were read out. One came from the then Minister for Justice, Sean Doherty. Peter was a garda in Granard and this was the reason for the Minister's telegram. This telegram caused impressed 'oohs' and 'aahs'. In keeping with the occasion I decided to promote Peter several ranks so I responded by saying: 'On behalf of my brother the Superintendent'. This brought the house down."

As the proceedings started to slow down the best man had to make a decision about whether to make the journey home to Newbridge or book into a hotel in Roscommon. A phone call was made to the Abbey hotel to see if there were any rooms available. However, it was not possible to make a booking over the phone because the receptionist steadfastly refused to believe that the great Dermot Earley was ringing her up two nights before playing in All-Ireland final! She nearly fainted with surprise when Earley and his wife strode into the hotel an hour later.

A few minutes later it was the Earleys' turn to be surprised when there was a knock on the door. The mother of the current army press officer, Wally Young, came in with a tray laden down with tea, biscuits and cake. Twelve years later that act of kindness is remembered as vividly as the All-Ireland final itself.

After training the next morning it was back to the hotel where a sea of good will messages for the team enveloped the foyer. A gift to Earley was a giant horseshoe in the Roscommon colours which remains a treasured souvenir to this day.

A large crowd awaited the team as they made their way to the train station. The air of expectancy was shared by players and fans alike.

Tony McManus remembers that day with great affection: "I have never felt so good as I did that day. I couldn't wait to get out on the field. I would be a lot more nervous now because I get very uptight before big matches. Tom Heneghan summed up the situation before the match well. Both semi-finals had been high scoring matches. Tom said the final would be a low scoring match. Twelve scores would win it."

As the train came into the station it carried a giant Roscommon flag on both sides. CIE also provided the team with a huge cake which was dispatched by Pat Lindsay to the supporters when the players had eaten their portion. Bonfires blazed along the railway line between Roscommon and Athlone.

A quiet evening in the hotel was agreed to, despite Harry Keegan's suggestion that they should go and see a Rocky film to psyche themselves up for the occasion.

Most of the players wanted to watch *Match of the Day,* but a few were interested in snatching a quick glance at RTE's special pre-final programme. The team tuned in as Jimmy Deenihan was being interviewed, by telephone, from the team hotel by Liam O'Murchu. The Roscommon team got a great laugh from one question and answer: "An raibh tú ag feachaint ar an clár?", "Ní raibh. Bhíomar ag feachaint ar *Match of the Day.*"

This Is What It Is All About

The All-Ireland final is not simply a football match. It is a major national event in social and cultural terms. This is evocatively portrayed in Brendan Kennelly's poem *A Religious Occasion:*

I was there for a purpose, not a lark,
I shall long remember
That Sunday afternoon, one mild September,
Standing with 89, 374 Catholics in Croke Park.

Hearing the Artane Boys Band play with verve and spark
The National Anthem and Faith of our Fathers
The Christian faces of the spectators
were proof of the hard spiritual work.

That goes to make true lovers of sport
I was part of that crowd, one with electric feeling
That turns a rigid stranger into an instant brother.

It was, dare I say it, a religious occasion.

Although all of Earley's sporting life had been geared towards playing in the All-Ireland final, he awoke to an initial disappointment.

"The day dawned dull, wet and windy. It was very frustrating. I always enjoyed playing in wet conditions but the wind made a lottery out of everything. Here I was, playing in the biggest game of my life but the weather was not very suitable."

The players prepared for the game in the normal way. Team captain Danny Murray tucked into his customary steak at midday. The other players had a light meal as was their custom. Then it was time for the journey to Croke Park.

"The only part of the build-up which I disliked was entering the stadium. There was (and still is) no players' entrance. You either went in by the turnstiles or at the main gates. I felt that was wrong. You had to mingle with the crowd which slowed you down. This is not being disrespectful to the fans but you wanted to get in and get psyched up. I feel very strongly that there should be a players' entrance. You are in a tense mood and you just want to get inside.

"A few years later I saw two Kerry players paying to get into the ground for a match they were playing in when they arrived at the wrong entrance. This is not good enough."

In the sanctuary of the dressing-room all negative thoughts were quickly dispelled.

"I felt absolutely great. There were many visits to the toilet, phantom visits but you needed to be sure. I met the same players on the way in each time and we shared a joke about it.

"I remember running through the tunnel and coming out onto the pitch and all I could see was a sea of blue and gold and I said to myself: 'This is what it is all about'.

"The first time I walked out on Croke Park was the Saturday evening before our All-Ireland minor semi-final against Derry in 1965. I remember standing with Adrian O'Sullivan on the 50-yard line looking into the canal goal and saying: 'You could point a 50 easily.' The stadium that day was empty. Now it was full of blue and gold. As it turned out I pointed a 50 in the match and as the ball went over the bar I thought of that moment again.

"I will never forget the sea of colour as I walked around in the parade. I remember saying to myself: 'David isn't here and everything is as it should be.' The parade is one of the things you remember about a commentary as a kid. As I marched behind the Artane Boys Band I never felt as tall as I did that day. I felt strong in my arms and legs. I was so proud to walk the pitch.

"I shook hands with Jack O'Shea and Sean Walsh as we waited for the national anthem. As I sang the anthem I kept my eyes on the flag and tried to be as poised as possible. As an army officer it is important to stand to attention.

"As the referee checked his watch there was a tingle in my toes. It was a special tingle that only went through me once. It almost gave me goose-pimples. The blood drained from my face. I was deadly pale. I stood on the top of my toes. My feet were prancing, ready to get the right jump. The game was on."

A Report From Our Correspondent

Much has been said and written about the 1980 All-Ireland final. One version of the story is that of a titanic struggle between virginal purity

(Kerry) and demonic evil (Roscommon) with the forces of light overcoming the forces of dark.

Twelve years on Earley watched the game again on video and wrote his own report. This was prompted by a casual meeting with Mick O'Dwyer at a function in Newbridge towards the end of 1991 in which O'Dwyer brought up the game again, summarising it in the following way: "Ye should have beaten us but ye were far too physical."

In the course of the All-Stars tour in 1980, Mick O'Dwyer made similar comments which are still clearly remembered by Tony McManus.

"Although Dermot said nothing at the time, it was the only time I have ever seen him really angry. There was reference made to the treatment of John Egan. The implication was that Harry Keegan (who marked him in the final) was a dirty player. Anybody who knows Harry Keegan knows that such a suggestion is completely false. Personally, that annoyed me more than anything. John Egan would be the first to admit Harry was not like that."

In the past, Earley has always 'bitten his lip' about such comments. For a long time he has waited for the correct forum to present his side of the story. He was intensely disappointed to lose the final but time healed the wounds. He was hurt by the way Roscommon's performance was portrayed, that hurt has lingered much longer and is periodically reinforced when the same one-sided account of the final is repeated.

Other Roscommon players share his annoyance. Tony McManus recalls his own experience in the final.

"I felt that those who criticised Roscommon so vehemently conveniently overlooked a few tackles that our forwards had to take. Every time I went for the ball that day, I had my jersey pulled. I accept that as part and parcel of the game, but then to hear Mick O'Dwyer's comments after the match you would think that all the sinning was all on one side and that Kerry were above reproach."

Mick O'Dwyer has said on the record: "In 1980, Roscommon had us beat if they played football."

Rather than answering O'Dwyers allegations on a general level, Earley has opted to correct the imbalance by reviewing the match and responding to all the disparaging remarks in the context of the following report. True to form it begins with a candid admission:

"This was not a great All-Ireland final. Both sets of defenders were well on top and scoring chances were at a premium. Marking was extremely close and this resulted in too many frees as a result of pulling and dragging. The referee booked three players from each side but it was not a dirty game. However, many of his decisions left the players bewildered, not to mention the crowd. Roscommon suffered more than Kerry in this area. We became frustrated and our game suffered as a result. Kerry deserved to win because they took their chances well. We had the winning of the game from placed balls alone but the concentration slipped and so did the opportunity for victory.

"Each time I have looked at the final again, I experience an excitement that I know should not be there but is brought on by the occasion of the final and that there will unfold before me the missed opportunities of scores and chances lost that would have made us All-Ireland champions.

"The start was magic – a goal from John O'Connor followed by sustained pressure from Roscommon and a further point from Seamus Hayden. Then Kerry took over and threw the ball around but our defence was good. Gerry Connellan and Mike Sheehy appear to be booked by the referee and then Tommy Doyle and I got our names taken. This happened as Kerry came forward. I turned hard to the left to follow the attack and bumped hard into the back of a Kerry player. He turned and let me have one in the face. The ref called us together as I got off the ground. The Kerry man was my former army colleague, Tommy Doyle. The referee booked me. I asked him: 'Why are you booking me ref?' He said nothing. He booked Doyle then moved away. Tommy and I looked at one another. We shook hands. There were no hard feelings but I was disappointed to be booked in my first All-Ireland final. Micheál O'Hehir in his commentary said: 'Tommy was a lucky man, he wasn't sent to the side-line,' but then the ref decided to hop the ball and O'Hehir wondered who hit who. Now I got frustrated as I felt doubly punished, i.e. booked and lost a free to a hop ball.

"Roscommon got going again and John O'Gara hit a good point from 50-yards. It was 1-2 to 0-0 with 12 minutes gone. The pace of the game seemed fast but there were a lot of frees some of which, if not called, would lead to open play. But the free was awarded and the defences had time to cover up. The game was very tight so far.

"Mike Sheehy scored a free after Harry Keegan fouled Ogie Moran and then Ger Power kicked a good left footed point from 45-yards. We moved forward again and Mick Finneran was penalised for holding the ball too long. We felt the free should have been to us. Micheál O'Hehir commented: 'There are those who think he held the Roscommon man a bit too long.' We got a line ball under the Hogan stand and Tom Donnelan drove it low, infield. Tom Doyle gathered, passed to Pat Spillane while running forward, drew the defence and slipped the ball to Mike Sheehy who hand-passed it to the net. It was 1-2 apiece. Our good start was gone. We regained the lead when I pointed a 50 and then Harry Keegan was penalised for a foul on John Egan. Nobody knew for what, as he had cleanly and with great skill, turned, trapped the ball with his left foot and let Egan run by. More frustration. Mike Sheehy points a free a few moments later – level again. There were no further scores in the first-half but a few incidents did occur."

Firstly, the linesman, David Foley, called for the attention of the referee and they both went to the Roscommon dug-out. Play was held up. We had the wind and we didn't want to waste time. Tom Heneghan was told to stay in the dug-out. Mick O'Dwyer was up on the line for much of the first-half and nothing was said to him. Time was being wasted and selective justice was administered – more frustration.

"Jim Deenihan won a free under the Cusack Stand. The free was taken and as Roscommon won the ball, the referee halted play as Mick O'Dwyer was on the side-line with substitute Ger O'Driscoll. It looked as if O'Driscoll was being introduced. The referee went to the line and discussed the situation with O'Dwyer. O'Driscoll was not introduced. The free was retaken. Roscommon did not win the ball that time. More frustration.

"Gerry Fitzmaurice and Pat Spillane were involved in an incident off the ball. It was also off-screen. Pat was on the ground and took an age to get up. Time went by and many efforts were made to assist his recovery, to no avail. Eventually he staggered up. Both players appeared to be booked and play resumed with a hop ball. Micheál O'Hehir wondered: 'Is Pat Spillane really hurt or is he in line for an Oscar?' Much time had been wasted again.

"Thirty-seven minutes after the ball was thrown in at the start of the game the first-half ended. Two minutes of extra time was played. Spillane must have been down for about 4 minutes not to mention the other stoppages. It was 1-3 all and now we had to face the wind.

"At the start of the second-half there were good bouts of play up and down the field and Aidan Dooley was short with a shot that Charlie Nelligan easily held. Then Mike Sheehy put Kerry ahead for the first time in the game from a free. The marking continued tight and it was hard to break down either defence. John O'Connor ran on to a great ball from Mick Finneran but arrived fractionally too soon and over ran the ball. The chance was lost. Spillane hand-passed over the bar. Shortly after Charlie Nelligan made a great reflex save from John O'Connor when he deflected his first time shot over the bar. The play looked good all this time and taking account of the wet and very windy conditions, and the closeness of the marking by all the players, the standard was quite high.

"Roscommon put on good pressure but we missed two frees by Mick Finneran and our efforts went for naught. At the other end Sheehy punished us with a free and it was 1-6 to 1-4 after 20 minutes. We scored two points in the next 3 minutes and missed a free too. John O'Connor's point in the 23rd minute levelled the match. It was to be our last score.

"Jack O'Shea gave Kerry the lead with a point. We scrambled a 50 when a goal was on and I drove it wide. Two further Sheehy frees gave Kerry two points. The final score was 1-9 to 1-6. Kerry won and deservedly so, before a crowd of 63, 854.

"As I pondered the result it stood out that the difference between the teams was Mike Sheehy's accurate free taking. He scored six frees and a goal from play. Although Roscommon scored 1-4 from play to Kerry's 1-3, we missed frees we should have scored. We should have been level at least going into the final moments and who knows what might have happened then.

"Our defence was magnificent, all six of them, but so were Kerry's rearguard. The midfield was even enough with both sets of midfielders on top at different times but O'Shea and Walsh probably shaded it a little. The closeness of the contest in each section of the field accounted for some of the frees but whereas much physical contact took place from both sides all through, it was not a dirty game. Yes, after a marvellous start, Roscommon seemed to change their style of play as the openings which were there in the first few moments were quickly closed off by the Kerry defensive unit. I have explained this change of play many times as a self-conscious feeling that Kerry would whittle down our early lead. What happened was that the fear of losing overcame the will to win. Roscommon were not dirty.

"I have two further observations to make. The first one concerns my own play. I was extremely disappointed when I saw the number of times I fouled an opponent in this game. It was always my policy never to foul and if I did foul during the course of a game I resolved afterwards to play more skillfully and disposes my opponent rather than foul him. In this All-Ireland final I stretched a jersey and grabbed at a ball in the hands of Sean Walsh but to mention two examples. I can only explain that the fear of losing dictated that my opponent would not be allowed go free and set up a move or score. I did not go out with the intention of fouling and did not realise until I saw the game recently on tape for the first time in 12 years that I had fouled a number of times during the game. The fact that this game took place 12 years ago does not diminish my disappointment at committing these fouls. The lesson at the end was that Mike Sheehy punished our fouls. We did not punish Kerry's.

"My second point relates to personnel in each dug-out. The cameras scanned both a number of times during the game. In the Kerry dug-out sat Joe Keohane, a selector and Frank King the county chairman. Two gentlemen – always friendly. In the Roscommon dug-out sat Michael

O'Callaghan the county chairman and Phil Gannon the county secretary. Two gentlemen and special friends of mine. All four looked anxious and concerned, 'wondering will their county win?' All four are no longer with us. May they rest in peace . . . Doesn't that put the whole thing into perspective?"

Another Kerry Angle

Although Mick O'Dwyer had been very critical of Roscommon's tactics this opinion is not shared by the Kerry players. Like O'Dwyer, Jimmy Deenihan frankly admitted that Kerry should have lost but he disagreed with him about the tactics which were used.

"It was a game we all acknowledge that Kerry should have lost. It was probably unfortunate for them that they went ahead so early because we had a long time to haul them back. We adapted our tactics for that game. Our backs played very tight and blotted out their 'star' forwards. If we hadn't adapted our tactics I am sure that we would have lost.

"The Roscommon defence marked very closely. At times they lacked discipline and were over exuberant but they were certainly not dirty. They were a very good side and did not need to resort to thuggery. They played hard and there were a few times when they went over the top but that happens in every tense match when there is so much at stake. I do not think it is fair to say that Roscommon resorted to underhand tactics."

Deenihan is genuinely puzzled about the story of a history of bad blood between Roscommon and Kerry going back to 1978.

"There were very close friendships between players on both sides, that of Eoin Liston and John O'Gara being a particularly good example. I for my part had great admiration for the Roscommon players, especially Dermot Earley. He was a tremendous athlete and a great disciplinarian. He had a great attitude and was unfortunate never to have won an All-Ireland medal. I never liked meeting him after beating him in a big game because I knew how much it must have hurt him to lose."

Ogie Moran is amazed and dismayed by the suggestion that there was hostility between the Roscommon and Kerry players.

"Myself and Eoin Liston struck up a great relationship with John O'Gara and Tony McManus. They used to come down and visit us for the Listowel races. I also had great relations with the Roscommon Gaels players on the team because of playing club matches against them with Shannon Rangers.

"We were lucky to win that All-Ireland and Dermot Earley was unlucky not to fulfil his dream and win an All-Ireland medal on the day. It was a tough game but I would not say that Roscommon used 'dirty tricks'.

Jack O'Shea felt that the shape of the game was determined by the conditions.

"It was a wet breezy day and not a day for either Kerry or Roscommon to play the type of attractive football they were capable of. The marking was very tight on both sides. The Roscommon defence set about their task with great determination. Maybe once or twice they went further than they should have but I am sure that they did not set out to be physical."

Tommy Doyle does not accept that there was any hostility between Roscommon and Kerry following the Ceannarus match in 1978.

"I would not say that there was bad blood following the treatment of our lads. I missed that match as I broke my arm against Roscommon in the 1978 semi-final. At the end of the day Roscommon won the match and I am sure their supporters were delighted, just as the Kerry supporters would have been."

In April 1992, the 1980 All-Ireland final was one of the topics of conversation between Doyle and Earley. Doyle's memories are happy ones.

"Last Easter Monday I played in the 'Mick Moran memorial trophy' in Ballybunion for our Kerry 'four-in-a-row' team against the All-Star selection organised by Ogie Moran and Eoin Liston. I met Dermot for the first time in five or six years and I must say that he looks younger than I. I would have to say that we were lucky to win the All-Ireland. Mike Sheehy won the game with his expert free taking. The Roscommon team must have been feeling very dejected and down-hearted because they came so close, and it is a hard thing to be beaten in a final after all the training. I would not say that Roscommon used dirty tactics. It was a wet windy day so there was not going to be open play, as the Roscommon backs were very strong and well prepared."

Holding Back the Tears

The final whistle did not simply end the All-Ireland it shattered Earley's life long ambition. The feeling of emptiness was almost overwhelming.

"I can remember turning around and shaking hands with Seanie Walsh. I remember Ger Power being close by and there was a clap on the back and a smile and an exchange of 'Congratulations' and 'Hard luck'. I turned around immediately because I was absolutely shattered and completely disappointed and I then walked to the dressing-room. Sean Kilbride who was a sub on the team that day caught me by the arm, I looked around and realised that the disappointment was there but you had to get on with your life and had to do things correctly.

"As the cup was presented to Ger Power, I thought – we were so close, we could have won the game. I would say that we should have won the game.

"There was not any jealousy there. Kerry deserved to win the game and had taken their chances well but for us there was nothing. Everything was gone. The whole effort that had been put in was not rewarded. Kerry took their trophy and everything was directed to them at that stage. The Roscommon supporters were absolutely drained of energy. The looks of disappointment as they came forward to console us will live with me forever."

In the post-match situation the losers have at best a peripheral role.

"I think there is a role for the losers after the match. I like the way they do it in soccer where the losers go up the steps for their medals. I know there was a faux pas in Wembley in 1992 when the losers were presented with the winners' medals by mistake. I feel it is appropriate to have medals presented at the end of the match and have them inscribed afterwards. At the very least the losers should walk up and shake the hands of the president of the GAA."

The Sound of Silence

After the game the Roscommon dressing-room was almost totally silent. Nobody wanted to talk about what had happened.

"I had been in many dressing-rooms after losing matches but there was nothing which came close to that day. Our defeats in three semi-finals were terrible but this was worse."

A number of fans came into the dressing-room to offer words of consolation. The disappointment on their faces was every bit as intense as that of the players.

"My father came in with Paul. The first words he said were: 'There will be next year'. His only comment on the match was that we had missed many chances and that I should have taken the frees. One of the things that he would always do when I played an important game, or before a big event in my life, such as going on a peace-keeping mission abroad was to take out a silver coin and spit on it and wish me luck. He did that on the morning of the final. He did the same thing in 1982 when I saw him for the last time as I headed off on a peace-keeping mission abroad. Just as he had offered words of encouragement to me as an 8-year-old, there he was with me in the worst moment of my sporting life with a positive message: 'Next year'."

Although the entire Roscommon team were weighed down with depression, nobody had an idea that this would be the end of their run of Connacht titles.

Tony McManus recalls his feelings at the time: "We were sick after losing but I thought I would be back again next year and many times afterwards. How wrong I was."

Earley did not know then that his only chance of winning an All-Ireland medal was gone.

"I thought we would come back. Even though we were beaten we had proved that we certainly were the second best team in the country and perhaps next year we would be the very best."

Nonetheless with the benefit of hindsight Earley now identifies the aftermath of the All-Ireland final as the beginning of the end of that Roscommon team.

"The thing that disappointed me most was that although we had been a very close unit in the build-up everyone went their separate ways afterwards. Some of the players returned some did not. I remember saying to Mary as we travelled back on the bus: 'We should all be together.' We had stopped being a team. We were never really together as a unit again.

"This disunity happened a lot with Roscommon. Win or lose, players went their own way afterwards, to celebrate or drown their sorrows with their friends. Often after a post-match meal at a hotel I would be leaving for home when some of the players would be arriving. This did not help the ultimate unity which you need to win matches.

"Although we got back to Croke Park the next year for the League final, the spirit we had in 1980 was gone. There were huge changes in attitude, preparation, procedures and personnel. The difference was really shown up when we went out in the first round of the championship against Sligo. Looking back now, I think the rot set in the evening of the All-Ireland final when we failed to stick together."

Ah Ref

A major controversy erupted immediately after the game about the standard of refereeing. The Roscommon county chairman, Michael O'Callaghan, was particularly critical of the referee Seamus Murray's performance and his comments were reported extensively in the media. "The referee had officiated at the classic 1977 All-Ireland semi-final between Dublin and Kerry. If he had the ability to referee such a match he was not a bad referee. You do not become a bad referee overnight. At the same time, referees too, can have their off days.

"I remember two incidents in particular. I tumbled Tim Kennelly to the ground with a perfectly fair shoulder and a free was given against me. In his commentary, Micheál O'Hehir said: 'That is the most ridiculous decision I have ever seen in an All-Ireland Final'. At the time I wondered what we had to do to get fair play. It was very frustrating.

"On one occasion Pat Spillane was down on the ground. He said himself he was not injured but was feigning injury as he was looking for his contact lenses. The referee stood over the ball and faced the Roscommon goal. It was not clear whether the referee was going to give a free-in to Kerry in a good scoring position or not. I thought that if I gave the referee an option, he might let us off. I walked up to him and said: 'Ref, is it a free out or a hop ball?' He looked at me uncertainly and said: 'Ah. It's a hop ball'. This gave us the opportunity to clear the ball, which we took.

"Afterwards Mary expressed her disappointment to Jimmy Smyth who was involved in the selection of referees at Croke Park. All the fifty-fifty decisions seemed to go against Roscommon that day."

A Long Day's Journey Into The Night

There was a huge demand for tickets to the function for the Roscommon team that night. The talk that night was of the 'might have beens'. The players themselves struggled to make conversation.

That evening a convoy of cars and buses made their way home. The normal buzz of chat and banter was noticeably absent. One of the songs that came on the radio was the hit single from Abba: 'The Winner Takes It All'.

Those five words said it all.

7. The Morning After Optimism

The best thing about this match was the final whistle.

This one comment typified the press reports in the daily papers the morning after the All-Ireland final. Anger and resentment displaced disappointment as the Roscommon players were given a synopsis of all the articles about the game at the breakfast table. All the blame for what had happened the day before had been put on Roscommon's shoulders.

The entire morning was to be something to be endured rather than to be enjoyed. Convention dictated that the players attend a repeat screening of the final with the Kerry team. Some of the Roscommon players required extensive persuasion to attend, causing the others to have a forty-five minute wait on the coach.

"As we arrived, the wife of one of the Kerry players said understandingly: 'This is your horror movie' It was a very appropriate comment because that was exactly how we found the experience.

"For me it was a very uncomfortable feeling watching the match, it is a difficult thing for a losing team to do. If I was in authority I don't think I would promote it. You have already lost the game and you don't want to be beside your conquerors watching them put one over on you the day after. I think it humiliates the loser and that the best thing would be to mingle with the winning team informally. "

There was no bitterness against Kerry but there was a frosty atmosphere between the Roscommon players and the media. Even Dermot Earley, who normally co-operated with the press to the fullest, responded to questions with monosyllabic answers. However, he did give a lengthy interview to Tom O'Riordan of the *Sunday Independent*.

The pained expression on Earley's face as he relates these events suggest that the wounds from this experience cut very deep.

"At the All-Star function that year I discussed the matter at length with Peadar O'Brien of the *Irish Press* and Paddy Downey of the *Irish*

Times. When I explained how I felt Paddy Downey came in on my side and agreed with me."

The press coverage of the match was also a topic of conversation on RTE radio that morning. Accordingly, David Davin Power requested an interview with Earley for the *News at One-Thirty*.

"I mentioned my disappointment that the first final I had played in was written up as a shambles. I said that if we had won the match the press would have written up the game another way.

"I also said that we were disappointed that Eoin Liston did not play and that it was a shame for any footballer to miss the All-Ireland final for any reason, but particularly for ill-health. We felt all along we could have beaten Kerry with him because in Pat Lindsay we had a full-back who could have held him.

"I got reaction all round the country after that interview. A few days later I was walking down the street in Newbridge. Somebody I never saw before came right up to me and said: 'Hard luck. I heard you on the News at One-Thirty. As usual you were very fair'."

The lunch was followed by speeches. The Roscommon contingent were very appreciative of the Kerry captain Ger Power's speech in which he pointed out that it would be difficult for anybody to understand what had happened in the match without being on the pitch themselves. Accordingly, it was unfair to be too harsh in the criticism of the game.

"It was a relief to leave the lunch. As I walked across the foyer Ger Power walked out with the Sam Maguire cup in a plastic bag. I thought to myself if only Roscommon had it, we would not treat it like that. Kerry accepted winning All-Irelands as natural."

Later that evening organised chaos prevailed. As the team waited in Heuston Station for the train journey home, an incident occurred which highlighted the unique popularity of Earley with fans of the game and offered a parable of the GAA – an organisation which can transcend rivalries and serve as a potentially unifying force in society.

"As I stood there, on a cold and dark September evening, I was still feeling very disappointed. A gentleman in an overcoat touched me by the arm and said: 'I just came down this evening to be sure to meet

Dermot Earley. As a Kerryman I am sorry you did not win yesterday because you deserve an All-Ireland medal.' I don't know what I said to him. He was gone almost as soon as he said those words. I cannot remember his name but I will never ever forget the gesture."

A Hero's Welcome

As soon as the team crossed the Shannon they got an early hint of the reception that lay in store for them. Bonfires blazed on the track from Athlone to Roscommon. The players were awestruck by the welcome that awaited them. Estimates of the attendance varied but 20,000 was the figure most often quoted.

The infectious enthusiasm of the fans brought the Roscommon team from the depths of despair to a communal emotional high. Roscommon town had never seen anything quite like it before. The speeches were passionate and elicited almost hysterical responses. Every time the words 'next year' were mentioned the crowd went into overdrive.

Roscommon's man of the match in the final, Harry Keegan, was identified on a number of occasions which brought rapturous applause. The overwhelming reaction from the crowd provided an uplifting postscript to the heart-break of the previous day.

As he began the long drive home at 2 a.m. the next morning, there was a poignant moment for Dermot as he passed Douglas Hyde Park – home of the Roscommon team and scene of so much blood, sweat and tears in the team's preparation. Despite all the sacrifices they had made, the team had not reaped the ultimate reward.

A few hours later he was making his way into work. Words of comfort were passed from familiar and unfamiliar faces alike as he journeyed through Newbridge out to the Curragh. His army colleagues were very supportive and encouraging.

An unpleasant surprise lay on his desk. Inside a brown official army envelope was a blank piece of paper with the following words poorly typed across the middle: 'Fair means or foul. Next time try the former.'

Realising that he might receive other such mail he resolved to check all correspondence for a signature. Those which were unsigned would be shredded without even being read. Over the next fortnight nine such letters were discarded.

Picking Up The Pieces

Sunday 5 October saw the resumption of the National League. Roscommon began their campaign with an easy victory over Kildare 3-14 to 0-8. The following Sunday an experimental Roscommon team was beaten by Offaly in the Ceannarus tournament semi-final.

The next major event on the GAA calendar was the All-Stars trip to America. In the first minute of the third match Earley was forced to withdraw with a pulled muscle. His difficulty was Paddy Quirke's opportunity. Quirke was a dual player from Carlow who never got the platform to show his immense talent to a national audience because Carlow were starved of success. Playing with the cream of Gaelic footballers on that day his credentials were plain for all to see – his exhibition of football earned him the 'Man of the Match' status.

On 12 November the Roscommon-Kerry rivalry was renewed in a League match in Tralee. A late Liam Tiernan point snatched a draw for Roscommon. It was another competitive game with both sides playing well. At one stage a Roscommon goal seemed certain when Aidan Dooley's shot beat Charlie Nelligan but the ball got stuck in the mud.

1981 started with Roscommon's defeat of Dublin in the National League by 0-10 to 1-5. A draw in their final match secured Roscommon a place in the National League semi-final against Mayo. The game was to be played in Hyde Park. A story circulating in Roscommon before the match suggested the reason the county had secured home advantage. The main priority at a meeting in Ballyhaunis to decide home venue was to get it over with quickly. Roscommon county secretary Phil Gannon was asked to write the names of both counties on separate pieces of paper and put them into a hat. The story was that he wrote Roscommon's name down twice.

"Knowing Phil Gannon as I did, I doubt very much if he would have done that but it was a good story. "

Roscommon went on to beat Mayo by 1-11 to 1-6 a match remembered for the brilliance of John O'Connor and a great goal from Earley. Roscommon had qualified for the second League final in three years. This time it was to be an all Connacht decider against Galway.

In March, Connacht football had received a major boost when the province beat Ulster in the Railway Cup semi-final. The game ended in whirlwind fashion. Connacht trailed by four points with just two minutes to go. A penetrating run through the Ulster defence brought Earley into the square where he was grounded. As cool as an iceberg Tony McManus dispatched the ball past Brian McAlinden in the Ulster goal. As the seconds ticked away only one point separated the teams. The Connacht fans who had been leaving the ground came streaming back following the almighty roar which greeted Tony's penalty.

As the crowd looked nervously at their watches Danny Murray made a great solo run up the field and was fouled. The referee informed the Connacht captain, Dermot Earley, that he must score direct from 40 yards out. His aim was straight and true. Connacht emerged victorious in extra time with a 2-19 to a 2-14 scoreline. However, they were unable to match Munster in the final.

With memories of the 1979 League final against Cork fresh in their minds, Roscommon fans made the now familiar journey to Croke Park. The dream of glory quickly turned to a nightmare. From the outset Galway took complete control. Brian Talty turned in a five star performance and received able assistance from Billy Joyce. A spectacular late goal from Earley, a thunderous left-footed shot through a crowded goal, only gave a veneer of respectability to the final score. Although Galway were forced to play with fourteen men for a long period, the final score was 1-11 to 1-2 in their favour. Much later Earley was able to take a morsel of comfort from the fact that his friend Billy Joyce had at last won a national honour.

Roscommon's performance was abysmal and was to prove an omen of things to come but even the most pessimistic primrose and blue follower could not have been prepared for the disaster that was to come next.

The Nadir

Sligo caused the upset of the year in 1981 when defeating Roscommon by 2-9 to 1-8 in the Connacht semi-final at Markievicz Park on a sunny June afternoon. The game was finely balanced with James Kearins and Earley swapping goals until Kearins broke through for a second goal.

The game was a personal triumph for Sligo's Barnes Murphy who was team manager and came on as a substitute in the second half. The result came like a bolt out of the blue for the Roscommon fans and players.

"Our preparation for the championship was very poor. The weather had been very wet and we were unable to cut the grass in Hyde Park. We were training in a meadow really and it wasn't going very well. Its not in my nature to be critical but I was a bit unhappy when our team captain, Tony McManus, went on a holiday. He had just qualified as a vet the year before and had been studying very hard and then he was working very hard in his new job and felt he needed a break. I was disappointed that he did. I felt we needed a leader with us in training. I can remember the evening he returned all bronzed and tanned. I was pleased he was back but something in my mind said perhaps it was too late."

Tony also remembers the problems in 1981. "We had problems with our build-up. I went on holiday for three weeks. Dermot was probably annoyed with that. If we had got over the Sligo match I felt that we would have got our act together and won the Connacht final but we did not put it together."

A number of changes in personnel and a series of positional switches were made from the 1980 side. Eyebrows were raised throughout the county when Gerry Beirne was recalled from oblivion to the county-side. He had formed an effective midfield unit with Earley in the Connacht final victory over Mayo in 1972 but had not featured in the Roscommon colours since a brief appearance against Armagh in the 1977 All-Ireland semi-final. To Roscommon fans his recall suggested a regression rather than an indication of better things to come. Earley was shunted from midfield to the half-forward line. The problems were not just at midfield but right through the team. To a large extent the problems were attidudinal.

"We had an 'it will be all right on the night mentality'. We had cruised through the League and had qualified for the final without playing well which sometimes can be the sign of a good team. We thought we would get through without putting in the work but you will never succeed without going through the pain barrier. Our League final performance was pathetic. There was a panic reaction to it rather than building on the strengths of the previous year. The drastic changes that were made afterwards caused doubts about the team and that was a significant factor in our defeat.

"As I look back on the whole thing now, I see the fact that we did not stick together after the All-Ireland final, as the beginning of the end. The organisation slipped a bit after that. Perhaps it was right that I was taken out of midfield, but maybe not. We did not appear to have a midfield partnership that would replace Seamus Hayden and myself. I did not think the writing was on the wall, but I felt the wrong decisions were made. I thought the mistakes would not be fatal but that the Sligo match would highlight them and we could learn from them. I expressed my strong reservations, privately, to Tom Heneghan. I felt that if we were to be successful we needed to bring new blood on to the team but that was not happening.

"As the game went on we reacted poorly and guys who had played well in previous years did not perform well. The championship is different from all other matches. No matter how good or how bad your opponents are, there is a high level of nervous tension which can inhibit a good performance. You have to hand it to Sligo, they took their opportunities well and deserved to win. We did not. We did not go in hungry enough. Complacency was the major reason we lost.

"After the match I went into the Sligo dressing-room to congratulate my old team-mate from St Nathy's, Barnes Murphy. The Sligo players were delighted to have won. Barnes put his arm on my shoulder and called for silence. The Sligo players gathered around me. He said that two of the greatest players ever to come out of Connacht were their own Mickey Kearins and myself. The Sligo players applauded. I did not want this to happen. I just wanted to speak to Barnes.

"When I got back to our dressing-room there was stony silence. It was the worst dressing-room I was ever in. Nobody spoke. They just stared ahead. Any words that day, no matter how magnificent and glorious, would have been lost. I can see the dressing-room now. People were sitting with their heads down or with their heads between their legs, gear half-off, boots still on, jerseys on the floor. I shook hands with Pat Lindsay and that was all that I could do.

"As always I was last out of the dressing-room. There were up to two hundred people outside. They all thought that it was my last game for Roscommon. Some people came up to shake hands with me. A few had tears in their eyes. There was sustained applause as I walked away. You take some sort of satisfaction from the respect people have for you, but it was only a glimmer.

"I did not allow the question of retiring to take over but it was at the back of my mind. It was at the end of a long period of success for Roscommon. I remember thinking our glory days were truly over."

Is it A Bird Or is It A Plane? No. It's Dermot Earley

After a few days of soul-searching the desire to continue playing returned with a flourish. There was to be a long wait until Roscommon's next significant outing against Mayo, in the semi-final of the Gael Linn Cup in 1981. Earley's problem was that he was due to play for his club Sarsfields in the Kildare county semi-final on that same day. Tom Heneghan was adamant that he should play for Roscommon later that evening. The match was important because it would bring the team back together and give them a goal to aim for.

The only way to ensure that Earley would get to Ballyhaunis in time for the match against Mayo was by air. His close friend Jack Boothman whisked him away from the pitch straight after winning the club match and drove him to an air-strip at a stud farm in Kildare where a small aircraft took him to Castlebar airport. From there Roscommon county secretary Paddy Francis Dwyer drove him to Ballyhaunis. The crowds going into the game were causing a traffic jam. He ran four hundred yards up the road and arrived in the Roscommon dressing-room just as Tom Heneghan was giving his final instructions.

Roscommon won by 1-8 to 0-9. The goal came from a spectacular twenty yard drop-shot from Tom Donlon. Five of Roscommon's points came from their 'jetsetter'.

The final against Galway in Hyde Park was scheduled for a fortnight later. However, the Kildare county final was scheduled for the same day. An additional complication was that Roscommon, unlike Castlebar, did not have its own airfield. Eventually a landing site (two big fields with a gap between them) was found. This meant that an even lighter aircraft would have to be used.

The pilot felt that the best course of action was to take off in Kildare with the same plane as had been used two weeks earlier and then land and board the lightest plane available at an airfield in Westmeath. As Jack Boothman again took Earley from the pitch following Sarsfields defeat by Raheens, a supporter asked if he was trying to smuggle him away.

The match had started as they flew over Hyde Park. A Garda escort was ready to ensure the quickest passage onto the field. The Sarsfields gear was replaced by the Roscommon gear in record time. There was sustained applause as he came onto the field and he immediately came on at corner-forward, where he scored two points. Roscommon lost by 0-7 to 0-11. For all Earley's efforts he had just two defeats to show for the day and no trip to America.

Thou Shalt Not Seek Publicity

The League campaign began poorly for Roscommon, going down to defeats by both Galway and Offaly. On 22 November Roscommon's fortunes took a turn for the better with the defeat of Kerry. Following an injury to Marty McDermott, Earley was moved out to midfield where he had one of his best ever displays for Roscommon, scoring five of the team's nine points from play.

The following Friday he was on his Command and Staff Course. The guest lecturer for the day was from the army press corps. Not surprisingly the subject for discussion was relations with the press. A repeated instruction was given that army officers should not seek publicity.

At lunch-time the *Irish Independent* was circulated. The 'Sportstar of the Week' was none other than Dermot Earley. All his class-mates ganged up on him and informed him he was in breach of army rules!

Roscommon's final game of the year was a League match against Armagh in Kiltoom. The home side led by a point when in the dying moments an Armagh forward raced through the Roscommon defence and appeared to kick the ball four yards wide. To the consternation of the crowd and disbelief of the players, the umpire put up the white flag for a point. In his enthusiasm to get the play going again so that Roscommon could manufacture a winning score, Gay Sheerin rushed to get the spare ball he had beside the goal, pushing the umpire out of the way in the process. The umpire called the referee's attention to the incident and Sheerin was booked.

The final whistle sounded moments later. The match ended in a draw. The Roscommon fans were very agitated with the decision about the equalising point. It was necessary for the Roscommon players, including Sheerin, to form a circle around the referee to ensure that he was protected.

Shortly after, Sheerin was summonsed to appear before the games disciplinary committee. Earley was also requested to attend as a witness.

"It was a bit of an ordeal. Ten or twelve people sat around a table. We had to wait a long time outside. Gay made his case and I was next. In Gay's defence the fact that he had come to the referee's aid when his safety was threatened and that his intention was to retrieve the ball and not to harm the umpire, stood in his favour. We had to wait a long time for the result. He was warned about his future conduct."

What's Another Year?

Roscommon failed to qualify for the knock-out stages of the League in 1982 but the campaign had uncovered some promising young talent. Among them was the captain of the 1981 Connacht champions minor side, Paul Earley.

"When I came back from my two year stint in the Middle East in 1977 Paul was a thirteen year old going to secondary school in Ballyhaunis.

He was playing great football for his school and his club. Unfortunately as I was in Newbridge I never saw him play but I heard a lot about him. Throughout the period 1977-81 he was doing his thing in relation to football and I was doing mine. When we met we talked about games but although he saw me playing, I never saw him."

The first round of the championship provided Roscommon with a welcome opportunity to lay the ghost of the previous year when they were again drawn against Sligo. Roscommon got off to a dream start.

Before the match Roscommon had worked on a new strategy in training. The plan was that should Roscommon get a free kick just outside scoring distance, that both corner-forwards would drag their men out to the sidelines and that Tony McManus would run forward from the number fourteen position while Dermot Earley would float the ball into the open space for Mick Finneran to run in and bury the ball in the back of the net. The plan worked to perfection and the team were a goal up in the first minute.

The Earley brothers combined later in the game to set up Michael Finneran for a second goal. The following morning a newspaper report cast doubt on the legitimacy of the handpass from 'the elder brother to the younger brother.' Roscommon ran out easy winners and qualified to play Galway in the Connacht semi-final.

Top Gun

Two days before the Galway match army duties took Earley to Baldonnel airport where he bumped into John Flanagan, brother of Mayo star Dermot, a pilot in the air corps and goalie with the army's footballing team. Earley decided to go on a test flight with his goalkeeping friend. It was not an experience he would forget in a hurry!

"I was kitted out in a flying suit, proper helmet, and oxygen. This experience was unbelievable, as for the first time in my life I went through all the hoops, and acrobatics he could muster. We ended up in Newbridge and I could see my house down below. Then he handed the controls over to me. The problem I had, was although I could steer perfectly well, the aircraft was gaining height steadily instead of staying at twelve thousand feet. John turned to Blessington lakes and we were flying an inch above water or so it seemed. He asked me did I want to go under or over Blessington bridge. We turned back to Baldonnel where we came in at 400 mph and then went straight up in the air and circled three times before landing. Although I did not get sick, when we went out of the plane and I looked in the mirror, I was as white as a ghost. At the time I was not sure if I would be able to play against Galway but a few hours later I was back to normal."

The semi-final was a dour match with very little between the teams, Galway winning by 1-9 to 0-9. The crucial score was a Galway penalty following a foul on substitute Tom Naughton. For Roscommon fans it was the same old story – failure to take chances. Tony McManus offers a slightly different explanation: "We had lost the habit of winning."

Nonetheless, Roscommon fans took heart from the improved performance by comparison with the fiasco of the previous year. Galway went on to prove that they were a very good side, crushing Mayo in the Connacht final and losing the All-Ireland semi-final against Offaly by just one point, the year Offaly won the All-Ireland with Seamus Darby's late goal.

Roscommon's future looked more promising as their under-21 side qualified for the All-Ireland final, losing to Donegal in atrocious conditions.

Mastermind

However, Roscommon fans plunged to the depths of depression again with the announcement of Tom Heneghan's resignation as manager of the senior side to pursue a career in America.

"Tom brought a great sense of professionalism to the way Roscommon organised and prepared itself. He did extraordinarily well with the under-21 side, guiding them to the All-Ireland in 1978. I remember being down in Ballinasloe when Roscommon won the under-21 Connacht final that year. I went into the dressing-room afterwards to congratulate the winning team. Everyone was over the moon. There was delight in my eyes because I could tell that some of these players were going to make it on to the senior team.

"Tom did not tolerate mediocrity or suffer fools gladly. Sometimes I thought he might have used more discussion to get the same short-term result but a better long-term effort. He was not prepared to do that on many occasions and perhaps rightly so. You don't want to expend all your energy trying to get agreement.

"We travelled together more than any other two players at the time. He was based in Mullingar working with Midland Tourism. I would travel across to meet him and we would go up and down to training together.

"In 1979 he was one of three Roscommon players to get an All-Star award, along with Danny Murray and myself. At a function one night organised by Mullingar rugby club, of which he was a member, they presented us with a wallet and notes. It was a great surprise to me but it was really their tribute to Tom.

"My attitude was always to be as co-operative as possible with the management. I rarely questioned his decisions. Sometimes we disagreed about things. I always felt that you should play your strong players down the middle. He thought that you should play some on the wing and spread the ball around. He wanted to introduce new ways of playing and if he had wanted me to play in goal, I would have played in goal. As I think back now, I believe I should have been a bit stronger in voicing my opinion where players should be played. Our strongest disagreement was about the treatment of the press in 1980.

"What made him great was his ability to plan everything down to the smallest detail, like who should help the goalie with his warm up before the throw in. He introduced new ideas which were very revolutionary at the time, like watching videos of matches.

"He was very concerned for his players, for example he wanted to make sure that anybody who had not a job would get one. Through his good offices a number of players did find jobs. His contribution to Roscommon's success was immense.

Jimmy Mannion who had played on the 1972 side and been a sub on the 1980 team became the new team trainer.

Roscommon's blues intensified with the news that Dermot Earley would miss the 1982-83 League campaign, due to service abroad on a peace-keeping mission. Roscommon had mixed fortunes in the League and despite some impressive performances failed to reach the knock-out stages.

When he returned to Ireland on 4 May 1983, Earley was thirty-five, but a demanding training schedule in the Lebanon had kept him in good shape. His secret ambition was to wear the primrose and blue in centenary year. Within a few days an invitation came to line-out for Roscommon against Laois, in Portarlington.

"I arrived at the pitch half an hour early. I was the first there. As I sat waiting in my car other players started to arrive, I am sure some of them must have thought: 'What's this auld fella doing here?' I was not sure if I was actually playing or not, but Roscommon did not have as many players as they expected and I was asked to turn out at midfield. I scored a goal from a pass from Tony McManus. I was delighted with my performance having marked John Costello who was a great player and played for London in the 1992 championship. I knew that other Roscommon players were happy with my display also."

However, in a series of challenge games, Roscommon's preparations for the championship did not seem to be going well. A victory over Clare was heavily outweighed by defeats against Dublin, Longford, Meath, and a bad defeat against Offaly. There had been a number of personnel changes, Tom Donlon was lost to the side when he decided to concentrate all his energies on hockey.

Roscommon began their onslaught on the championship on 12 June against Mayo in Castlebar. Mayo's winning margin of 0-9 to 0-7 did not tell the full story. They completely outplayed Roscommon and should have won by a much larger scoreline having missed a penalty.

Playing at full-forward Earley scored four of Roscommon points but the side looked poverty stricken and bereft of ideas.

Captain Fantastic

Roscommon's 1983-84 campaign mixed the good with the awful. Matches were lost which should have been won, culminating in defeat in a play-off against Tyrone for a place in the knock-out stages of the League. There was some disquiet among the players with the way things were going. As team captain, Earley was very aware of this disaffection.

"There was a willingness on the part of all players to co-operate with all the managers. Jimmy Mannion had a very tough job trying to fill Tom Heneghan's shoes. We all wanted to give him every assistance we could. Although we were getting some good results in challenge games, coming up to the championship it was obvious that we were not really progressing as a team. There were constant changes in the team itself, even in the course of particular games. It was obvious that there was widespread discontent with the manager but it was simmering beneath the surface. Nobody said anything in public.

"A problem I had at the time was that our county chairman, Michael O'Callaghan, told me privately that he felt that too much was being said in the dressing-room before matches. As captain I had always tried to get the players going as much as possible but I complied with Michael's wishes and left the talking to Jimmy.

"Things came to a head in a match against Louth to mark the opening of Padraig Pearse's new pitch. We tried Eamon McManus in a new attacking role and it was working brilliantly. Eamon was winning a lot of ball. At half-time a big number of changes were made. Five of the forwards were switched around. I felt this was a mistake and I said so, because we seemed to have no continuity.

"There was a feeling that something was lacking in the preparation of the team. There was frustration creeping in. As we came on the field we tried too hard and when things did not work out, we played as individuals. Our fuses were shorter and we got more and more frustrated."

The cumulative effect of all these changes were plain for all to see in the Connacht semi-final against Galway the following month. A generation of Roscommon fans, who did not remember the dark days of the sixties when the team was starved of success, witnessed the kind of massacre which is normally the preserve of London in the Connacht championship, with Galway winning by 1-17 to 0-7. Although Roscommon fans had endured a diet of disappointment since 1981 nothing had prepared them for such abject humiliation.

Earley, playing in his best position, midfield had contributed five points but his dreams of glory in centenary year had ended in ignominy. The team's inadequacies was reflected in the fact that in the second half they only managed a mere point.

"Morale was atrocious. We were annihilated. The Galway players were just throwing the ball around casually in the end. The entire team seemed to play as individuals and that was something that was evident in all our play in those days.

"Perhaps the problem was that Jimmy Mannion had played with all of us and did not have the same objectivity that Tom Heneghan had.

"The dressing-room afterwards was even worse than after losing to Sligo in 1981. For the fourth consecutive year we had failed to qualify for the Connacht final. Our run of misery was extended still further.

"There was a major question afterwards about how many of our senior players were going to retire. I didn't know what I was going to do myself. As I left the dressing-room I was joined by Galway's Brian Talty. He asked for my jersey. I hesitated about giving it to him because I thought at the time it might be the last one I would have. I told him that and he said: 'No. No. You will be back again next year'."

There is a special bond between Tony McManus and Dermot Earley based on a potent cocktail of friendship and mutual admiration. Each speaks of the other in glowing terms. Criticism of the other is never offered but has to be carefully extracted.

In reviewing this barren period in Roscommon's history, Tony Mc eventually overcame his reticence about criticising Earley.

"The only black mark against Dermot was that he was much too tolerant of incompetence on the sideline. Unfortunately we were hamstrung by decisions made by management, particularly in the 1977 All-Ireland semi-final against Armagh and many times after Tom

Heneghan left. I felt that there were a lot of decisions made in those years which did not benefit the team."

When Earley was informed of this criticism he agreed with it immediately. However, he offered two arguments in his defence.

"I was there to play, not to be squabbling with selectors. I thought that the best way I could lead my players was by example on the pitch. Secondly, I always felt a team needed a plan; even a bad plan was better than no plan at all. I was always prepared to go along with what management decided and give as much encouragement to other players as I could. I suppose I always feared that any criticism I might make could do more harm than good.

"I always wanted harmony in the dressing-room. There were times, especially in my later years, when I wondered if other players on the team thought that I was too 'prima donnish'. That was one reason why I kept silent when perhaps I should have spoken out.

"Looking back, I should have said: 'This is ridiculous. We are going nowhere fast.' Now nothing but the best is expected from the manager. Special expertise is often brought in today. Perhaps we needed special expertise to take us to a higher level than we reached in 1980.

"I would say that Tony's criticism is fair enough. I did become frustrated and speak out eventually. I was also critical of players who were not showing enough commitment, so I did not simply criticise the manager.

"With the benefit of hindsight I should have said something earlier. To miss out on a game is disappointing for any player but to miss out on two years of success was horrendous. Most of the players on the 1983-84 team formed the basis of the 1990-91 side. We failed not because we did not have the players but because we did not use them properly.

"I should have taken action earlier. Looking back it's a great disappointment to me that I allowed the situation to go on."

The Boss

Centenary year did bring a major honour to the Roscommon captain when he was appointed player-coach to the Connacht side for the Railway Cup matches. He scored six points and Connacht beat Leinster

McDonagh Barracks Medical Services Cup Winners 1978

l to r: M. Freyne (captain), P. Collins (referee), J. Smyth (Armagh captain),
Phelim O'Broin (Chief Stewart), [1977 All Ireland Semi-final]

Roscommon – National League Finalists – 1974
Back Row: (l to r) Sean Young, J. O'Gara, J. Mannion, P. Lindsay, J. McDermott, D. Earley,
H. Keegan, D. Watson, J. Kelly.
Front Row: T. Heneghan, T. Donnellan, M. Freyne, J. Kerrane, J. Finnegan, G. Mannion,
T. Regan.

Roscommon Co. Minor Team – 1965 Connacht Champions
Back Row (l to r): D. Earley, J. Nicholson, V. Glennon, M. Silke, J. Keane, J. Cox, T. Rock
P. Finneran, B. Mescall, J. Beirne
Front Row: F. Fallon, M. Kelly, P. Callaghan, M. Cox, A. O'Sullivan(capt) L. Dufficy,
B. Carberry, P. Clarke, C. McGuinness, J. Kelly

Roscommon All-Ireland Under-21 Champions – 1966
Back Row: (l to r): P. Nicholson, J. Cox, F. Fallon, J. Nicholson, N. Daly, P. Reynolds,
R. Sheerin, W. Feely, F. O'Donnell, S. Beirne, M. J. Keane
Front: D. Earley, J. O'Connor, P. Clarke, M. O'Gara, J. Finnegan, J. Kelly, C. Shine (capt.)
T. Heneghan, G. Mannion, J. Keane, P. Moclair, M. Cummins

Roscommon vs Galway
Back row: (l to r): T. Heneghan, J. Finnegan, G. Beirne, H. Keegan, D. Lindsay, D. Earley,
T. Hunt, J. Kerrane
Front: G. Mannion, M. Freyne, M. Flanagan, A. O'Sullivan (capt.), J. Neill,
J. Mannion, J. Kelly

Army Gaelic Football team beaten by the Garda team, 5-8 to 0-22
(Matt Connor beat us on his own)

Michael Glaveys – Roscommon Intermediate Champions 1970

Dermot presents Gerry O'Malley – Roscommon's greatest ever footballer – with his Hall of Fame award

Take them on Jigger!

Tackling the Best

Sarsfield – Kildare Champions and League winners 1986

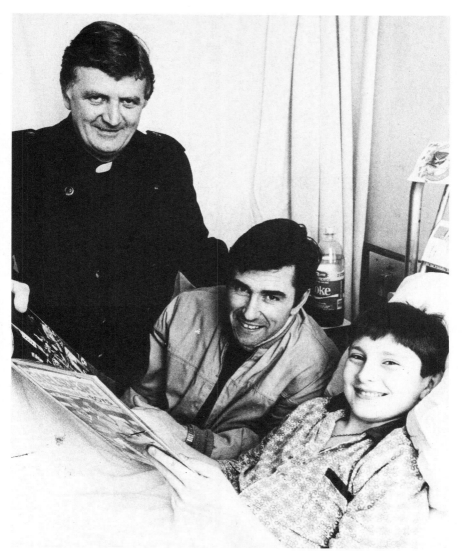

Dermot and Fr Jimmy Ryan visit a 'true' Roscommon supporter – young Martin Nolan, from Doohan, Ballydangan who lost his brave battle against cancer two years later in (1984)

"I swear by Almighty God that I will be faithful to Ireland and loyal to the Constitution..."

Carrying the Cadet school colours at the Commissionary ceremony of my senior class (1966)

Receiving my 'Commission' from Mr Michael Hillard T.D., Minister for Defence (1967)

Mam and Dad

Páipc Chuimneacháin Uí Mhaolmhochéirzhe
Eanna Ó Cionnaith T.D.
Aine Stáit Oideachair azur Saothair azur
Micheál Ó Ceallachain
Cathaoirleach Bhord C.I.Z. Rorcomáin a o'orcáil
ar an 18 ú Bealtaine 1986

**EARLEY MEMORIAL PARK
OFFICIALLY OPENED 18TH MAY 1986
BY ENDA KENNY T.D.
MINISTER FOR STATE AT DEPT, OF LABOUR & EDUCATION
& MICHÉAL O'CALLACHAN
CHAIRMAN ROSCOMMON C.A.A. CO., BOARD**

Memorial stone dedicated to my father

Western Sahara 1987 – a long way from Hyde Park

"For Better or Worse" 1971

*With my wife Mary and family (l to r) Conor, Dermot, David,
Paula, Anne-Marie and Noelle*

Roscommon Manager, 1992

0-15 to 1-9. In the final he scored 1-3 but that was not enough to prevent Ulster winning the title 1-12 to 1-7.

The appointment as player-coach to the Connacht team in subsequent years, was particularly gratifying because Earley had disagreed publicly with them in an incident involving the first compromise-rules series between Ireland and Australia.

Apart from the test matches, the Australians were scheduled to play games against provincial sides. A match was arranged against Ulster and the Ulster team got together for a number of training sessions. However, none of the Connacht players received notification about playing against Australia despite press reports that a match against Connacht was scheduled.

A phone call to the Connacht Council by Earley as to whether the fixture would go ahead or not yielded an ambiguous answer. Almost immediately he received a number of phone calls from prominent players on the Connacht team expressing disappointment that the Connacht Council had decided to allow an Irish selection to represent the province rather than a Connacht side. Some of the players involved said that they would never play for Connacht again.

"I was very frustrated when I realised that there was not going to be a Connacht team, even though I felt that if we could get a Connacht team at that late stage then that team would give a good account of themselves. I felt that the Council's decision was a grave error of judgement.

"The following year, when I selected the players who had been offended by the incident, I asked them to forget what happened the previous year. To a man they did, and they all performed very well."

The controversy has not in any way soured Earley's passionate interest in Connacht football nor his enthusiasm for the experiment with the compromise-rules.

"I am 100 per cent in favour of compromise-rules. We need an international outlet. However, I feel we have to make more adjustments on our side. There is great interest in the games here but not the same interest in Australia. They have made great sacrifices in their game.

Perhaps we should go further and play with an oval ball on these occasions to build a bridge between the two games. We would have to be prepared to sacrifice winning in the short term but in ten years time we could have a great game established. I think that it is good for our game here, that players like Paul, Dermot McNicholl and Tom Grehan have gone over there and come back with a greater range of skills."

In 1981 Earley bit his lip and remained silent when the Connacht Council allowed a H-block banner to be displayed in Hyde Park during the H-block crisis. The decision provoked controversy at the time.

"I can see the banner still. I was disappointed that the GAA was being used in this way. I felt that this should not be allowed to happen. I thought that it was reinforcing the stereotype of the GAA as a republican organisation. As an army man I am loathe to get involved in political debates. We try to stay above and beyond politics. I can see reasons why in the north of Ireland the GAA might take a political position but I would like to see sport separated from politics."

The Good, The Bad And The Ugly

1984 also saw the introduction of a new open-draw competition introduced to the GAA calendar for the centenary trophy. Roscommon were drawn against Kilkenny in the first round which provided all Roscommon players with their first opportunity to play in Nolan Park.

The attendance was particularly small and Kevin Heffernan's story of going down to Kilkenny to play them in a match was recalled. Even though the 'Dubs' were at the height of their popularity at that stage they were surprised to find thousands of people were at the ground. The curtain raiser to the game was a club junior hurling championship match. When Dublin took the field there were only ten people there!

Roscommon won the game easily. It was a game in which Dermot Earley could do no wrong – kicking six points from play and three from frees. After the game he was besieged with Kilkenny players and mentors asking him for his jersey. However, if he gave away his jersey the whole set would be spoiled. Discreet inquiries were made to the county secretary to ascertain if this gesture would be allowed. Eventually, in the special circumstances of the day, approval was given on condition that everybody kept quiet about it. Unfortunately this instruction was not adhered to and the Kilkenny mentors went wild with delight at gaining such a prized possession.

"I went down a few times to coach football teams but found that half of the Kilkenny hurling team were there. Some of these guys had five All-Ireland medals and I was a little in awe of them. Of course Roscommon and Kilkenny have good connections because Eddie Keher has Roscommon parentage. We always claim him as one of our own. "

In the second round Roscommon were drawn away against Cavan. The contrast with the Kilkenny game could not have been starker. As the close physical match drew to a close Earley sustained a severe blow to the eye and collapsed to the ground. As he lay on the ground he was struck again, by a different Cavan player who was sent off immediately, much to the dismay of the home fans. Although he could not see with one eye he resumed his normal position. The first time play came in his direction he saw two balls zooming at him instead of one. Only then did he realize how serious his eye injury was.

He was taken off the field and examined by a doctor in the dressing-room. He instructed the doctor to open his eye only to discover that the eye had never been closed.

The doctor advised him to get to the Eye and Ear Hospital in Dublin immediately. Mary and the children had continued to watch the match in the stand, not realising the extent of his injury and had to be called to the dressing-room. The game ended in a draw and went into extra time with Cavan winning easily.

The geography of the Cavan pitch meant that it was necessary for Mary to drive by some of the Cavan fans to get out off the ground and on to the main road. Even though extra-time was not completed the result, was not in doubt. Cavan would run out easy winners. However, a small minority of the Cavan fans who were still agitated with the sending off decision shouted abuse and kicked and thumped the car as the Earley family slowly made their way out of the ground.

"I was very disappointed that this should happen, particularly with my wife and children in the car. The kids wanted to know what was going on. We passed it off by saying that they were people who knew me and just wanted to say hello."

The injury was diagnosed as a burst blood vessel which clouded his eye and prevented him from seeing. Although the problem was serious it was in itself not an eye-threatening situation. The real danger was that if there were any sudden movement of the head, it might trigger secondary bleeding. Should secondary bleeding occur, the eye would be lost.

The injury necessitated a ten day stay in hospital. During his stay he was visited by a host of Roscommon fans and the former Cavan footballer Garret O'Reilly at the request of the Cavan county board.

His stay in hospital coincided with his club Sarsfields' successful defence of their All-Ireland 7-a-side club title. The team called in to visit him in hospital with the trophy. Under normal circumstances he would have been disappointed to have missed out playing but on this occasion he was happy just to be able to see them.

Little Things Mean A Lot

The 1984-85 League series saw Sean Young back in charge of the side and brought an end to the now familiar pattern of Roscommon's inconsistent form. Two victories were noteworthy as much for what happened afterwards as what happened on the field. On 11 November Roscommon beat All-Ireland finalists Dublin in Croke Park by 0-8 to 0-6. The biggest cheer of the day came in the Roscommon dressing-room when the news came through from Athleague that Roscommon hurlers had beaten Dublin and a Dublin double recorded.

In February, Roscommon beat Mayo in Charlestown. Michael Commins in the *Connacht Telegraph* of 23 February recorded the following postscript to the game in an article entitled: 'Touching Moment.'

> *It was one of those days when the east wind seemed to penetrate every fibre of the body and to lodge in every corner, and as Dermot Earley eased his way out among the frozen crowd from the pitch in Charlestown, a hot*

shower and getting dressed must have been uppermost in his mind. Suddenly there came a little shuffle and through the crowd poked the head of a small physically handicapped boy. He nudged the Roscommon man and was given a kind ear. As best he could the boy explained the purpose of his action.

Dermot understood, and a tiny hand guided him to the wheelchair of the boys younger and more physically handicapped pal. People stood fascinated as Dermot lifted the little twisted body into his arms and carried him into the Roscommon dressing-room.

In that simple gesture the dreams of two boys were realised and the gracious heart of a great footballer and their hero stood out.

'Even though we lost', a Mayo supporter told me, 'I walked from the field in Charlestown prouder that the GAA had produced a player like Dermot Earley'.

Roscommon went on to qualify for the League quarter final but lost to Down. Their preparations for the Connacht championship were impeded when Earley was struck down by a bout of hepatitis. Desperate situations call for desperate remedies.

"Gerry Connellan told me that there was a man in Meath who had a cure. I went to him and got two five naggin bottles of black stuff. It was absolutely horrible but it did the trick. I went over to London to play in the first round of the championship and brought a bottle of the stuff with me."

Although Earley came on as a sub in the match he did not score. He was surprised the next day to see the papers crediting him with scoring four points. In fact those points were scored by Paul.

After the draw with Galway in the Connacht semi-final and Roscommon's subsequent victory in the replay, the stage was set for the prince of Connacht footballers to crown his career in the West with another Connacht medal. It was only fitting that the man who wore the primrose and blue with such distinction since 1963 should leave the Connacht football stage in a blaze of glory.

The only problem was that Mayo forgot to read the script.

8. Learning To Be A Spectator

"I have just heard of your decision to retire from the inter county scene. (Interview with Jimmy Magee). For the tremendous enjoyment you have given to all of us over the past 21 years a very sincere 'buiochas'. May the quality of your football and the excellence of your sportsmanship be an inspiration to others to follow. I felt a little sadness in your voice today. Understandable. A very happy retirement."
(Ordinary GAA fan)

This was the message on a postcard from Bournemouth addressed to 'Dermot Earley, GAA Roscommon, Ireland', following his emotional interview with Jimmy Magee after Mayo's defeat of Roscommon in the Connacht final in 1985. It was just one in a hundred of letters, postcards, Mass cards, Thank-you cards and retirement cards sent to Earley after he announced his retirement.

Some were typed. Most were handwritten. Some were short. Others were tomes. Some were written by friends. The overwhelming majority were from ordinary football fans, who had never met Earley in person. There was a great variety of addresses. Only a handful had his home address. A few were written to 'Dermot Earley. Roscommon footballer'.

Some of the correspondence was formal such as a letter from Roscommon County Council informing him that they had passed a vote of congratulations to him to mark his retirement. Others were heartfelt expressions of thanks.

It is an incredibly moving experience to read these letters. In explaining why Earley was revered so much, people shared their own stories. A Tyrone mother described how her football crazy sons used him as their role model when they played football. Some time later when Earley was giving a training course in Tyrone he saw a lady approaching him as he came off the field. Although he had never seen her before he knew straight away it was that same lady, because she had become a regular correspondent.

The emotion in Earley's radio interview was replicated in the letters written to him. A correspondent from Galway commented:

"I must say here and now it brought tears from my eyes. It certainly brought back memories to me of a young Dermot Earley appearing for the first time as a minor in the Connacht championship game against Castlebar. Isn't it strange but we knew then that a new star was emerging from Roscommon. I remember Padraig Carney arriving in 1946 and Mick O'Connell in 1955 . . .You will certainly be missed from the Connacht Championships, Earley the motivator, Earley the accurate free taker, the mighty catch, the baffling solo runs, the kick, and the score."

Many of the letters commented on the one honour that passed him by – the elusive All-Ireland medal.

"As a dyed-in-the-wool Galway supporter I congratulate you on a long and distinguished playing career. Of course, you infuriated me often as I held you responsible, and rightly so, for many a Galway defeat. I am sorry that the All-Ireland medal never came your way but, as you said yesterday that medal isn't everything. Any man who played throughout a long career with drive and skill, and always within the bounds of sportsmanship, as you did, is assured of the respect and affection of Gaelic followers everywhere . . . and not least in Galway.

"Thanks for the memory. On no account, are you to acknowledge this. It would bankrupt you to pay for stamps to reply to all the messages which I am sure you will receive!"

What is most striking about the letters is the fact that so many people effectively bared their souls to a complete stranger. They shared their dreams, their stories, and their aspirations with a man they only saw on the playing fields.

One of the most touching letters came from an eleven year old schoolboy who followed a long line of young Roscommon lads who wanted to be Dermot Earley:

"My dream when I grow up is to become the new 'Dermot Earley' of Roscommon football. I much prefer Gaelic football to soccer, and

Dermot Earley to any Ian Rush or Frank Stapleton. When I was in bed the Sunday night you retired I started crying to think such a good player as Dermot Earley had gone from the game."

In similar vein was a letter from a young girl who described herself as a 'lady footballer and a Leitrim pal'. She wrote:

"I was so glad when ye reached the All-Ireland final in 1980 against Kerry. You had a great display at midfield. I prayed for ye that whole week. I still feel sad when I think Dermot of you never winning an All-Ireland medal. Would you please answer all these questions Dermot. I would be very interested in them all."

Her 48 questions included the following: "What occupation have you? What is your wife's name? What year did your father die and what age was he? Favourite person outside Gaelic football? Do you drink or smoke? What height are you Dermot?"

When a reply to her letter was not forthcoming within a month, another letter arrived, enclosing a pound for postage. The second letter was broadly similar to the first except this time there were 53 questions to be answered!

Some of the good wishes came with requests for signed autographs. An army colleague was philosophical:

"I listened with somewhat a little sadness to your farewell address on Sunday 14 July, as it brought home that Father Time has a devious way of keeping in touch with us all."

Another letter recalled Earley's own philosophy: "I got out of the game what I put into it."

Although the letters and cards came in many different sizes and shapes, of varying degrees of literary merit and grammatical precision, there was one unifying thread in them all – sincerity. Each had a common desire to pay homage to a great man.

One note which embodied all the goodwill that was apparent in all the correspondence came from Earley's friend and family doctor, Michael O'Connell:

"Commiserations on a small defeat. Congratulations on a great career. After listening to you yesterday I was moved to write the following small tribute to you.

Motto of a Young Footballer
To play the game with skill and flair
But most of all
To play it fairly,
To learn to win and lose with grace
To play the game
Like Dermot Earley

The Final Curtain

Having taken Roscommon to great heights in his 20 year career it was a cruel disappointment for Earley to have to end his days in the primrose and blue, not in a blaze of glory but in a damp squib. Roscommon entered the Connacht Final as hot favourites but their dream of emulating the glories of the late seventies on the home turf were torpedoed by their Mayo visitors.

The roar of the Roscommon supporters faded into a whisper as Mayo took the game by the scruff of the neck and outplayed Roscommon in every sector of the field. The scoreboard showing 1-9 to 0-1 at half time and final score of 2-11 to 0-8 told its own stark, sad tale of woe.

In fact it was not until the twenty-fourth minute, by which time Mayo had built up a score of 1-5, that Dermot Earley registered Roscommon's first score, a point from a thirty yards free. Roscommon were not to get their second point until the fifth minute of the second-half.

Teams

Mayo: E. Lavin, M. Carney, P. Ford, D. Flanagan, F. Noone, J. Maughan, J. Finn, T.J. Kilgallon, W.J. Padden, H.Gavin, J. Burke, N. Durcan, K. McStay, S. Lowry, E. McHale. Subs: P. Brogan (for Gavin), D. McGrath (for Brogan), B. Fitzpatrick (for McHale).

Roscommon: G. Sheerin, H. Keegan, P. Lindsay, G. Connellan, A. Garvey, G. Fitzmaurice, P. Hickey, S. Hayden, S. Killoran, D. Earley, T. McManus, P. McNeill, T. O'Brien, P. Earley, E. McManus. Subs: G. Wynne, (for Keegan), P. Gaynor (for Garvey) P. Doorey (for Hayden).

Scorers:
Mayo; K.McStay (0-7), S.Lowry (1-0), E. McHale (0-2). N.Durcan (1-1), H.Gavin (0-1).
Roscommon; D.Earley (0-5), S.Hayden, T.McManus, and T.O'Brien (0-1) each.

In his diary Earley's own comment on the day of his retirement was brief and to the point:
"Rosc V Mayo. Connacht Final 1985 at Hyde Park.
Rosc 0-8. Mayo 2-11. Scored (0-5 frees)
END."

Mistaken Identity

Although disappointment lingered long after the Connacht final it was possible for the family months later to look back on the game with a sense of satisfaction. Dermot's younger brother Paul was one of the few Roscommon players whose high fielding had caught the eye that day and who came out of the game with an enhanced reputation. His performance in the Connacht championship helped him win a coveted All-Star award that year for the full-forward position.

An interesting postscript to this story was that Paul's award was reported in the Bank of Ireland's internal magazine *Banktalk*. Paul became the bank's first employee to win such an award.

However, the magazine reported that: 'Dermot Earley (U.C.G. Branch) from Roscommon became the first Bank of Ireland Bank of Ireland All-star if that makes any sense!'

It was difficult enough to explain what was meant in the first instance, but the confusion was added to when they got the name wrong!

In fact in recent years Paul is increasingly mistaken for his older brother much to his annoyance and Dermot's delight. The sequence is reversed when some people think Dermot is Paul's father. Consequently Paul is asked: "Does your father still play for Roscommon?" On one occasion when he told somebody that his father died a few years earlier the person said: "Gosh that's terrible. Imagine he was only playing for Roscommon a few years ago."

Regrets. I Have Had A Few

The discussion about Paul brought back less happy memories for the doyen of Roscommon players. He saw his younger brother play for the first time in an under-age game for Michael Glaveys. Earley winces at the memory.

"I remember him as a juvenile playing in a final in Castlerea. My father had told me the game was on and I made a special effort to attend. Paul's team were not doing well, the other team were much stronger. I had expected a lot from Paul because of the stories I had heard about him. In that situation I felt that they needed something special. When the half-time whistle came Daddy asked me to go in and say a few words. I told Paul that he needed to make a major effort in the second-half. I was critical of him for not being more mobile on the field. When he got the ball he was very skilful and made some great passes and got some great points from frees. I gave out to him. I told him he was lazy. This was not the way to approach an 8-year-old. He was very shocked that I had spoken like this. I know it was the wrong thing to do and I have regretted it many times since. 'Mól an óige agus tiocfaidh siad' would have been much better."

There were two other unsavoury incidents in Earley's career which make him cringe with embarrassment and shame. The first was in a match against Longford when Roscommon were badly beaten and he played the proverbial stinker.

"I played absolute rubbish. When the full-time whistle went I was absolutely disgusted with my performance and annoyed that Longford beat us so easily. I was marking Sean Mulvihill, Liam's brother, and he had not allowed me a touch of the ball in the whole game. He was a player I knew very well, having spent a year with him in Strawberry Hill and we won the All-Ireland seven-a-side together. I would have considered him a good friend. He held out his hand for me to shake but I was so sick with my inability to play well that in frustration I walked away without shaking hands. I am still haunted by that memory."

A second painful memory was a League match against Kerry in Tralee, playing full-forward on John O'Keefe. Earley was unable to cope with the mastery of his opponent. In the final moments in a gesture of pure frustration Earley struck him a blow in the stomach. There was little force in the blow but the aggression was out of character.

"As soon as I hit him I regretted doing it. John's reaction was that of a gentleman. When the full-time whistle blew I apologised to him and I can remember him saying: 'I know that's not like you'. Somehow this made me feel even worse. It was something that I regretted very much."

Blood Brothers

Although the Earley brothers first experience of being on a football pitch together was an unhappy one this position was reversed when Paul gained a regular place on the Roscommon side in 1982. For both brothers, who had lived essentially separate lives up to that point, this brought them close together on personal terms as well as in a football sense.

Paul had only been a toddler when Dermot went to join the army and because of Dermot's football commitments and his marriage in 1971 the only time they were ever together was at Christmas. They were almost strangers. Inevitably such a lack of real contact was not conducive to a close personal relationship. All this was to change when Paul became Dermot's team-mate. The brothers that play together stay together.

"We didn't get to know one another until we played together. I enjoyed playing with him. I consider him to be a far faster and more skillful player than I could ever be, even though he was often playing in my shadow. He had a great ability to distribute the ball which I felt we needed at the time. He was a great utility player. To this day he can still play for Roscommon at midfield, centre-forward, or full-forward. It was great to get to know him as a person. We became very close and went fishing together.

"In addition it was good to have somebody to confide in about my frustration with my own game. He had different opinions about other players and about the game and I found this interesting. We talked about other aspects of life and this was very enriching for me."

Roscommon has seen a series of brothers playing together on successful Roscommon teams down through the years, the Murrays, the Feeleys, and more recently the McManuses. The Earleys situation was unique because there had never been such an age gap (17 years) between the brothers. One career was in its twilight years while the other was in its infancy.

The situation was particularly difficult for Paul. When he did something well, spectators passed comments like: "He learned that from his brother." When he made a mistake the comments were: "He will never be half the man his brother was." The Roscommon fans found it hard to see him as a player in his own right and not simply "Dermot Earley's baby brother".

The burden of the Earley name was a heavy load to carry. For his part Paul tried hard not to let it get to him.

"It was said many times to me that I never would be as good as Dermot. The only time it ever got to me was after playing one of my best ever games for Roscommon when a man came up to me and said: 'You played very well out there today but still you will never be the great player your brother was'."

The Roscommon players welcomed him as an injection of much needed new blood. Tony McManus saw Paul's difficult predicament at first hand.

"When Paul came on to the team in 1982 I looked on him simply as a good acquisition for the team and not as Dermot Earley's younger brother. It was a burden for him to have been in Dermot's shadow. He has been judged too harshly because he is Dermot's brother instead of being assessed on his own terms. I would have suffered in the same way if I had been in his shoes."

The physical similarities between the two brothers are striking. However, there are more subtle similarities. In conversation they use identical mannerisms, gestures, facial expressions and hand movements to emphasise points. Although their opinions diverge on a number of points their thought processes are virtually the same. They even have the same handshake.

Paul observes the central importance of football in his relationship with Dermot even to the present day: "Football has moulded our relationship. All my early memories of Dermot revolve around football. It was either watching him play football, talking to him about football or hearing others talking about games he played in. When I started playing I tried to model myself on him: to have his style, his high catch, to take frees like him, to be both skilful and powerful as he was. I always wanted to play on the Roscommon team with him. It happened sooner than I expected but when it did, the fact that he was there was just a bonus. What mattered most at that stage was that I was a county player in my own right. I just wanted to be the best player I possibly could for Roscommon and develop my own skills to the maximum."

Contrary to expectation Paul did not experience having to live in the shadow of a more famous brother as a burden or even as a mixed blessing.

"Having a brother who was a star was tremendous. I always was very proud to be associated with him especially when I was going to post-primary school in Ballyhaunis between 1977-81. Roscommon were one of the top teams in the country in those years and never lost to Mayo in the championship which was great for me because I was going to school there. Roscommon were in the spotlight, Dermot was in the spotlight and because of this I was in the spotlight also. When you have a brother playing on the team it is a lot more intense watching the team playing than it is for the casual observer. There were times when I got physically ill before games.

"There were no negatives really except sometimes spectators would give out about Dermot during matches. I took this criticism very personally. There was one occasion when I was waiting in the casualty ward in Roscommon hospital and I was talking to an elderly man about football. It was in September 1977 after Roscommon had lost to Armagh in the All-Ireland semi-final. Although Dermot had played well in both matches he missed a few scorable frees in the first game. The man in the hospital did not know who I was and blamed Dermot for Roscommon's defeat. I wanted to respond but I knew that Dermot would have let the comment pass so I said nothing. I was sorry afterwards to have let the comment go unchallenged but that is what Dermot would have wanted.

"Both of us have been described pejoratively by our playing colleagues as 'nice guys' and criticised for not being physical enough. We don't retaliate, intimidate or 'put ourselves about'. We both share the same ideas about the way the game should be played. One part of Dermot's philosophy which I have made my own is that the best way to repay an act of aggression was to get a score. We both believe that skill will always win out in the end. I remember once Dermot got annoyed with me on the pitch for throwing my weight around. It was a Centenary Cup match against Meath in 1985. I was just back from Australia where you intervened if one of your opponents used unfair means against one of your team-mates and I ran twenty yards to challenge a Meath player who had struck one of our lads. Dermot was furious that I should respond in this way because apart from anything else it was counter-productive. All that it achieved was to encourage more Meath players to step in.

"There was one time I remember Dermot breaking his own rules. He had played in a controversial club match for Michael Glaveys which ended in a draw. After the match one of the spectators assaulted the referee. Dermot raced forward and flattened him. He hated anybody attacking the referee.

"On the other hand perhaps there were times when Dermot was not assertive enough. I suspect that in his latter years with Roscommon Dermot lost a bit of confidence because he was losing his pace. He didn't want to be seen as a 'prima donna' so he did not make any comments about the direction of the team. Perhaps one or two players might have misread his attentions if he had done so but the majority would have loved to have heard him saying the harsh things that were necessary about the shape of the team and the team's problems – but they were left unsaid. No action was taken and the team suffered as a consequence."

Earley Retirement

As Roscommon prepared for their first League game of the 1985-86 season against Tyrone, a major psychological readjustment was necessary for Roscommon supporters. A county side without a fit Dermot Earley was as inconceivable as Hamlet without its prince.

Inevitably the readjustment was all the greater for the player himself. A number of approaches were made to enlist his services as an assistant to the management team. Those soundings were steadfastly resisted and he resolved to temporarily distance himself from the Roscommon side in the "post-Earley era", in order to allow the team to forge a new identity and allow new leadership and new stars to emerge.

Having comfortably ensconced himself in the armchair beside the radio at his family home, the dulcet tones of Jimmy Magee introduced the *Sunday Sports Programme* on Radio One. Jimmy opened by giving the 'menu' for the programme. He listed all the venues where RTE would have reporters, including Hyde Park for the division one match between Roscommon and Tyrone.

Unfortunately because of a technical hitch the Roscommon match was never mentioned until the closing sequence. Having fidgeted nervously, bitten his nails to shreds, and paced around the living room for two and a half hours he was strongly encouraged by his family to go to the next match against Kildare. Whatever about Dermot himself, the family were certain that they could never go through that particular ordeal again!

The next game against Kildare was played in Newbridge.

"As I was living in the town I felt that it was my duty to welcome the Roscommon side. I was greeted enthusiastically and invited to join the team on the sideline. Without making any fuss I drifted away to the stand because it was not my show anymore.

"Living in Kildare I knew the county players well and knew both sets of supporters or thought that I did. I had been at All-Ireland semi-finals and finals that Roscommon had not played in, but this was my first time to stand with the Roscommon fans since I was seventeen.

"I groaned at what I was hearing. The criticism was very harsh from both sets of spectators. When somebody did well he was praised inordinately but if a player made a mistake there was no limits to the abuse he got.

"Harry Keegan was playing particularly well and one Roscommon supporter felt that Harry should be everywhere. When Roscommon got a fourteen yards free or a fifty, Harry should have been brought up to take it but when our goal was under attack Harry was the man to be there. All Roscommon needed were 14 other Harry Keegans and everything would be all right then.

"I felt the comments were very harsh and I remembered back to another occasion when I thought spectators were excessively critical. It was the 1982 Leinster Hurling final between Offaly and Kilkenny, the year after Offaly had beaten Galway to win the All-Ireland. I was in the Cusack stand among Offaly supporters on a beautiful day. I can still see a ball that was going wide being policed over the line by the Offaly goalie, Damian Martin when Matt Ruth raced in and with a flick of his wrist drove the sliotar across the Offaly goal and an incoming forward got an easy goal. I can also see Damian the year before making a fabulous save which kept Offaly in the match. Now he was hounded by his own fans. When the criticism persisted I reminded the Offaly fans of his performance the year before. I was told in no uncertain terms to mind my own business.

"I find it distressing that there is so much abuse of players. When a player makes a mistake encouragement, not abuse is needed. I try to sit quietly and not to shout. The game that I became most passionately involved in was the 1991 All-Ireland semi-final against Meath when Roscommon performed so magnificently. I was going wild with excitement.

"The other time I got carried away was watching the 1991 Connacht final in New York when Derek Duggan pointed a monstrous free kick to bring the sides to a replay."

Right up to the Connacht final of 1986 Earley was still struggling to come to terms with the new status. On a wet Sunday in July, Galway stood in the way of Roscommon winning the Nestor Cup for the first time in six years. Roscommon entered the match as hot favourites having beaten Mayo in the Connacht semi-final in Castlebar in a match memorable for the midfield brilliance of Willie Joe Padden and the class of Tony and Eamon McManus.

The win brought sweet revenge for Roscommon's disappointment of the previous year particularly as Mayo were expected to win the Connacht championship and make a serious bid for the All-Ireland following their outstanding displays against Dublin the year before. However, tragedy struck Roscommon when their star player, Tony McManus, was ruled out of the game with 'flu the day before the final. Dermot Earley had his own thoughts about this situation.

"1986 was a great year for me football wise. I was free of the burden of travelling up and down to Roscommon for training. As player-coach of Sarsfields I was still training hard but I was home for the main news every night instead of at 1 a.m. when I trained with Roscommon. I felt as fit as ever. In May, my father's and my former club, Michael Glaveys, opened a new pitch called 'The Peadar Earley Park'. In these special circumstances I played for Roscommon. In the dressing-room beforehand I explained that I was honoured to play this special day for the Earley family but that I hoped I was not depriving any of the young players of staking a claim for a place on the championship side. I played wing-forward and felt I played well. Appropriately enough we won with a last minute goal from Paul.

"When Paul told me the evening before the Connacht final that Tony was out, I thought to myself that the solution to this problem was that I should play at full-forward for Roscommon the following day. The next day I walked into the ground before the match and wished the players well but I did not go into the dressing-room. As I took my place in the stand a lady passed a remark: 'He is a very young looking 37 year old'. The thought stuck in my mind again that I should play in the final. I felt strong and wet conditions were ideal for me. I did not know it at the time but I found out four years later that lying in his sick bed Tony McManus was having the exact same thought."

Tony recalls: "I felt that Sean Young should have persuaded Dermot to come back for the championship. Even if we didn't use him for the whole match he would have been a great sub to be able to spring when the going got tough. I still believe that if Dermot had played in 1986 we would have won the Connacht final title that year."

The match itself was a tense scrappy affair illuminated by two superlative performances. The 'new veteran' on the Roscommon team Harry Keegan, had yet another outstanding match at corner-back culminating in a surging run from his own goal to the half-way line which whipped Roscommon fans into a frenzy. The performance played a substantial part in Keegan winning his third All-Star award that year.

His only other serious rival for the 'Man of the Match' award was a second-half substitute for Roscommon, John Newton whose high fielding earned Roscommon almost total dominance in the centre of the field. Sadly the Roscommon forwards were unable to capitalise on this possession.

Roscommon were so much in control that it was difficult to imagine them losing but late in the game Harry Keegan had to leave the field with an injury and with the consequent chaos in the Roscommon defence, Stephen Joyce, a Galway sub, scored the winning goal.

It was yet another title that got away. Roscommon fans filed the game away in their now bulging 'should have been' file.

Mercs and Perks

Earley's disappointment with the fortunes of the Roscommon team were to some extent offset by the success of his club side Sarsfields. At the time he was commissioned in 1967 he was informed that Sarsfields would be delighted to have him should he ever wish to transfer to a Kildare club.

By 1978 travelling down to train with Michael Glaveys had become an excessive strain. He no longer felt in a position to commit himself totally to the club. Moreover, he no longer knew the Glaveys players very well on a personal basis. A generation gap had emerged. He knew their parents well but not the sons.

At this stage Dermot had a family of his own and was thinking ahead to their possible football futures. He felt that he should make a commitment to a club before his children were ready to play. Of the two clubs in Newbridge he chose Sarsfields ahead of Moorefield because they had approached him first.

There are great apocryphal stories about the inducements offered to players to switch their allegiance from one club to another. Earley candidly admits that he did get a perk from his transfer to Sarsfields but not of the kind to boost his bank balance.

Having played his first championship for Sarsfields against Kilcullen Earley walked home with his wife and two children. As he passed O'Connor's shop a queue of people had formed to get ice-cream. When he joined the queue Earley was recognised by the son of the proprietor, a stalwart of the Sarsfields club. Immediately he was brought to the head of the queue. This was his one perk from joining Sarsfields!

Earley helped the club to become Kildare senior champions in 1982. 1986 was a special year for Sarsfields, winning the League and championship double for the first time in 30 years. The county final against Leixlip was played one week before the All-Ireland final which put Leixlip star Jack 0'Shea in a difficult predicament. As rival fans talked about the duel between Earley and Jacko in the build-up, local experts described the clash as the 'battle of the blow-ins'. Jacko was due to line out for Kerry against Tyrone the following Sunday. He came on as a sub with 15 minutes to go against the explicit wishes of the Kerry management. Although predictably Jacko made a positive contribution it was not enough to turn the tide with Sarsfields winning 0-11 to 0-8.

"When Jacko came on he inspired us to perform better just as much as he inspired Leixlip. The first ball that came in our direction was won by our midfielder Des Bergin. He made an unbelievable catch and that spurred us on to greater things."

As player-coach Earley played a key role in Sarsfields double. His interest in coaching had begun at the end of the 1960s at a time when the GAA were actively promoting coaching programmes, particularly in the aftermath of Joe Lennon's coaching book. Coaching courses in

Gormanstown were introduced under the tutelage of former greats such as Joe Lennon, Eamon Young and Jim McKeever.

Attending one of the first courses Earley remembers the fact that the only topic of conversation for the entire week was Gaelic games and one specific incident.

"I woke up at 6 a.m. the rain was teaming down outside. Although rising time was still an hour and a half away most of us were awake for some reason. We were all sleeping in a big dorm. The only person who still seemed to be fast asleep was Jack Mahon. One of the lads went over to him and shook the daylights out of him, shouting: 'Jack, Jack. It's a day for the gloves.' We all collapsed with laughter."

When It's Not a Funny Old Game

In the 1970s in the light of his growing reputation as a coach and his PE qualifications, Earley was invited onto the GAA's coaching panel and later on to the National Coaching Committee becoming involved in policy making in relation to coaching. His only fear about the increased popularity of coaching was that it sometimes led to an excessive emphasis on physical fitness rather than the skills of the game. Although he finds coaching extremely enjoyable it also brings its own hazards.

"In June 1992 one of my players from Sarsfields got a blow in the soft tissue between his hip and his rib cage, across the kidneys. He was quite sore for a few minutes and was unable to continue playing. When I was talking to him in the dressing-room after the match he suddenly went absolutely pale. His eyes rolled in front of him and he went into a faint. I panicked realising that the injury was more serious than I had had thought. As I went to look for his pulse there was none to be found. I put his head between his knees to get a flow of blood back. After a few seconds he moved his arm in a convulsion and at last I was able to find a pulse. We called an ambulance and he was discharged from hospital the next day as good as new. It was a very frightening experience for me. It shows how things can go wrong and emphasises the need for proper back-up."

Having checked with the hospital the next morning that the player had made a good recovery during the night, Earley left his home for work. However, he was quickly transported from the sublime to the ridiculous when the father of one of the players pulled up outside. The father was extremely agitated that his son had been substituted the previous evening. After some less than complimentary words about Earley's judgement, the irate father informed him in the most categorical fashion imaginable that his son would never play football for the club again.

The next evening as Earley drove to training he saw the player in question walking to training. He stopped and gave him a lift but there was no reference to his father's torrent of complaints.

This Is Your Life

1986 was Earley's most successful year as a coach to date but that year brought many other moments which he will treasure forever. In February of that year the Roscommon county board arranged a special presentation for both Pat Lindsay and Dermot Earley at a sell-out function in Roscommon. Both players received a special 'This Is Your Life' eulogy. The closing citation for Earley read:

"Dermot Earley you were not only a classic footballer, you were a true sportsman, a shining example to all. Dermot you are a man amongst men whose love and pride of the blue and gold is near to being unique, and above all you have led by your example Dermot, you are one of nature's gentlemen."

The organising committee presented Mary with a bouquet of flowers and Dermot with a stunning piece of crystal which retains pride of place in the Earley sitting-room to the present day.

Many letters of thanks had to be written afterwards. Among them was a letter to one of the organising committee which had the following 'P.S.' attached:

"I have admired the crystal on my own each night this week and as it sparkles in its magnificence I remember the games, the wins and the losses. Wet days in the Hyde when winning took away the gloom and great days in the Hyde when winning didn't matter, just to play did. Sincerely. Der."

A Touch of Class

28 April 1986 is a date which Earley will never forget. It was the occasion when he ended up marking one of his heroes, perhaps the greatest soccer player the world has ever seen, George Best in a celebrity match. This match took place in front of 1,500 people in Collins Barracks. The occasion was organised to help promote a forthcoming match between Shamrock Rovers and Manchester United, a benefit for former United and Irish International, Shay Brennan.

The Collins Barracks Celebrity side featured John O'Leary, Ciaran Fitzgerald, Tony Ward and Earley while the opponents, a Liam Touhy side, featured Best, John Giles, Eoin Hand, Ray Tracey, and Pat Crerand.

Despite the thickness around the waist Best still displayed a few magical moments. Although he was not trying very hard, Best's immediate opponent, Dermot Earley, was trying extremely hard to keep Best from scoring or doing any fatal damage to his team.

Best did not appear for the second-half. To this day Earley claims that Best did not reappear because he knew he would be as outplayed in the second-half as he was in the first. In fact the real reason was that George had to leave hastily to catch a plane back to England!

In the speeches afterwards Jimmy Magee commented that in years to come a good question for a quiz would be: "When did Dermot Earley mark George Best?"

Earley's admiration for George Best's genius is tempered with disappointment that Best never fulfilled all his potential. Unfulfilled potential is not just a soccer problem. Earley cringes as he thinks about two immensely talented Roscommon players who never fulfilled their potential, John O'Connor and Mick Finneran.

One of the most depressing obituaries for any club player is the kindly dismissive comment: 'He was a great minor.' For Earley a major reason for this phenomenon is the fact that star minor footballers play too many games, minor, colleges, under-21, junior, and sometimes senior.

Another problem he identifies is the excessive emphasis on physical fitness at juvenile level which is to the detriment of the young players enjoyment of the game. He feels that it is important to nurture a correct philosophy of sport, particularly where young people are concerned.

"I would like us to get the message across to the next generation of players that winning is not everything and that is more important to play fairly than to play to win at all costs."

In Earley's eyes one one of the biggest blights on the game today is the level of physical and verbal intimidation on the pitch. The look of disgust on his face as he talks about the problem conveys his own discomfort more eloquently than any words could. He recalls more in sorrow than in anger an incident from one of his last matches with Roscommon. Ironically the other player involved was someone he considered to be a friend.

"I shook hands with my opponent. After the national anthem was played I turned around again to wish him well because we were good friends. As I turned his arm was swinging ready to punch me but because I turned and held out my hand he froze. I was disappointed. There is an attitude now that you take out your opponent and then get on with your own game."

This opinion is shared by Jack O'Shea: "When I started playing there were always hard players and crunching tackles. In the last ten years though I have noticed a big change. There is a lot more physical aggression on the ball and some players set out to intimidate opponents verbally."

A Personal Disappointment

In Autumn 1986 Earley got the opportunity to put his footballing philosophy into practice when he finally yielded to pressure and became assistant to team manager Sean Young. It was a decision he made reluctantly because there is always a complication coaching players that one has played with oneself. However, he felt that having made the decision he should give it total commitment.

Having immersed himself in the task he gradually discovered that there were serious problems. His role was not clearly defined, particularly in relation to team selection. Frequently, decisions about the team did not reflect his own thinking. Obvious weaknesses in key positions were not remedied, much to his frustration. As the team built up for the first round of the Connacht championship against Sligo in 1987 there were significant differences between Young and Earley. The magnitude of the malaise confronting the Roscommon team was exposed when Sligo won the match. It was a chastening experience for all concerned. With the benefit of hindsight Earley now recognises he made the wrong decision in accepting the position.

Less than a month later the Earley family were packing their bags before moving to America. Happier days lay ahead.

9. Simply the Best

What makes a great player? Is it natural talent or the ability to inspire others? Alternatively, is greatness essentially a question of spirit or attitude, a 'never-say-die' mentality, an innate drive to overcome all the odds, to give every ounce of energy to the glory of the team? To what extent is greatness a matter of style, does a great player shape a football match in the same way as a great artist uses paint on a canvas? Is physical presence a factor to be considered? How long does a player have to maintain the highest standards on the playing fields to be considered a 'great'? Can the quietly effective player attain the same status as a gifted 'star'? Who decides? And who decides who decides?

Greatness, like beauty, is an extremely subjective concept. One person's 'great' might be somebody else's 'average'. The problems of identifying the 'great players' are magnified when one attempts the hazardous task of selecting the greatest team of one's era. Undaunted by all these difficulties Dermot Earley set out to select the fifteen players who would form his ideal team.

The following criteria were used to determine selection: "In selecting your best fifteen you are taking into account the fact not only that they might have been in your opinion the number one person in that position on the field, but also that they would have the ability to gel with the other fourteen, so that in addition to the fifteen best players you would get the best possible team."

The Men Behind Dwyer

Although players from every county in Ireland were considered for inclusion, special attention was given to the Kerry team of the 1970s and 1980s.

"In selecting a 'greatest' team you would have to consider, without reservation, all the players who played for Kerry between 1975 and 1986. The Kerry team of that era must go down as being the greatest team of all time and therefore all the players who contributed to their success must be considered for the best fifteen that anyone would select."

"I would also have to consider all or most of the players from the Dublin teams of the same period. I would also have to take into account the performance of a number of players from counties who 'threatened' at those times, that is Offaly, Meath, Cork, Armagh, Roscommon and Galway."

Although he has an in-depth knowledge of the history of Gaelic football, in particular of the great players of the 1920s, 1930s, 1940s and early 1950s, he did not consider players without actually having seen them play himself.

The Last Line of Defence

In choosing his best goalkeeper Dermot was spoiled for choice. His first candidate for selection was former Galway great, Johnny Geraghty.

"Goalkeeping is an art that has changed a lot in Gaelic football in recent years. I think that the change in the style of goalkeeping came about when Galway came on the scene in the 1960s. The man I credit with bringing about this transformation is Johnny Geraghty. He was small in stature but exerted enormous influence over the goal-mouth area.

"All the goalkeepers I had seen up to that time had cleared the ball as far from the danger area as possible. Johnny brought a new dimension to the game, by linking up with his team-mates as no goalie had ever done before. An attack was set up immediately from the goal line area and this revolutionised the whole game.

"He was also very agile, almost cheeky when he got the ball. Forwards would come in on top of him and he would side-step them and give a pass to a corner-back. The crowd would almost moan, because the ball was not cleared quickly enough and then possession might be lost and Galway might concede a score.

"I can see him in the goal-mouth on the top of his toes. A lot of the time he wore an American baseball cap, particularly if it was sunny. He looked great. He was also captured in great photographs. I remember one in particular in which he was completely off the ground, almost like a swallow, swooping through the air. He was bent, arched, hands fully stretched scooping at the ball. This was something we thought came from soccer. We saw very little soccer at the time. Of course the fact that he was beaten so seldom added to his reputation."

Listening to the way Earley talks about these players is itself instructive. As he speaks his eyes sparkle, his hands gesticulate and his voice is animated with passion. He transmits enthusiasm like electricity.

The Day the Crossbar Broke

Inevitably in any discussion about goalkeepers, the conversation turns to Aidan Brady of Roscommon. One of Dermot's happiest childhood memories is an incident which has become part of GAA folklore, the day Aidan Brady broke the crossbar in the 1962 Connacht final in Castlebar between Roscommon and Galway. Roscommon trailed Galway by five points with less than ten minutes to go and looked a beaten side.

"As I look up the field in Castlebar I can still see that sight in MacHale Park today. I am looking up the field through the people and I see only parts of the pitch. I can see a Galway forward taking a shot and putting Galway six points up. As the ball was cutting like a bullet over the crossbar, Aidan Brady, a big man, jumped up and hung on the crossbar and then the crossbar broke. I can remember the waiting, the players sitting on the pitch and the crowd being humoursome and taking it as a great joke and then another crossbar coming in and the game being resumed."

As he talks about the game, Dermot does not simply remember it, he relives it. He replays each incident in his mind. His facial expression betrays all the emotions of the game itself.

"All I can remember after that, and maybe it's not all memory, maybe it's a reaction to the stories that I have heard about it, is Gerry O'Malley taking the game by the scruff of the neck. I remember O'Malley soloing the ball down the field, a high solo run; when he soloed the ball, it was with a style peculiar to him. It was not neat and tidy, but out in front of him. I always felt he could be easily dispossessed but he never was. He came down the field and made a goal for one of the Feeleys. The next scene I have in mind was Gerry O'Malley coming up with the ball and setting up a goal for Cyril Mahon. Then from the kick-out O'Malley came forward through all the Galway players and set up the winning point."

Gerry O'Malley recalls with relish the way in which the breaking of the crossbar disrupted the Galway players' rhythm and allowed Roscommon to snatch victory from the jaws of defeat.

"I remember talking to Sean Purcell while we were waiting for them to fix the crossbar. I said to him: 'It's probably gone from us. We cannot turn it around now'. Then I thought to myself 'maybe not'. I went up to Eamon Curley (who almost twenty years later was to become manager of the Cavan team) who was playing at midfield and told him to swap positions. Fortunately we got two goals to tie things up. When we equalised I ran over to the Roscommon fans who were on the sideline and asked them how much time was left. They said that time was up. Luckily, I won the ball and put Feeley through for the winning point."

Taking on the Terrible Twins

MacHale Park was also the venue for one of the most outstanding displays of goalkeeping Earley ever witnessed: "It was a Connacht Championship match between Galway and Mayo. Playing for Galway were 'the terrible twins', Frank Stockwell and Sean Purcell, two of the greatest players who ever lived but whom I only saw in fleeting glances. They were legends, everybody talked about them and I looked on them in awe.

"The other two players who stood out that day were the Mayo goalkeeper Mick Corkery and right-fullback Willie Casey and the reason that they stood out was that they were magnificent in defence even though Galway were on top for all of the game and won easily on the day. Corkery made great windmill-like saves that day even though Sean Purcell scored a goal from a penalty against him. He was as rock-like as the Mountains of Mourne. As we say down in the West, he had a 'whale of a game'."

The Octopus

In considering the goalkeepers Dermot played against, Dublin's rock of dependability, Paddy Cullen was a serious candidate for inclusion on his ideal team.

"Paddy Cullen, like Jimmy Kevaney, had played for Dublin for many years before the Dubs came to prominence in 1974. He could stop the ball all sorts of ways. He probably had the best kick-out of any goalkeeper in that he could place the ball exactly where he wanted it. I experienced that first hand when playing with him on the All-Stars tour against Kerry. I was playing on Sean Walsh. When Paddy kicked out the ball, he would place it so much to my advantage that I usually had no difficulty winning it on that day. I often think how great a contribution the goalkeeper can make in kicking out the ball. Why is it necessary to kick it ninety yards up in the air, where anybody could win it, when someone like Paddy Cullen could place a ball at its most advantageous position for his midfielders?"

One vintage Paddy Cullen performance is recalled with particular affection by Dermot Earley. It was a charity match following Paddy Cullen's retirement, which featured a number of well-known personalities and leading players.

"It was played in a very light-hearted manner, but everybody wanted to score a goal against Paddy. All the shots that were fired at him – he saved. He blocked shots by putting up a hand, or by turning his elbow or sticking out his leg. It did not make any difference at what speed or angle the ball came against him, he blocked them all. One time after he had made a spectacular save somebody said: 'Cullen – he is like a bloody octopus' and this really typifies the way he played as a goalkeeper. In the great penalty save against Liam Salmon in the All-Ireland final of 1974, he just leaned in the direction of the ball, with his knee almost touching the ground but his hand was outstretched and with the palm of his hand he deflected the ball out for a 50. He would use all his body parts and I think the octopus tag is particularly appropriate. Dublin were very lucky that when he retired they had a goalie of the calibre of John O'Leary to replace him."

Another goalkeeper who impressed Dermot Earley was Kerry's Charlie Nelligan: "He was a class goalkeeper, a brave goalie and a great man to go down on the ball. He never flinched from the close-in shot. The hardest ball for any goalkeeper to save is one that is right down on the ground at the butt of the post. He has to bend and get down to the ball. In an upright position the reflexes of your hand can help deflect the ball away but having to put your body down on the ground and bend and at the same time cover a distance is very hard to do, but Charlie Nelligan could do that extraordinarily well. In addition he had a monstrous kick-out. He had great reflexes and of course I remember his reflex save from John O'Connor in the 1980 All-Ireland final, when John O'Connor pulled on the ball and Charlie just raised his hand and deflected the ball over the bar." The sudden emergence of a pained expression on his face as he recounts this story confirms how vividly he recalls this save.

My Ideal Goalkeeper

Having considered all the possibilities, Billy Morgan emerged as the choice for the goalkeeping position.

"Billy Morgan was the next edition to Johnny Geraghty. He was brave, catlike, had good hands and again like Paddy Cullen had a good kick-out, which was used to the best advantage of the team. He worked with his defence much more than any other goalie. The qualities which made him great were his ability to deal with every kind of ball. His ability to deal with a ball being crossed from the wing was superb. He constantly read the game well and could deflect crosses away from the goal-mouth and out of the danger area. He was the complete goalkeeper in my opinion. He would have to be my number one."

The Footballing Trinities

In a consideration of great full-backs and corner-backs the initial discussion was on units of defence such as Offaly's Paddy McCormack, Greg Hughes and John Egan; Dublin's Gay O'Driscoll, Sean Doherty and Robbie Kelleher; Galway's Enda Colleran, Noel Tierney and John

Bosco McDermott; and Roscommon's Harry Keegan, Pat Lindsay and Tom Heneghan (and later Gerry Connellan): "They stood as a particular unit, that would play very well together, knew all about one another's play and both corner-backs would cover for the full-back in a particularly effective way."

The decision about the right corner-back position involved three possible candidates: "You would have to choose somebody who played in his particular unit with distinction but who could also fit into any other unit. Such a player was Paddy McCormack, a great corner-back for Offaly in the 1960s and who went on to win two All-Ireland medals at full-back for Offaly in 1971 and 1972."

Another serious contender for inclusion in this position was the lion-hearted Jimmy Deenihan, an impassable rampart in the Kerry defence, a player whose career ended tragically in 1982 following a serious injury. Mick O'Dwyer has always maintained that Deenihan's absence was a significant factor in Kerry's failure to win the elusive five-in-a-row in 1982, because he argues that Deenihan would never have allowed Seamus Darby to score that celebrated goal in the dying moments, which cost Kerry their victory.

Jimmy Deenihan and Dermot Earley were opponents on a number of occasions: "He was a very tight marker, very strong, well set to the ground and could move left or right very quickly. He had strong hands that would not push a player away or foul him but would have the strength to stop a forward from lunging past him. Deenihan had the ability to mark well and that is very important for any defender, to be able to shadow your man all the time and whatever turns or twists that your opponent tries to make, you have to be able to react immediately and be almost in unison with your opponent."

Perhaps the most telling testimony to Deenihan's efficacy as a corner-back is the statistic that in the six All-Ireland finals in which he played, the combined scoring total of his six immediate opponents was a derisory two points.

Although Jimmy Deenihan's claims for selection were very strong, Earley chose a man whom he played against and under: "The man I would consider to be the complete corner-back would be Enda Colleran of Galway, who won three All-Ireland medals with his county. He was a great footballer, strong on the ball, a good marker of a player, not a fouler and he had a great left foot. Not alone was he a great player, he was a great leader. He captained Galway to two All-Ireland's and he captained Connacht to the last Railway Cup they won in 1969. "

Rugged and Indestructible

In his lengthy footballing career, Dermot Early came up against a number of rugged and indestructible full-backs. No less than five players were seriously considered for this position.

"One of the men who I think of straight away when I think of great full-backs is Nace O'Dowd of Sligo. I saw him play as a kid, but the reason his name stands out is hearing his name on the radio through Micheál O'Hehir. He always seemed to play a great game. Inevitably the star in the Sligo defence would have been Nace O'Dowd."

Another member of the impenetrable defensive screen that constituted the great Galway full-back line of the 1960s was also considered because of his majestic high fielding.

"Noel Tierney had a tremendous jump for the ball, from a standing position. He always seemed to be standing behind his marker, his chest was almost resting on the back of an opponent but he could rise high above him and catch the ball."

One of the most formative influences on Dermot's footballing career was former Roscommon full-back John Lynch, a colossus figure in his own locality.

"John Lynch played full-back for Michael Glaveys, the club founded by my father. We always talked of him in awe as: 'John Lynch, the county player'. In fact when I started playing football I only wanted to play a full-back because Lynch was full-back. All my early football was played at corner-back, and it was only in my college days when I was switched to midfield in a challenge match, that I was introduced to a whole new dimension of football, which allowed for much great creativity in my play. I suppose a lot of full-backs might be very insulted by this idea.

"I remember watching John Lynch in a league game in St Coman's Park and he was up against Frankie Stockwell and Sean Purcell. Lynch was now playing his football with Tuam Stars because he was living and working in Tuam and was a team-mate of the 'terrible twins'. I remember him holding Stockwell that day to a point. People talked about it for a long time afterwards how John Lynch held Frank Stockwell to just one point, because Stockwell was the greatest full-forward of that time, possibly of all time. I can remember Purcell feeding the ball to Stockwell and Stockwell toeing it on his toe, being forced by Lynch out the field, left-right, left-right, until they were forty yards out the field. Then Stockwell got half a yard and kicked the ball over the bar. It was a tremendous example of full-back play and also of full-forward play. Lynch forced him away from the danger area, but Stockwell got a fleeting glimmer of a chance and scored a great point."

Big Bird

John O'Keefe's ability to police his man and reduce him to virtual impotence made him a strong contender for the full-back position. He was known affectionately by his team-mates as 'Big Bird' and oozed authority and confidence.

"Kerry wanted a full-back. They had a great midfielder in John O'Keefe and put him in at full-back. He was an exceptional fielder, stopper, blocker and a great team player. His outstanding characteristic was his ability to come forward quickly to the incoming ball and win possession.

"My choice for this position would be another player converted from midfield to full-back, Jack Quinn of Meath. I suppose I would have him there because of his complete all-round play, his ability to jump so high and field the ball and the combination he had with another great Meath player of the time Bertie Cunningham. The two of them had an almost telepathic understanding and made a great defensive unit. He was very spectacular, very strong, and very athletic. He gave the best full-back displays that I ever saw.

"Speaking of full-back displays, you would have to hand it to Micheál O'Muircheartaigh, one of the great authorities on the game who said that the greatest display of football he ever say was by Sean Purcell at full-back for Galway in the 1950s. I never saw Sean Purcell play at full-back."

Sharp as a Razor

There were three main candidates for the left full-back position, John Egan of Offaly, Robbie Kelleher of Dublin and Tom O'Hare of Down.

"John Egan was as sharp as a razor in the Offaly defence in the 1960s. He was a formidable opponent and would have to be considered.

"Robbie Kelleher was a tremendously intelligent footballer, very clever and very fit. He was able to shadow an opponent, perhaps allow him to take possession, but keep him in a position where he could do very little. He was also a great man to set up an attack. I can remember him coming up in various games and having a shot. He was the attacking mould of a player, as soon as he got the ball he came forward and set up an attack.

"However, my choice for the left full-back position would have to be Tom O'Hare of Down. He was an All-Ireland winner with Down in 1968 and was a great player of that time. He was very sure, very strong and a great man to clear the ball. He also had a tremendous free-kick and if I remember rightly he would come up the field to take Down's frees. His frees were magnificent. Invariably he would find a colleague with a radar-like pass. He always impressed me as having total control of his position at all times."

Fear Crua

"I would have to consider three players for the right-hand back position. Firstly, John Donnellan who captained Galway to their All-Ireland final victory over Kerry in 1964. (Later he became a Fine Gale TD for Galway West, which is one of the competitive constituencies in Ireland). His single-minded determination in many a rip-roaring contest was invaluable to Galway. Secondly, Eugene Mulligan of Offaly. He would have to be considered for one reason alone, that is, he was the first ever automatic choice on an All-Stars team. Only a top class player could earn this distinction."

In the end the final choice was Kerry's Paudie O'Shea, one of the greatest characters of the modern game. His willingness to go through fire and water for the good of the team and his insatiable hunger for Kerry success have become part of GAA folklore. One story about him which epitomises his unquenchable spirit goes back to the time when he was captain of the Kerry team in 1985. The story is that he was so pumped-up with fervour that when he was exhorting his team mates to heroic feats just before they went out for the All-Ireland final against Dublin, he hopped the ball so hard that broke the lights on the ceiling.

"One of my clearest memories of Paudie O'Shea was his response to a suggestion in an interview that he was a 'fear crua'. Paudie answered that he played hard on the ball but never stooped so low as to play the man."

Paudie is part of an illustrious quintet (sometimes known as 'the magnificent five') which includes Ger Power, Mike Sheehy, Ogie Moran and Pat Spillane who played in ten All-Ireland finals between 1975 and 1987, winning eight.

The Flying Dub

All experts agree that the centre-half back position is the pivotal position on any team. On the one hand he needs to be a sterling defender and on the other hand he has to extricate himself from the attention of opponents to set up the forwards attacking moves. He is the nerve-centre of any team, acting as a conduit between the backs and forwards. In the modern game the centre-back is very involved in forward play. No one has done more to revolutionise the centre-back position than Kevin Moran because of his ability to scythe his way into open space and instigate a dangerous move.

"I recall Kevin Moran's run at the start of the All-Ireland final in 1976 when he just took off from mid field and ended his run with a rasping shot at the Kerry goal. It would have been an outstanding goal had he scored. Kevin Moran to me was an outstanding footballer. He was very athletic, with tremendous fitness and he could cover a lot of ground. He had such speed on the ball that even if he were in a very defensive situation, the danger was done almost as soon as he got possession. His attacking qualities were special.

"Another player who impressed him in the number six jersey was Sean Meade of Galway who won three All-Ireland medals in that position. He linked very well with his forwards and defence. He was particularly adept at interpreting dangerous balls coming in, but he was never as spectacular as Kevin Moran."

Death of a Friend

A new range of emotions comes to the fore as Dermot considers one of the other leading contenders for the position of centre-half back, the late John Morley of Mayo. The normal flow of his speech is impaired. Pauses appear between sentences. His tone is not of simple admiration, but of sadness and regret. He speaks with obvious pain, as befits a man who has experienced an enormous personal loss. Theirs was a friendship that transcended inter-county rivalry.

"John Morley was a player whom I played on many times, who I knew very well and who tragically lost his life in my parish at home on the 7 July 1980. I remember that date for many reasons, but particularly because it was Dermot, my son's second birthday. John was a tremendous footballer who could play in almost any position for Mayo. It was mainly at centre-back that he played most of his inter-county football. I remember hearing a lot about this up and coming footballer John Morley, particularly when he was in St Jarlath's College, Tuam.

"He came on as a sub for Mayo in a game I saw in Charlestown in the early 1960s. He kicked very long and high with his left foot. People expected a lot from him and they were given a lot but his kicking was a little wild. I cannot remember him kicking wildly, but I do remember the comments to that effect around me. In later years he gave great displays with his cultured left foot.

"One incident in particular stands out in my memory about John Morley. It was a League final when Mayo beat Down. John was playing at centre-half back, when a Down player grabbed him and tore his shorts. Just as he was about to put his foot into a new shorts, the ball came close by, he abandoned his shorts and in his swimming trunks fielded the ball and cleared it magnificently down to the field to the adulation of the crowd.

"We played together for Connacht and having won the Railway Cup in 1969, we went out to New York to play in the Cardinal Cushing games. In our first game against New York in Boston, I was playing very well in midfield. On one occasion the ball was hanging in the air. I went into the clouds, or so I thought, to catch the ball. I touched the ball and then it was wrenched from my hands. As I reached the ground, I turned around quickly to be on the defensive, but I looked around to see that it was my team-mate John Morley with the ball tucked in as tight as could be, ready to set up another attack. You would have to consider him as being one of the great players."

Inevitably when discussing John Morley's career, memories are rekindled of his death. The man who gave every ounce of energy on the playing-field for Mayo, was also prepared to put his life on the line to honour his professional duty and uphold law and order regardless of any risk to his personal safety. The bravery which he had so often exhibited in the green and red of Mayo was to manifest itself even more strikingly in the dark blue uniform of the Garda. A hero in life became a hero in death.

Earley speaks about John Morley's death with difficulty. The passion and sheer excitement of reliving Kevin Moran's great run is totally dissipated. His eyes moisten. It is evident that he still feels a pronounced sense of personal loss. His voice drops to a whisper.

"It was coming up to the 1980 Connacht final, I remember because we were preparing for the Connacht Championship. I used to come home from work, get something to eat then get in the car and drive down to Roscommon to train. I remember that particular evening hearing that an incident had happened and that Gardai had been shot. I thought immediately of the two people who were Gardai in Castlerea whom I would speak to often. One was John Morley and the other Derek Kelly. I can remember listening carefully to the Five-Thirty bulletin to find out what had happened and then hearing that it was John Morley and Henry Byrne who were killed and that the other man in the car was Derek Kelly.

"Derek Kelly, from Mayo, was based in Loughglynn and played at centre-half forward for my club, Michael Glaveys. He was a great footballer. John Morley, like Henry Byrne, was from the Knock area and had been based in Ballaghadreen where we got to know him well. Before that he had been a stalwart on their football team and was keenly involved in the local community, organising all kinds of community activities. John was then based in Roscommon town and was also involved in the community there. He was accepted and admired by everybody. Finally he was transferred to Castlerea and was involved in everything worthwhile in the area.

"A robbery had taken place and the squad car encountered the get-away car at the crossroads outside Loughglynn on the way to Ballaghadreen. Shots were fired and Henry Byrne and John Morley were fatally wounded. In the telling of everything that happened subsequently, a retired Garda from Loughglynn, Garda Kneafsey emerged as the central figure. He had returned from Limerick to live in this area. I knew him very well from his interest in and support of our football ambitions.

"Apparently he was the man who came on the scene after the shooting and spoke to John Morley on the side of the road. John had been badly wounded and was bleeding. I can recall in detail Garda Kneafsey, God rest him now also, speaking on television and being asked what had happened. He said that had he recognised the footballer. John said to him: 'I am getting awful cold', which would have been an indication of loss of blood. Then he said an 'Act of Contrition'. Shortly after the ambulance came, but it was too late to save John".

"The human tragedy had a huge effect on Connacht because the Connacht final was just up the road, the next Sunday, in fact. It was between Mayo and Roscommon, between a county that John had played for, for many years and the county that he had lived in for many years. Everybody in both counties respected him. That Connacht final totally reflected that feeling. Fr Leo Morahan, who had been involved with Mayo football for many years, but who is now based in Connemara, was on the Connacht Council at the time, and gave an oration before the throw-in. I remember that clearly.

"In the west of Ireland there are two things we are noted for. One is for saying 'mighty'. If something good happened 'it was mighty','you're mighty' or 'we were mighty'. The other thing we are noted for, is that we generally refer to people we admire, even though we may never have met them, by their surname. If you go into any GAA setting in the West of Ireland today, indeed all the West of Ireland is a GAA setting and you say 'Morley', everyone will know the name. He remains known by that name with affection and admiration.

Spellbinding Brilliance

In the end the man who won the number six jersey was Offaly's Nicholas Clavin whose spellbinding brilliance illuminated many a match in the late 1960s and early 1970s.

"Nicholas was like Kevin Moran, but before Kevin Moran. He was taller than Kevin and had, I would think, almost perfect skill. He commanded the position totally. He could take out the ball from defence, with a swerve or feint, and as soon as he had won the ball, he could feed it to a team-mate with unrivalled accuracy. He was one of the stars of the great Offaly teams of the late 1960s and early 1970s. It was a great pity that he did not play on because he could have made a major contribution to Offaly for many more years. However, his pastoral duties as a missionary priest took him to the west coast of the United States."

Of all the positions on the team the selection of a left-back proved to be the most problematic. "I have been lucky enough to see some great left-backs in my time. The name which comes to mind first is Donegal's

Brian McEniff. He was a very classy player who combined great skill with the right attitude. I remember watching him play for Donegal in an All-Ireland semi-final. My heart sank for Donegal when he had to leave the field injured. If there was one player you would not want to lose it was Brian McEniff."

When Kerry won their first All-Ireland under Mick O'Dwyer's stewardship in 1975, the 'Man of the Match' award in the final went to their left-half back, Ger Power. The son of the legendary Limerick hurler, Jackie Power, Ger electrified Croke Park on many occasions with his phenomenal speed.

"Ger Power was one of the best half-backs I ever saw. As I speak of him now I can see him go from stationary, to running at almost a hundred miles per hour, then stop suddenly and go one hundred miles per hour in the other direction, leaving everybody for dead behind him.

"His ability to link up with his team-mates was uncanny. Support-play was the forte of all of that Kerry team but Power exemplified that quality more than any other."

However, the final choice for this position was a player who had an economy of style and, like a gifted athlete, an economy of movement, as if he were conserving his energy for a major explosion, Martin Newell, a star of the Galway three-in-a-row team.

The discussion on Newell's footballing abilities is deferred as Earley recalls a story about Newell's professional duties as a Professor, in University College Galway.

"This story was related to me by P J McGrath, the All-Ireland referee from Mayo. Apparently one evening a number of army officers who were attending UCD needed extra direction from Professor Newell. He agreed to help them out. Having spent an hour with them Martin left for home. It was a cold damp evening and the rain was getting heavier by the second. As Martin prepared to cycle home, the officers who had been in his tutorial passed by in their mini-bus almost splashing him. They were being driven home and when they got back in dry condition there would be a hot meal ready for them in a nice warm house. On the other hand when Martin got home he was soaked to the skin. He had to put on the fire and get something to eat. The contrast speaks for itself."

"I would have to include Martin in my team for his style alone. He was a prince of wing backs whose tight viligant covering left very little leeway for forwards. He was a deceptively tenacious and unyielding defender."

The Man from Valentia

An assessment of the greatest midfielders of all time must begin with Mick O'Connell. His status and legend demand no less. No event testifies more to the O'Connell mystique than the tumultous reception he received when he appeared on the pitch in Croke Park before the 1969 All-Ireland final between Kerry and Offaly. Before the match the rumour factory had gone into overdrive with tales of injury to Mick O'Connell. The prevailing wisdom right up to the appearance of the Kerry team on the pitch was that O'Connell would not play. Novenas and rosaries were said in both counties for opposite petitions. When O'Connell strode majestically on to the hallowed turf, a new sound level was reached in Croke Park. The crowd's reaction said it all. He had no peers.

"Mick O'Connell was probably the most skillful player that I ever saw, having the ability to do almost anything with the ball using both his feet. Of course the hallmark of his performances was his ability to field the ball high in the air.

"I came up against him for the first time in the All-Ireland semi-final of 1972. Three things stand out about him that day. He was a legend, coming into the game following his performances for Kerry in the 1950s and 1960s. His feats were known throughout the country and again Micheál O'Hehir brought them back vividly to me, as I listened to him on the radio, in the kitchen at home. Now I was going to play on him.

"Gerry Beirne and myself were the midfield partnership for Roscommon and John O'Keefe and Mick O'Connell for Kerry. At one stage, John Kerrane, the right half-back for Roscommon passed the ball over the head of a Kerry player to me. The ball hung in the air and was an easy ball for me I had no doubt when I jumped for the ball that it was mine. But, as I jumped and my hands reached for the ball, it was not there. O'Connell, without ever touching me, or brushing against me, had won the ball. That was an extraordinary piece of skill, particularly as I did not even know he was robbing the ball off me.

The O'Connell Enigma

"The other famous incident in the game arose when, because his boots did not fit him properly, he sat down in the middle of the park for seven minutes and re-laced them. Effectively Kerry were playing with fourteen men during that time. I suppose there was some resentment on the part of the Roscommon players and supporters that a player would do this and not go to the sideline and adjust his boots temporarily and wait until half-time but O'Connell was a perfectionist in his performance and therefore everything had to be right.

"There was another time I saw him leaving the Kerry team to try out his leg when he took a tumble. He stood in the dug-out and practiced solo running until he was absolutely certain that he could perform with skill before going back out on the field. This incident highlights his perfectionist streak. He wanted to do everything properly.

"In that 1972 All-Ireland semi-final, I can remember the ease with which he would come into the ball and score almost at will, both from frees and from play. His ability to drive the ball a great distance with incredible control made him almost the complete player. Of course he formed a great partnership with John O'Keefe.

"The only drawback that I think he had was when the games were very close and you had to use your body weight, not in any foul manner, to jostle your opponent and force your way through. Mick O'Connell did not take part in that kind of football. When it did get that tight he was not involved."

Many stories were told about Mick O'Connell. The classic story, though there were many variations of it, revolved around the celebrations following Kerry's victory over Galway in the 1959 All-Ireland final. O'Connell was captain of the team, but he left the Sam Maguire Cup behind him in the dressing-room and had gone home on the train and was rowing a boat out to Valentia Island before anyone knew where he was or even that he was missing. One theory was that he had gone home to milk the cows!

No footballer before or since has ever attracted the same level of interest and comment as Mick O'Connell. One of RTE's earliest celebrated documentaries was entitled 'The Man and the Myth', which proported to reveal the real Mick O'Connell. However, O'Connell remained as enigmatic a figure afterwards as before. Dermot Earley had the opportunity to talk to Mick O'Connell on a number of occasions and is in a position to offer some tentative opinions on the O'Connell enigma.

"He was a very quiet, shy person. I remember one time reading that he had gone to England to look for work. To me it was a huge disappointment that Mick was not going to be around anymore, and that maybe we were going to lose him for good. I also remember our Irish teacher in St Nathy's bringing in the Irish paper, '*Inniu*', from which we would read Mick O'Connell's articles. Here was a man who was so shy and lived on Valentia Island and yet he would come out and write so fluently in Irish about Gaelic football.

"I met him once or twice on tour with the All-Stars and on one occasion I played with him. He wanted to do everything absolutely perfectly and play the ball at all times. I think it was because he was such a perfectionist and such a shy person that people were desperate to get to know him and that this accounts for his decision to skip celebrations. He was such a quiet individual, that his only ambitions were to play football and live in Valentia. I would have loved to have heard more of his opinions when he was a player but it was not to be."

A Childhood Idol

"When I was a child if I was asked who I would most like to emulate when I grew up, it was Mick O'Connell. He was my hero. Again Micheál O'Hehir was responsible for this. He brought all these great players into your mind. The complete player to me was Mick O'Connell. The only thing I would have against him, and the reason why I do not pick him on my team was that, he did not have the necessary 'aggressiveness', that is, the ability to fight fairly for the ball and win it, especially when the chips were down. Others might think that he more than compensated for this deficiency with all his other skills, but I feel this dimension is essential."

Midfield Mastery

Although Mick O'Connell dwarfed the stature of any other midfielder, there were a number of other nominees for the midfield positions.

"You could not discuss midfielders in Connacht without discussing Billy Joyce of Galway who was a direct opponent of mine on many occasions and gave me so much trouble so often. He was a tremendous 'horse of a player' if I can describe him in that way. He would go anywhere for the ball and give every last ounce of energy to the team. He had so much heart in him, that on several occasions Roscommon found themselves in a commanding lead only to be hauled back by the sheer power and tenacity of Billy Joyce.

"In Ulster great midfielders have come forward and the one midfielder who is spoken about with reverence is Jim McKeever. He was so magnificent in the 1958 All-Ireland semi-final and final that many people would have spoken about him as a suitable midfield partner for Mick O'Connell on the greatest team of all time. His ability to jump and catch the ball were the hallmarks of his play. Apparently he would jump so tidily, that he would be almost like a gymnast in the air, toes extended and fingers outstretched as he grabbed the ball, way above the heads of anybody else and then he would hit the ground, turn and play.

"I never saw him play, but again he was known to me through Micheál O'Hehir before I ever got to know him personally. Micheál was able to describe every move he made so correctly and vividly that you felt you knew who Jim McKeever was, even though he lived up in Derry and you were a hundred miles away.

"In Leinster, the name of Bernard Brogan of Dublin immediately springs to mind. He covered closely and tenaciously but it was his cutting runs through defences which set him apart from others. I suppose that celebrated goal he scored against Kerry in the 1977 All-Ireland semi-final goal will never be forgotten."

Keep an Eye on the Fisherman

"In Munster, Declan Barron of Cork was a magnificent fielder. During the Championship games he fielded balls that were almost in the clouds. There was one incident in the 1979 League Final against Cork, which we won, that I remember particularly well. We were in control of the game all the way through, when Jimmy Barry-Murphy scored a goal and Cork put us under a bit of pressure. They forced a 50 in the last few minutes of the game. Declan Barron to us Roscommon players was a great player, but there was a lot of curiosity in Roscommon about Declan Barron's occupation.

"You would often read stories in the papers that Declan Barron was not available for Cork on a particular day. So, everyone wanted to know what Declan Barron did for a living. One story was that he worked on the oil depot at Whiddy Island. Others said that he was a farmer. Another story was that he was a fisherman and that he would be out fishing for days and would miss a number of games. Still another said that he worked in England and that he moved back and forth. To this day I still do not know what he did for a living.

"As we faced up to the 50, Pat Lindsay was orchestrating our defence. Declan Barron started to make a run to the small square. In the tension of the moment, Lindsay shouted out commandingly: 'Keep an eye on the Fisherman'. I can still hear Lindsay's voice ringing in my ears. Although the mystery of Declan Barron was never resolved in Roscommon, as far as Lindsay was concerned he was a fisherman."

My Ideal Partnership

In selecting his two ideal midfielders Dermot Earley opted not for the two outstanding players in that position, but the two players who would form the perfect partnership.

"I always thought that the ideal midfield partnership would be a strong player, who would also be a good fielder contesting every ball that was dropping in the air, and a good runner who would cover for the big man.

"My first choice would be Jimmy Duggan of Galway, a player of approximately my own age. He went to St Jarlath's and I went to St Nathy's and we were great rivals as we grew up. We clashed in football at College, once in minor football and many times at senior level when he played for Galway and I for Roscommon.

"He played for that great Galway team at the end of their winning streak of All-Ireland's and won an All-Ireland medal in 1966. To play such a prominent role in Galway's victory showed him to be an outstanding player. I always considered him to be a most skillful player. In 1969 we played together at midfield on the Railway Cup winning team. He was a joy to play with. He gave great encouragement and great leadership. He had all the ability that you needed, the ability to thrust forward and get a score or set up a score, as well as gracefulness. He was a great team player and performed magnificently for Galway up to the late 1970s.

"Jack O'Shea has been consistently brilliant for Kerry over the last fifteen years. His outstanding quality is his mobility. He could crop up anywhere either to save Kerry or to cause havoc for the opposition. He had a phenomenal work-rate, which was complemented by exceptional levels of skill, strength and speed.

"If I could pick out one quality that he has that Mick O'Connell had not, it was his strength and ability to fight for a ball and win possession in a crowd. He is a whole-hearted forager who can jostle for the ball and win it or jostle hard for the ball and lose it, but who keeps jostling and so puts his opponent under pressure. He may not have the same level of skill as O'Connell, but I would rate him as a midfielder of extraordinary class, because of the all-round ability he has, making him the complete player.

"We had a good few battles in our time, though not enough for my liking. I would have liked to have played on him on more occasions. I suppose that as I am ten years older, while his talent was developing and getting stronger, I was going downhill. It was a great honour to play against him and Seanie Walsh in the All-Ireland final in 1980 and in other games.

"In selecting my ideal midfield partnership I would consider all the players I have mentioned, as well as other great midfielders such as Mick Garret and Mick Reynolds of Galway, Sean Ferriter of Donegal and other great midfielders from the contemporary scene such as Gerry McEntee and Liam Hayes of Meath. However, I think the ideal combination would be Jack O'Shea and Jimmy Duggan. They would probably be the hardest combination to beat."

A Footballing Artist

Only one player was considered for the right-half forward position, Matt Connor of Offaly, whose footballing days ended at the zenith of his career, following a horrific car accident on Christmas Day 1983. As a footballer Matt was gifted with a vast array of talents. As a forward he was addicted to scoring.

Matt Connor's injury robbed Gaelic football of one of its greatest exponents. It would be easy to talk about his accident as a modern day tragedy. Much too easy. Greatness is most obviously manifest in the face of adversity. A lesser man would have hid himself away following his accident. A lesser man would have fallen victim of the bitterness of the 'what might-have-been' syndrome or the futility of the 'why me?' mentality and thus become paralysed by self-pity. Not Matt Connor. He has overcome his personal misfortunate and continues to play an important role in the development of Gaelic games as as a selector with the Offaly minor team. Few players will ever surpass Matt Connor's ability on a football pitch. Yet, in his resilience in coping with his nightmare experience, Matt Connor has eclipsed his greatness as a player, by his greatness as a man.

"You do not need to talk about him. His scoring feats, his skills on the ball, his free-taking ability, his power on the ball as well as his speed of movement and thought. I remember him scoring two goals and nine points for Offaly in the All-Ireland semi-final in 1980 against Kerry, when the final score was 4-15 to 4-10 in Kerry's favour. Of course I remember the free kicks he took in the 1982 final when Offaly were under pressure and clawed their way back.

"I remember seeing him play for Walsh Island in Newbridge, in a Leinster Club match. They were under pressure and needed a score. Matt Connor collected the ball twenty-five yards out from his own goal and went the length of the field on a solo run. He left everybody that came to tackle him behind, stretched on the ground, without any of them even touching him, where he swerved, feinted, sold a dummy, slowed up or accelerated to lose his man. I can still see him in the green and white hooped jersey that day in Newbridge being in total control. As the ball went over the bar I can see some of the players he had beaten up the field were still on the ground. Some were picking themselves up. One or two were on one knee. All were pictures of dejection, beaten by superior skills.

"I have spoken to him many times since his accident. He came back to be involved in County Board activities, to be a selector of the Offaly minor team. He also resumed his professional duties as a Garda. He must be admired as much for adjusting so well, as he was admired as a footballer."

Matt Connor was the consummate footballing genius, driven almost by a lust for scores. His talent will never again grace Croke Park, but the memories of his footballing artistry will linger forever.

The Forty-Yards Man

"When you come to speaking about centre-half forwards you are talking about the man who is going to lead the attack. Another term that I used to hear as a young man was 'the forty-yards man'. My earliest memories of that phrase is of my father using it as the team lined out for junior matches in West Roscommon.

"One man who immediately comes to mind is Jim McCartan of Down. Like his son James, he played with tremendous determination and strength. The feats of McCartan were well known to all young lads playing football in Roscommon and each feat enhanced in the telling.

"The one thing that we all remembered when we were small about James McCartan was that, he was supposed to have scored a goal having fielded the ball in the square, turned in the air and then hit the ball in the net with his foot, before he hit the ground. I am not sure if that story is true or not. I remember as a boy trying to emulate the feat at home, without opposition - setting up the chance time and time again, trying to catch the ball in the air, turn in the air, and kick it before I hit the ground. I do not think any of us ever pulled it off but perhaps James McCartan did do it. He was a legend as far as we were concerned. Again the man who put those thoughts into our head was Micheál O'Hehir.

"Another man who must rank as one of the great centre-half forwards was Packie McCarthy of Leitrim. I remember seeing him play in a number of Connacht Championship matches, but particularly in a Railway Cup game in Ballinasloe against Leinster. I remember it because I nearly got squashed at the gate when the game was over as the crowd left the pitch. I was close to the wall and as the crowd left I was pushed towards the pillar because I was so small, and looking up I thought I was going to be trampled on. After one or two little yelps I was immediately freed and released from the crowd. Before that I can see Packie winning the ball from the midfield position, turning, soloing the ball and then from about thirty-five yards out driving it with immense power almost like a rocket and the hands going up vainly to grasp for it as it went over for a point. Packie was still playing when I started to play for Roscommon. He had a great understanding with another exceptional Leitrim forward, Cathal Flynn.

"We were both subs on the Connacht team in 1967. I travelled down with him to Galway for our match and that was the first time I got into conversation with him. It transpired that Packie was playing at inter-county level when I was only two years old. I thought of that day much later on, when my brother Paul first played for Roscommon. I had played for Roscommon when he was only two.

"In modern day football, one of the players who contributed most to Dublin's team-work was Tony Hanahoe. I think you need a play-maker at centre-half forward. Tony Hanahoe was certainly a play-maker. He contributed a lot to the smoothness of the Dublin forward line by his ability to get the best out of every ball and his ability to link with other forwards, particularly (the Blue Panther) Anton O'Toole. Their potent combination caused big problems for defences.

"The man that I put in at centre-forward could not be ignored for one reason alone – he won eight All-Ireland medals in that position, Ogie Moran. Anyone who can do that must be regarded as a tremendous player. He was a pillar in the Kerry team and to hold the same position in all of their wins was an outstanding achievement. The qualities that I admired about him were his outstanding speed, his great skill, but above all his total unselfishness. I think that is an awful drawback in a lot of great players, who only see the goalposts and do not see their team-mates. If Ogie had a fault it was that he did not see the goal-posts often enough and only saw his team-mates, but that worked to great advantage for Kerry. His unselfishness and tremendous work-rate singled him out from other players. He would have to be my centre-half forward."

A Scoring Machine

On first sight the selection of the player for the number twelve jersey seemed a foregone conclusion, insofar as there was one outstanding candidate who seemed an automatic choice. However, other names emerged that also merited serious consideration. The first of these players was Sligo's great scoring machine, Mickey Kearins.

"He could play with the best of footballers but he only won one Connacht medal for Sligo in 1975. His skill, free-taking, and point-taking were immaculate. In a 1972 Railway Cup match in St Coman's Park in Roscommon he scored thirteen points against the combined universities. In the 1973 final in Croke Park with the combined universities leading by 3-9 to 17 points, Connacht got a line ball forty-five yards out in the dying seconds and Mickey drove it over the bar to earn Connacht a replay. He was a thorn in Roscommon's side whenever we played against Sligo and would have to be rated as one of the the greatest footballers ever."

Following Kerry's defeat by Down in the 1961 All-Ireland final, no less a person than Mick O'Connell described the Down number 12 that day, Paddy Doherty, as 'the best footballer of all time'. His claims for inclusion could not be ignored.

"Peter McGinnity of Fermanagh is another player I must consider for this position, even though he also played a lot of football at midfield. I always think of him as 'Peter of the left foot' because he was predominantly left-footed. I remember playing against Ulster in the Railway Cup semi-final in Ballybay in Monaghan. It remains one of the windiest days in my memory. The wind blew from one goal to the other so that one team had a distinct advantage. Connacht won the toss and elected to play with the wind. I think the score at half-time was Connacht 2-12 and Ulster something like two points. It was a huge margin but perhaps not quite enough given the breeze and skill of the Ulster men. In the second-half Peter took control of the game and scored two goals. I can still see him swinging that left foot and burying the ball in the back of the net. It was an outstanding display by an outstanding player. He nearly beat us on his own!"

Ironically it is that very same match which provides former Donegal star, Brian McEniff, with his enduring memory of Dermot Earley." "Connacht were under siege in the second-half. One time when we were on the attack Dermot got the ball, burst his way through, and scored a great point despite kicking into a gale force wind. There was only one point between the teams at the final whistle, that was the point that turned the game. Dermot broke our hearts that day."

Fleet as a Deer

In the end the claims of Pat Spillane for the number 12 jersey were too overwhelming to be ignored. His name is synonymous with sporting excellence. He was the engine in the great Kerry forward line which attacked like a pack of starving wolves. On the move he was as 'fleet as a deer' and his brilliantly intricate approach work and swashbuckling style was responsible for many great scores.

"I think one could not exclude Pat Spillane from any team that you would pick because he has been a whole-hearted, skillful, unselfish player for Kerry over the last seventeen years and because he has thrilled crowds in Croke Park on so many occasions. He had the ability to cover the whole field. I can remember one occasion in the 1978 All-Ireland

Final when Kerry were temporarily without a goalie and the man who went in goal was Pat Spillane. If Kerry were in trouble the man who would turn up at corner-back was Pat Spillane. The ball might be bobbling out in the defence and the next thing, like a knife through butter, Spillane would come away on a solo run going the length of the field, linking up with the other Kerry forwards and the man who would pop-up to finish the move off with an important score would be Pat Spillane.

"He had the ability to take scores from difficult angles, mostly with his right foot. He was a quick thinker and his release of the ball was always excellent. Above all he was an inspiration to those around him. When things were going against Kerry, Spillane would be the man who would pull something special out of the bag whether it would be a catch, or a run, or a pass, or a point. It would lift the team again and establish Kerry on top.

"One of the things you would have to remember about him during his long and fruitful career was that although he had received a serious knee injury, his determination was so great that he was able to come back and perform at the highest level again, wearing that distinctive blue knee brace that everyone became familiar with. On one occasion I saw an opponent deliberately swiping at Spillane's knee with the obvious intention of re-injuring it, but nothing like that ever worked against him."

Let's Make a Switch

One of the most familiar scenes in Gaelic football when a team is suffering a heavy defeat, particularly in club games, is the dejected face of a corner-forward who is substituted even though he had no opportunities to have any significant impact on the game. The corner-forward is not the problem and replacing him achieves no constructive purpose if the team is under siege at the back. The fact that such substitutions are commonplace reflects a widespread misconception that the corner-forward is the weakest player on the team. In recent years a number of players have exposed this myth for the lie that it is.

"Another man who has defied the medical experts and has come back from injury to perform with such class, power and craft that he must be rated as one of the best forwards of all time, is Colm O'Rourke. The way in which he came back from a serious injury is a sign of his incredible dedication and commitment.

"One of the things I remember especially about Colm O'Rourke was a game against Australia in Croke Park in the Compromise Rules series. Ireland were not doing well and badly needed a score. He won a ball out in the middle of the field and turned on an explosive run. Here was an amateur footballer, recovered from a serious knee injury, up against professional and semi-professional Australians, who were ready to pounce on him. He went on a seventy yard solo run and I do not know how many players attempted to catch him. In the end they attempted to trip him, by diving after him and tapping his heel. None of them caught him and he stuck the ball into the net. Those six points brought Ireland back into the game and made it a great game.

"It was a great pity that he could not play in the 1991 All-Ireland final. I know illness prevented him from doing so but it makes one wonder what would have happened had he played. You must admire the turn-around he created and the way the Meath players responded to him when he came on. Sitting there in the Hogan Stand I can recall the excitement as he warmed up and got ready to come on. There was a buzz in the crowd and then when he came on I suppose every Meath supporter stood and cheered. The rest is history. He almost did it.

"Jimmy Barry-Murphy was a player who impressed me a lot, particularly because of this temperament. Most players when they get the ball in front of the goal think they have scored the goal even before the ball is in their hands. They have jumped and often the ball is left behind and the chance is lost. Jimmy Barry-Murphy seemed to have complete calmness in any situation, which gave him acres of room that appeared to allow him to put the ball anywhere he wanted it. The other thing about him was that I never saw him strike the ball with thunderous force. It always appeared to be placed delicately. I always thought that if I was in those situations I would have blasted the ball and goalkeeper into the roof of the net, but he kicked the ball with the utmost economy. The fact that he played both hurling and football to such high levels is a tribute to the ability of the man. I always think that if he had concentrated as much on football as hurling, that he would have achieved as much as a footballer, as he did as a hurler.

"In the great Dublin team the performance of Bobby Doyle at corner-forward was outstanding. But, perhaps he would not be recognised as a true corner-forward in that he rarely stayed in that position. He was a player who used the whole field, coming back to midfield and beyond and the next moment turning up to get an important score. As a roving corner-forward he had the ability to adapt to any type of game or play that Kevin Heffernan wanted him to perform. He was a vital cog in the Dublin machine.

The Chess Player

Despite the quality of the other contenders the choice for the number thirteen jersey was Kerry's Mike Sheehy, a ruthlessly efficient scoring machine. His ability to clinically take defences apart was the product of a footballing brain which was overflowing with ideas. His approach to football seemed to borrow heavily from chess, insofar as he always seemed to be thinking three moves ahead of his opponent.

"He was probably the outstanding forward on the Kerry team. He could do almost anything with the ball. The scores he made and got are legendary now, especially the famous free kick when he chipped Paddy Cullen during the 1978 All-Ireland final."

Earley recalls with affection a personal memory of playing against him in the 1979 League quarter final. He laughs more at his own naviety than anything else.

"A penalty was awarded to Kerry, I thought harshly against Roscommon and I said to Mike Sheehy as he placed the ball for the kick: 'Mike, that penalty should not have been awarded to Kerry. In fair play now you should send it wide'. He looked at me and smiled and then he thundered the ball into the back of the net. That was his answer.

"I remember another time, we were training hard to play Kerry in the 1980 All-Ireland football final, we heard a story about Mike Sheehy playing in a club match for Austin Stacks the week before. He was supposed to have scored twelve points, six were sideline balls on the left and four were line balls from the right. This only went to prove that he was of such calibre that there was nearly always exaggeration and embellishments concerning his play; no doubt to enhance his already magnificent reputation, as would be normal for anybody of such greatness.

The Square Man

"In my years in New York I saw many games in Gaelic Park. The commentaries there are given by Tommy Smith, a Louth man and in that distinctive Louth accent, he calls the full-forward 'the Square Man'. I had never heard that before and I always found it funny.

"Full-forwards are a special breed. Some full-forwards are target men. Some are both target men and scorers. Others are disruptive players who cause havoc for defenders. Some full-forwards are very big; while others are very mobile.

"Jimmy Keaveney was one of the best full-forwards I have even seen. I can remember him taking tremendous scores for Dublin from long-range. He was so accurate with either foot and so confident on the ball that it really did not matter what position he was in, you were sure it would go over the bar. This is a tremendous asset to any team."

The Human Sky-Scraper

"Eoin Liston was a huge man of immense mobility and skill. Apparently Mick O'Dwyer worked on him for a long time to get the requisite level of fitness. Liston was a great exponent of the running game. I suppose my enduring memories of him are of all the great goals he scored. It may sound strange to Roscommon supporters, but we were genuinely very disappointed when we found out that he could not play in the 1980 All-Ireland final. We wanted everybody who should have played for Kerry on the field, so that there could be no excuses if we won. Unfortunately he got appendicitis the Wednesday before the final and was unfit to play. He received a tremendous ovation from the crowd when he took his place with the Kerry team for the photograph before the match. That reception crystallised the high esteem in which he was held, both in Kerry and Roscommon.

"The man, I have picked as full-forward is Sean O'Neill of Down. He started his career as a half-forward in the 1960s but when he went in at full-forward in the 1970s he really made teams tick all around him. His alertness was his forte. He had the ability to react to any situation, to link up with other players and to take a score.

"I remember playing with him a few times on All-Star teams. When you turned after catching the ball you would see him with his hand outstretched and he would be five or six yards ahead of his man. All you had to do then was to kick the ball in the general direction of the outstretched hand and he was going to win it. He had created so much space for you, that then even with a bad kick forward, if it went in his general direction he was going to get it. His quickness off his marker and his ability to read the game are qualities which I think are marks of greatness in Sean O'Neill."

Beginning from the End

Earley prefaces his consideration of corner-forwards by recounting a conversation he had with former Cork dual-star, Denis Coughlan, in the UN cafeteria in 1989. Although they were in one of the most important nerve centres of world affairs, the time was spent discussing great football and hurling games of the past rather than the dramatic political events of the period. Denis related the story of how in the 'later' Christy Ring era the Cork selectors at one stage would select their team by beginning from the left corner-forward position and working their way back to the goalkeeper!

An obvious candidate for this position because of the consistently high standard of his performances is dismissed immediately. Tony McManus' strong claims are rejected because he is from Roscommon.

"In picking such a team I think it is accepted practice that you do not pick players from your own county otherwise you are immediately accused of being biased. I think everybody would agree that Tony should be considered for selection, as I think they would also agree that Gerry O'Malley should be considered for the centre-half back position, but I think it would be inappropriate for me to pick any Roscommon players on this team of greats.

"One of the players you would also have to consider for this position is Bernard Flynn who has performed so effectively and brilliantly for Meath. You can have great ball-winners, great runners, super-fit players, but if you do not have scorers you are not going to win games. Bernard Flynn is a scorer, he can do great things with either foot, as he showed in the 1991 All-Ireland final."

The One that got Away

"However, my choice for this position is Kerry's John Egan. Everyone will agree that one of the best forwards Kerry had was John Egan. He had great skill, great strength and a great attitude. I spoke to him on a number of occasions and for a man of such stature in the football world, he was a quiet gentleman. Apparently he had to work very hard to stay fit because from time to time he would get a little heavier than Mick O'Dwyer liked him to be. Of all the players that you might want to captain a team to win the five-in-a-row, it would have to be John Egan, but, in the end it was not to be and it did not bother him. I think that it is another example of the kind of personality he had, that he was able to handle the whole thing and still get on with his life."

God so Loved the World that he did not send a Committee

An important new innovation in Gaelic games in the 1970s was the emergence of managers of Gaelic football teams. The convention was that the selection of a team was made by a committee system of selectors. The problem with this system was that it was difficult to get consensus. With the extraordinary success of Kevin Heffernan and Dublin, managers became very fashionable. It is sometimes said that the appointment of managers has concentrated too much influence in the hands of one individual. However, Dermot Earley is an enthusiastic supporter of the managerial system.

"In Gaelic games the standard of fitness and skill required to win at national level is almost on a par with any professional game. If you are to get the best results you need to have a professional background team to achieve the level of success you desire. I do not feel that we are following the English soccer system, rather we are putting in place the proper organisation to identify people who are responsible and to put the structures together to help the team win.

"The problem arises when managers become better known than the players. It may be a criticism of the system that some managers appear to take away the publicity from some of the teams or individuals on the teams. The media are attracted to some managers who have the ability to put forward their opinions in an attractive manner. I see nothing wrong with that as long as the whole-hearted direction of the manager is to the advancement of the team and that the development of the managerial system makes for a much better organisational unit than the loose system of before."

However, one man who has made the transition from star player to manager, Dublin's Paddy Cullen is worried that we have followed the trend in English soccer and created the 'cult of the manager'. High profile managers like Tommy Docherty and Brian Clough are often much better known than any of their players.

"To be honest I feel the importance of the manager in Gaelic football is over-rated. As I found from personal experience, a manager can only do so much. In the final analysis you are completely dependent on your players to implement your ideas. It can be so frustrating sitting on the bench feeling powerless to actually turn the match around."

The success of Sean Boylan and Eugene McGee have established that it is not necessary to have been a great player to be a great manager. For Earley there are four essential qualities which any prospective manager requires: organisational ability, leadership skill, flair for motivation and tactical know-how.

"The organisation is the most important. If you can get the organisation right you will achieve some limited success almost immediately. It is not necessary to be an authoritarian sort of person to be an effective leader. A good leader is one who gets the best out of his players individually and collectively. Motivation is an integral component of this process.

"Many people will say motivation is unnecessary. They will say that the winning of an All-Ireland final or a National League is motivation enough. However, when you are in a situation of intense competition, nervousness and unfamiliarity with the occasion can reduce your ability to perform and you need something special to lift you out of the trance that you are in. When I was growing up I heard all sorts of stories about great motivating speeches given to teams in Croke Park. Motivation was always necessary at half-time when you were six points down and going out to play against the wind. I remember when I went into the dressing-rooms for the first time in Croke Park, as a minor with Roscommon in 1965, one of the things I looked for were the holes in the ground or the broken tables that would have been there following the great half-time speeches by people like Christy Ring which lifted teams. I think everybody heard stories about players who would seize a hurley and use it to hit an almighty belt on the table, breaking it to remind them of the fact that they were going out to represent their county.

"A story I heard about Christy Ring was that he was leading his team out of the tunnel one time, and when they were half-way out, he turned them back to the dressing-room. Then he took off his jersey held it up and asked his players to look at the colour and what it meant to them. After that the team went out with fire in their bellies and played out of their skins."

Many of these stories have been added to and may bear no resemblance to what actually happened.

"Motivation can come in different ways. Some players respond to the thumping fist on the table. Others need to be taken individually and almost punched to get their gander up. Then others need to have a hand placed on their shoulder and to be told quietly that they are the players the county is depending on. There is a dormant leadership within that person which can lift a team when they go out to play.

"I remember in my minor and under-21 days getting encouragement from the late esteemed County Chairman, Dr Donal Keenan. He would always give a rousing speech and then he would come to a few players, myself included, and say: 'I am depending on you. You are my man. You can win this game for Roscommon'. With that personal identification you went out with a greater intensity and with an in-built desire to honour his request.

"There is a lovely story told about the Notre Dame American football team. Their fortunes had declined enormously and their playing standards had reached rock bottom. The school decided that the team was not worthy of wearing the traditional Notre Dame colours. For years they played in their second strip. Then a team came together and qualified for a major final. In accordance with the custom in American football the team went out and were introduced to the crowd. Then they went back into the dressing-room for their final instruction. There, hanging on every player's peg was the traditional jersey of Notre Dame. To me that would have been a magnificent motivational ploy when the coach told them to throw away their old jerseys and put on the traditional colours. I am not sure if they won or not but it was certainly an inspirational motivating factor.

"A good manager is also a good tactician. You must know the strengths and weaknesses of your own team and that of the opposition to be able to adjust quickly to strengths and weaknesses of both sides. I think the greatest tactician of all time was the late Tull Dunne of Galway who was up and down on the field of play more often than any coach I have ever known. He would run up in his overcoat, with his hat on the back of his head changing the Galway team around when they were in difficulty and his changes always seemed to work. You can only do that if you have great players and if you have great players all over the place there are very few tactical changes necessary. Think of how few tactical stitches either Mick O'Dwyer, Kevin Heffernan or Eugene McGee had to make because they had a whole series of talented players. It is when you do not have the amount of great players that you have to be tactically astute.

"The rivalry between Mick O'Dwyer and Kevin Heffernan in the 1970s fascinated the nation. Shortly afterwards Eugene McGee emerged as a great manager. He came and worked with the Offaly team for a number of years, with set-backs all the way, gradually building a team, first winning a Leinster title in 1980 and finally the famous 1982 All-Ireland. Each manager had a different emphasis. Kevin Heffernan raised the level of physical fitness in Gaelic football to a new plane. Mick O'Dwyer got his players to a high fitness level early on in the year and then concentrated on working with the ball to develop the skill-factor. I saw McGee training the Offaly team a few times. He was going through patterns of play without opposition on a continuous basis, which was very repetitive but in the heat of the game, the players could do what McGee wanted automatically."

In recent years two managers whose paths have crossed frequently in important matches, including three All-Ireland finals, are Meath's Sean Boylan and Cork's Billy Morgan.

"Sean Boylan's genius is his organisational and motivational qualities. Most of the input on tactics would come from senior players. Colm O'Rourke told me that at half-time in the 1991 All-Ireland semi-final against Roscommon, when Meath were facing a much sterner test than expected, it was the senior players on the team who decided the way Meath played in the second-half. Meanwhile Sean Boylan was making switches in personnel. Like Boylan, Billy Morgan is a good organiser and a good motivator. He also has the ability to read the game. He got great performances out of the Cork team because they looked up to him and because of his reputation as a former great player. They were keenly aware that he knew what he was talking about.

"In any consideration of great managers one would have to acknowledge that the better the players, the easier the manager's job. The appointment of two managers in recent times has had a marked effect on the counties in which they managed. P.J. Carroll's involvement with Leitrim has transformed them into a serious contender for the

212

Connacht title. In 1990 and 1991 they pushed Roscommon very closely. John O'Keefe took on what could be described as a mediocre bunch of Limerick players and moulded them into a team that almost beat Kerry in the 1991 Munster final. It was a magnificent achievement and must be considered as a vindication of the managerial system. Obviously Peter McGrath has worked wonders with the Down team, guiding them to their first All-Ireland in twenty-three years in 1991. John Maughan took Clare to an All-Ireland B Championship in 1991 and they were extremely unlucky to lose to Meath in the League quarter-final in 1992, particularly as they finished with only thirteen players and of course he guided Clare to the shock of the century when they beat Kerry in the 1992 Munster final. Brian McEniff, of Donegal and Ulster, Marty McDermott of Roscommon and Eamon Coleman of Derry amongst others have also done tremendous work in their roles.

"On performance alone to pick a manager for my ideal team, I would have to pick Mick O'Dwyer. He has taken a team to ten All-Ireland finals and won eight. The man who could do that would have to be the automatic choice for manager. Living in Kildare I have seen at first hand how his appointment as manager of Kildare lifted not just the county team, but all the teams within the county."

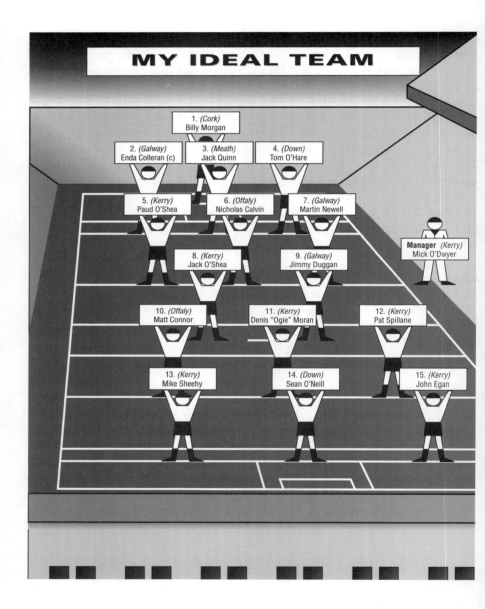

Having omitted all Roscommon players from his greatest team, Earley decided to select his greatest Roscommon team. Again, only players who wore the Roscommon jersey in his time were considered. The players on the 1962 and 1980 All-Ireland final sides form the nucleus of the team. Some of the players like Gerry O'Malley and Tony McManus were automatic choices. The most problematic position was full-back with two outstanding candidates Pat Lindsay and John Lynch. The fact that Lynch was from the same club and was Earley's childhood idol swayed the decision in Lynch's favour. Another major dilemma was the goalkeeping position – whether Aidan Brady or Gay Sheerin should get the nod but Brady just shaded the decision.

The team in full is:

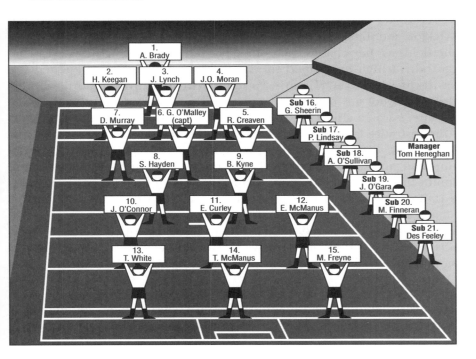

10. The Killing Fields

"Oh my God, what have I done wrong? This was the thought that came to Dermot Earley on a crisp April morning in 1975. He had been working in the army training ground in the Glen of Amal with his physical training class. Despite the unseasonal chill the class and their instructor had worked up a good sweat, following a series of demanding exercises, involving hill walking, river crossing, and mountain climbing. Out of the blue a summons came to officer Earley to report back to his base in the Curragh immediately. Such a summons was unprecedented in his ten year army career. Normally this type of instruction indicated that the officer had been guilty of a serious breach of discipline and was to be 'carpeted'. Only trouble could result from such a request.

As Earley drove back silently he was blind to the beauty of the Wicklow countryside around him. The newly born lambs which speckled the fields as they chased each other playfully barely caught his eye. The daffodils which enveloped the lawns like yellow blankets elicited no smile of pleasure. His mind raced with possibilities and sought desperately for any memory of a transgression of any army procedure.

There was a slight tremor in his stomach as he knocked on his Administrative Officer's door. He feared the worst.

One of life's most irritating and exciting qualities is its unpredictability. Although for long periods life can run smoothly and follow the projected direction, events arise out of the blue which involve a radical readjustment. The next few moments would result in major changes for Earley's professional, family and sporting life.

As soon as he entered the door he was greeted with the news. There was no exchange of pleasantries or preliminary conversation, just a simple matter of fact statement: 'You are going to the Middle East'.

Blessed are the Peacemakers

The overwhelming majority of army officers and soldiers volunteer for overseas peace-keeping work with the UN forces. The experience of serving actively in a conflict situation and the opportunity to travel are two of the principal attractions. In addition there is also the prospect of making some extra money; an important consideration for those who are hoping to get a mortgage for a house or those hoping to send their children to college. There is also an altruistic motive. Ireland has earned a tremendous reputation world-wide for the peace-keeping efforts of its soldiers. Most Irish soldiers want to be part of this proud history.

Irish involvement in UN peace-keeping projects dates back to 1958, when a contingent of Irish officers went as military observers to Lebanon to monitor the border between Lebanon and Syria.

However, in 1960 Ireland really established itself as a major figure on the world peace-keeping stage when we sent a force to the Congo. It was an event which captivated the attention of the Irish public, attracting enormous media attention. Paradoxically this interest intensified with the tragic death of Irish soldiers in the course of their duty. Martyrs for the cause of peace, their return from duty touched a deep chord in the psyche of the Irish people. Few events this century have precipitated such a grounds well of sympathy.

The initial departure of troops had created great enthusiasm. An example which illustrates this is the fact that the women in the Curragh camp came together to sew Irish flags for the soldiers before they left.

Adversity brought even greater unity among the families and nurtured a steely resolve to continue with the task. There were major practical difficulties in achieving the peace-keeping goals in the Congo. In 1960 communications were very poor by today's standards, both in terms of travel and telephone contact. The biggest difficulty though was the novelty of the experience. Inevitably with such a major departure in Irish military history there was a number of teething problems. However, the Congo experience and that gained in many other locations such as Angola, Cambodia, Central America, Iran-Iraq, Kuwait and Afghanistan has enabled Ireland to become world leaders in peace-keeping activities.

Peace-keeping is not actually part of the UN Charter, but peace-enforcement is. Peace-enforcement is the taking of forcible action such as in the Gulf War, to restore peace to a region.

A number of definitions of peace-keeping exist. One is: 'The positioning of military forces between two belligerents in order to keep them apart to allow the peace process to continue'. However, General William Callaghan gives a different nuance with his definition: 'Peace-keeping is the use of military personnel to assist the parties involved in a conflict to solve their problem if they want to'. If neither side want to make peace then no peace-keeping efforts will bear fruit.

The Promised Land

On 2 July 1975, Dermot Earley set off to take up his post as a military observer with UNTSO, the United Nations Troop Supervision Organisation on the Golan Heights. Arriving in Jerusalem was an enormous cultural shock.

"I remember distinctively the size of Jerusalem, a magnificent walled-city. People dressed differently, not unlike the images I had gleaned from films of the area. It was a bustling city with narrow streets and people crowding in the markets. And yet within minutes of the old quater there were parts of the city that were very modern and recently built.

"The first thing I think of every time I remember the Middle East, is the journey from Jerusalem through Jericho up to Tiberius through the Jordan Valley. The reason I remember this so vividly is the heat of the journey. It was much hotter than anything I was ever subjected to. The Jordan Valley is almost below sea level and in some places it is below sea level, so the temperature can be well above the hundreds, as it was on that July day.

"The other thing I remember is the sand colour everywhere, the lack of vegetation and finally, the fact that the region I was going through had an enormous military presence. The Israeli army on the Jordan border was very much in evidence. That manifested itself in the number of patrols that were on the road, and the security check-points that we went through as we travelled along the border.

"Of course the other noteworthy aspect was the history of the place. All through my school days and at Mass every Sunday I had heard stories about the Holy Land, now I was actually to see them with my own eyes. Jerusalem itself is steeped in biblical history. Then to leave the city and see the Sea of Galilee and to swing left to the town of Tiberius. There was an expectancy about the place and I was not to be disappointed. There are incredible views from some of the hills. From Tiberius I could see the Golan Heights where I was going to work."

As he looked at the Golan Heights the lines of a poem his father had taught him about the Irish boglands, when he was in third class flashed through his mind.

> The purple heather is the cloak
> God gave the bogland brown
> but man has made a pall of smoke
> to hide the distant town.

On the surface these lines seemed very opposite of the Golan Heights.

"If you were dropped onto the Golan Heights and left there for a few moments you might think you were dropped into a tiny part of Ireland's bogland which was flat, wide, and stony, but that it was an extraordinarily hot day by Irish standards. The purple colour is the cloak which gives a misleading sense of familiarity.

"The Golan Heights is very different though from Ireland. It is a plateau made up of black volcanic rock on which a very harsh thistle grows and with the heat of the day and the heat rising off the rick, the ground in general gives a very purplish colour. Since the Golan is composed of volcanic rocks you have the craters or towers of the volcano all around the area. These locations give you panoramic views of the area. These pimples, as it were, are dotted all over the Golan Heights."

Professionally life in the Golan Heights necessitated a major readjustment of work practices. An essential prerequisite to conducting his tasks was to familiarise himself with the background to the peace-keeping area.

In 1967 Israel invaded Syria. The invasion became popularly known as 'The Six Days War'. The Israelis had gone into Syria and pushed towards the capital, Damascus. They also went into the Sinai desert and pushed on towards the Suez Canal. When that war ended, the Golan Heights was in the hands of Israel.

This position remained until a further war in 1973 when Egypt, Syria and the Arabian countries attacked Israel. When that war ended a new situation existed which led to the creation of an area of separation between both Syrian and Israeli armies. Neither side was allowed to bring military personnel into the area. Under the terms of the treaty, the separated area came under Syrian sovereignty. The Syrians retained administrative control. The result was that a force of Israelis and Syrians faced each other with the UN in between.

A feature of the area was that the landscape was despoiled by war debris. Although to some extent the wars had faded into the memory, their legacy remained. The desert sands were the graves of the wreckage of battle tanks and armory. The strewn fragments of military equipment hinted at the human tragedies which must have complemented this destruction.

Although these poignant pictures brought home the cold harsh face of war they also provided a potent reminder of the danger confronting the UN soldiers.

An intrinsic part of the observation requirement was the patrolling of the separated area. However this was fraught with danger unless soldiers adhered closely to particular tracks. As a site of the battlefield, the area had been heavily infested by mines. Straying off the tracks meant that there was every likelihood that an observer would be blown to pieces.

This created enormous problems for the nomadic shepherds and the Bedouins, who were looking after sheep and goats in the area. The animals themselves were frequent casualties of a war that had long since been concluded, as they unwittingly treaded on unexploded mines. It was a disturbing sight and sound, even for the hardened professionals.

"On one occasion I saw a mine going off under a herd of goats and two or three of them were killed. Once I saw a donkey being blown up. There were a number of occasions when I was involved in arranging emergency hospital relief for shepherds, in some cases, young boys or girls who were very badly injured by mines exploding. My task was to use our communications system to arrange emergency medical evacuations."

An Uncivil War

The most enduring problem of the 1973 war and the most heart-tearing one, was the fact that families and communities were divided by an arbitrary borderline. The separation zone was equivalent to the Berlin Wall in Germany to the extent that families and friends were split up without any consideration of the human factor.

Consequently the UN had the extraordinary task of allowing these people to speak across to their families and friends through a megaphone. Although they only lived three or four hundred yards apart, periodic conversations via a megaphone was their only contact. It was impossible not to be touched by the human cost of the border. The location for this extraordinary scene was a settlement in the northern part of the Golan called Migdal Shamms.

"To a casual observer there was a relaxed atmosphere and little danger of hostilities breaking out. But beneath the calm exterior a deep distrust remained which led to sporadic bouts of tension. In such a tense atmosphere, the smallest incident could spark a major incident, even all out war. For example, some shepherds might move too close to the fence on the Israeli side. This would be interpreted by the Israeli's as an attempt to test their defences and warning shots would be fired to keep the shepherds away. On one occasion shots resulted in the death of a shepherd in a situation close to me.

"Another time there was a flurry of activity on the Israeli side and we had no idea what was going on. It was only when we listened to a report on the BBC World Service that day, that we discovered what had happened. An infiltration of what the Israelis called 'terrorists' had been intercepted by the Israeli army and they were killed.

"Another day I remember carrying out a fortnightly inspection of the military forces when I saw everybody scrambling for cover. The radar screens picked up incoming aircraft and sure enough, almost immediately a Mig fighter came very close to the Israeli side of the cease-fire line and then turned away. This was an attempt to test the Israelis and to see what the Israeli response might be. After that there was an all out alert by the Israeli soldiers. Had these aircraft crossed even one centimetre of their borderline, all hell would have broken loose."

As the example of the outbreak of World War I illustrates, a relatively trivial incident can spark off a major war. So there was a constant requirement for the UN delegation to be on continual alert in order to mount a fire-brigade service, if necessary, to keep tension to a minimum. Moreover it was vital to ensure that agreements entered into in 1974 were scrupulously adhered to.

Although army training in the Curragh provides excellent training in dealing with conflict situations, it can only do so through simulations. In emotional and psychological terms there is the world of difference between the training ground and the real situation. Practical experience rounds off the officer's military education. You have to see and more importantly feel the tension at first hand.

"One of the first things I learned was the sight of two armies being deployed against one another. You can imagine what it must be like, but you really have to experience it for yourself.

"Likewise you can read about tragic situations of grief, stories of brother fighting brother, families being destroyed by wars like the Vietnam War, the horror of the use of napalm, the tragedy of people being displaced but now I was actually seeing the reality close-up. The very concrete evidence of the tragedy that war brings was something I learned at first hand, particularly the cruel division of families which meant that they could only communicate with each other through a megaphone."

The Diplomacy of Taking a Penalty

"The one thing I would like to think I learned was how to be a good peace-keeper. This involves understanding both sides. What is required is not to say one side is right and the other is wrong but to stand with both sides and negotiate a solution to the problem.

"One of the other things you find is if you can communicate and establish a relationship with the person you are dealing with, then you can achieve much more than if you were very formal and stand-offish. It is an enormous help to get behind the personality that's confronting you when you are dealing with a particularly thorny problem.

"There is one great incident from the Golan Heights which illustrates this. Some of my colleagues went on an inspection on the Syrian side of the Golan heights and they went to a particular camp where the Commander would not allow them to go into the military camp. Of course this was contrary to the agreement. After much negotiation they were brought to the Commander's tent.

"There he had pictures of many beautiful girls on the wall and he had also pictures of great soccer players particularly goalkeepers from the English first division and Europe. Among the collection were Liverpool's Ray Clemence, Peter Shilton, Bobby Charlton, Denis Law and Johann Cryuff. Immediately they started talking about football. The next thing a football was produced from behind a desk. The Commander explained that he was a goalkeeper himself and he invited them outside to show off his skills. Goals were set up and a penalty competition was introduced. As the Commander stood tall and erect in the goal his 'goal-posts' were two stones, just like we used in the west of Ireland years ago.

"The event had caught the imagination of the camp and everybody was crowding around the 'pitch'. There was a great carnival atmosphere. An Irish officer was designated as the penalty taker. One of the other observers whispered into his ear saying "Perhaps this is an occasion you should miss". The penalty taker faced a tricky situation. If he scored the Commander would be diminished in the eyes of his soldiers. Yet if he was seen to miss on purpose the Syrians would be very insulted. A further complication was that the Commander did not look very agile. His ability might not match his interest. The easiest kick for a goalie to save is a shot that is waist high and is right in the centre of the goal. The ball can be hit very hard but all the keeper has to do is to stand up straight and put up his hands. With this in mind the Irish officer blasted the ball straight at the Commander. It looked a great save and he was delighted. All the Syrian soldiers were ecstatic; it was like winning the World Cup itself.

"That penalty save completely diffused a potentially difficult decision. The Commander was higher in the estimation of his troops than ever before and savoured his moment of glory. The UN officers left confident in the knowledge that relations would be smoother with that particular camp in the foreseeable future."

Apart from learning the art of peace-keeping it was also important to get the best possible understanding of the psychology of the Syrian and Israeli soldiers.

"The Israelis knew what they were all about. They were very highly motivated, knowing exactly why they were there. The state of Israel requires them to be there. There are nationalistic reasons. The Syrians are a bit different. Initially they are as fired up with enthusiasm as the Israelis. But, the ordinary Syrian soldier in the trenches may lose this enthusiasm as boredom sets in. They may ask themselves after a period of time: 'What are we doing here? Is it all worth it'? The one thing both armies have in common is a deep hatred of each other."

A 'them and us' mentality prevails in this situation in this context. It is important for any peace-keeper to establish that there is no hidden agenda. This task is easier for an Irish officer because of our status as a neutral country.

The sensitivity for the rights of both parties must be matched by a meticulously even-handed approach. Neither side must suspect that the other is getting preferential treatment. The perception is as important as the reality. All points of view must be seen to be taken seriously and appreciated.

"I always describe this to our students in the Curragh by getting them to imagine a situation in Ireland. Suppose there was a border between Dublin and Kildare, or Mayo and Roscommon. Imagine, that if you wanted to travel from one county to another that a soldier from Finland could call you to a halt and ask you to open the boot of your car and to produce your ID, how would you feel?"

"To be a good negotiator and diplomat you have to have the ability to never ever say no – but you must never ever say yes either. What you want to do is to get agreement. It is equally important that you never upstage the conflicting parties. The complete and utter result for the achievement must go to the conflicting parties and that is the most important of all."

A familiar adage is that 'we learn by our mistakes'. Earley was to get some valuable insights into the 'do's and don'ts' of peace-keeping from the actions of his fellow officers. In particular he was to see the destructiveness of thoughtless bureaucratic behaviour.

On one of his first missions on the Golan Heights he was accompanied by a Liaison Officer who on this occasion was to take charge of their encounter with the Israeli Commander they were due to meet. The conversation went well until the UN duo were leaving and the Israeli officer made a simple request. He politely asked if one of his officers might be given a lift in the UN vehicle to the first town on their way back. Taking the passenger would not have involved the UN vehicle in any detour.

"Our man made a big scene about it and wouldn't let him travel with us. I felt that this was a grave mistake. Here we were trying to win their support but metaphorically we were slapping them in the face. The right course would have been to say certainly. Should other approaches be made requesting greater favours, then you would have to reconsider and exercise your judgement. The observer in question outlined in no uncertain terms the reasons for his refusal. Although he was following the letter of the law I felt the correct option in peace-keeping terms would have been to accede to the request.

"There was another day when we had to cross into Syria from Israel. This necessitated going through four check-point gates, initially an Israeli gate, then a UN gate, then a second UN gate, and finally a Syrian gate. Sometimes there could be a delay at a particular gate as the soldiers would correctly leave nothing unchecked. On this particular day the officer I was travelling with got extremely impatient, even aggressive, with the Israelis. That impatience should never have been expressed. In practical terms all that was achieved, was a further delay. However, if you saw there was a problem and said you appreciated their problem, then ninety-nine times out of a hundred you were let through quickly. It's all about patience and approach."

Far-Away Hills

In the course of Dermot's nine months stint in the Golan Heights a substantial part of the time was spent on some of the observation posts along the border. A four day stint at a time was the standard practice for observation duty. Normally an officer was accompanied by a colleague from a different country. Both lived and worked there, scanning for trouble and keeping headquarters informed of any new developments.

Tension can be created by people losing their head and taking reckless steps. The movement of extra soldiers into an area is seen by the other side as an aggressive gesture and they respond by moving a similar or greater number of troops into the area and perhaps heavy armour as well. As soon as the first side responds not just in kind, but with an even larger reinforcement, a chain reaction is sparked off. The domino effect of a small movement can be astronomical and out of all proportion with the initial action.

The cumulative measures and efforts at 'one-upmanship' inevitably escalates tension dramatically. All that is required is for a soldier with a hand on a rifle to accidentally flex a finger and in his highly charged atmosphere a shot is fired that might thereby precipitate a war.

Nevertheless, the natural frame of mind of a peace-keeper is an optimistic one, always seeking out new possibilities and opportunities to build bridges.

"Although some of our efforts have been going for long periods without total success it is not the fault of peace-keepers that these situations have not been resolved. I would blame the lack of motivation of the conflicting parties to achieve a lasting solution.

"Were UN troops to get out of Cyprus for example, the possibility of loss of life on both sides would divide the community even further than now and would prevent the possibility of a lasting peace."

The Body Beautiful

In the tension of the peace-keeping mission it was important to avail of the limited opportunities for relaxation that presented themselves. While continuous monitoring of observation points was essential, the system of observers working in pairs allowed individuals to get some time for leisure activities.

The life of the Military Observer is a sedentary one, observation, radio monitoring and writing reports, feature prominently. Many officers also take some measures to keep themselves in shape.

The American singer Paul Simon once said 'One man's ceiling is another man's floor'. Earley's aim was not simply to keep his body in reasonable shape but to return to Ireland when his two year term was complete in 1977, fit enough and skilful enough to resume his inter-county career with Roscommon immediately. For this reason a vigorous physical training programme was necessary. A Gaelic football had been part of his luggage as he journeyed from Ireland. That football was itself a casualty of the Middle East conflict. It was completely worn out by the time he returned to Ireland from constant use. The football was a constant companion on any journey which involved him leaving his base for more than a day.

"Everywhere in the Golan Heights there are thick walls around the living accommodation. Every day I took out the ball and kicked against the walls, high, low, to the left, to the right, over my head, on the ground, high catch, low catch, pick-up and block down - hard off the wall to see if I could stop it from passing me by.

"I got great enjoyment from the whole thing. If there was a flat area that was conducive to running and would allow me to run a solo run for a mile or two up the road, I would do so. If not, I would try to find an area that had a suitable stretch of three or four hundred yards and I would do ten or twelve solo-runs back to back.

"One thing I had to be very aware of was not to cause panic to either the Israeli or Syrian forces. There was a very real danger that the conflicting sides might misinterpret a running figure for an enemy and take a shot. Perhaps a young soldier, new to the situation, might lose his head and fire at you.

"There was one observation station, on the southern most part of the Golan which overlooked the point where Israel, Syria and Jordan met. Down below me was a river and a railway line. Stories of *Lawrence of*

Arabia were told and re-told about his movements in the valley. This observation post was on a huge height above the valley and on one occasion while playing with the football I made a magnificent save and deflected the ball around the post in my mind. To my horror the ball bounced hard and then soared over the wall and down the valley, a couple of hundred feet below."

This situation posed a tricky dilemma. Should he risk climbing down an extremely hazardous path or could he stay sane without his football? His self-preservation instincts told him it would be a foolhardy thing to do but his love of football sent him a conflicting message. As he tried to objectively weight up the danger of making the descent, the image of the Roscommon jersey came into his mind. After that there was no question of a dispassionate appraisal of the risks. There was no going back.

He explained his plans to climb down to his partner. His fellow officer looked at him in disbelief and pointed out the difficulty of getting back up. Earley decided if he was able to get down he would be able to get up, an opinion that a mountaineering expert might not have agreed with.

Looking down over the valley was an environmentalist's paradise and wildest fantasy. There were gazelle, wild board and exquisite low-flying eagles. Despite the captivating beauty of the flora and fauna, Earley only had eyes for his football.

Having successfully retrieved the football in a climb that was physically shattering rather than dangerous, he sat admiring the spellbinding view with the sweat pouring out of him. As he sat there he realised that if he were to make the climb every day it would be an excellent way to retain an exceptionally high level of fitness. So after that when the spirit was willing but the flesh was weak, he deliberately forced himself into the climb by kicking the ball down the valley.

"I was constantly playing Connacht Championship matches, club matches, All-Ireland finals, and replaying matches I had actually played myself years before. I was just like a school boy. The Liaison Officers on both sides thought I was weird but they left me alone."

Their puzzlement is understandable. If only 'mad dogs and Englishmen go out in the midday sun', what kind of eccentric goes on a two mile solo-run in scorching heat?

Dermot of Arabia

After a nine month period in the Golan Heights Dermot was transferred to the Sinai desert. The operation headquarters were in Cairo. He lived in Cairo but worked out in the desert.

This was a completely different situation to that which prevailed on the Golan Heights for a number of reasons. The physical environment was very different. Instead of the vegetation, tarmacadam roads and hills, the landscape was comprised simply of rock and sand. The only exception was areas with oases. The image of oases which Irish people get from films like *Lawrence of Arabia* is extremely misleading. The popular notion of luxuriant growth and picturesque palm trees is far from the reality. In fact, often all that is there are small holes in the desert from which water appears intermittently.

In military terms there was also a significant difference. The Israeli and Egyptian armies faced each other across a desert instead of a UN border point. The political situation was also very different. At that time, in 1976, negotiations were under way to have the area handed back to Egypt. In fact some regions such as Abu Rudeis and Abu Zenama had already been returned to Egyptian control.

The UN observers had an additional difficulty in this area which was not shared by those on the Golan Heights. There were certain areas and roads which the Israelis had control of for part of the day and which the Egyptians took control of for the other. It was essential that the established time frames were scrupulously adhered to. The timing of the check-point change-over had to be second perfect. Supervising this sensitive transition was Earley's first task in this area.

He then returned to more conventional observation duties such as liaising with the Israeli and Syrian forces and patrol duty.

Although he lived in Cairo, his work in the Sinai desert entailed a 100 km drive from the Egyptian capital and a trip on a UN aircraft to the observation post. A rota system operated. Officers worked for a seven to eight day period and then returned home.

It was here that Dermot saw oil-fields for the first time. It was a real eye-opener to see the procedures. Many oil-wells were unmanned but pumped oil continuously by means of a generator. The oil travelled via a pipe and it would end up eventually in somebody's car, perhaps even in Ireland. It was also an awesome sight to see the huge number of oil tanks in the area.

"One day I was just 10 km away from an oil-field. All of a sudden the ground shook. I thought a war had started, it was so ferocious. Then a pall of smoke rose into the air. Later on that day I went to the scene of the explosion, it burned like an inferno, just like the oil-wells in Kuwait during the Gulf War. The lucky thing was that there had been no oil in the tanks close by, as they were almost completely melted down. What had happened was there had been some welding going on and someone had been careless in a repair operation. So the tank blew up and one tradesman was killed."

Not surprising rain was a novelty. "On one occasion towards the end of my time in Sinai, I was driving from Suez back to base when it started to rain. The rain was the lightest drizzle we would ever experience in Ireland, the sort where you might have to turn on your wipers for a minute now and again. I asked my Liaison Officer how much rain he expected. He indicated that there would be no more. That was their total rainfall for a year.

"I would say that the single thing I missed the most was the rain. I can remember writing to my father and telling him that when I came home that I would stand out in the garden for the first shower. When I returned I did and it felt magic."

Although deserts are synonymous with sand they can be very interesting visually. In the Sinai desert there are some impressive mountain ranges which break up the skyline. There were also a number of military camps dotted around the landscape. Even the oil-fields, although not very aesthetically pleasing, helped to break the monotony of the sand.

On the coast there was a greater variety of sights to be seen. Ports, piers and the movement of machinery made a refreshing contrast to the sand. There was also a beach, though pollution from the oil-fields had defaced it significantly.

"In the desert you could drive for a day and only see sand but because it was so new to me I found it very interesting especially in the first few months. There was always the possibility of seeing something memorable. There were also some great places to visit such as the monastery at Mount Sinai, which marks where God handed Moses the ten commandments."

Home Thoughts From Abroad

The working life of an observer almost by definition entails a lot of monotony. In such circumstances it is necessary for the army to take steps to keep morale high.

In light of this, one of the most important objectives for the army is to enable their personnel to keep as close a contact with people and news of home as is humanly possible. For this reason the Irish army has established a system whereby a telex or fax is forwarded to a senior Irish officer at every single UN post where Irish officers are serving. This takes the form of a news digest which outlines the principal headlines of the day from Ireland, the army news and sports news. This document is a prized possession among Irish soldiers. In some cases people drive great distances to get it.

The papers arrive later and allow people to read articles of particular interest in greater detail. This was particularly valuable for GAA fans who wanted to follow the progress of their county team.

"In 1975 I had played in the Connacht championship against Mayo. Roscommon got to the Connacht final in 1976. I got the result of the game that evening. The boys back in army headquarters knew I was interested so they sent out a message informing me that the game ended in a draw. The replay was played on a day I was in the Sinai desert. I had left the day before and was not due to arrive back for seven or eight days.

"Of course I thought of Roscommon on those days. You wonder what the day is like, if the wind is blowing and who is playing on the team. You look at your watch and it is 3.15 p.m. and you think the team will be getting ready to go on the field now. Then you remember that you are in a different time zone and it will be hours before the match starts. You think of the dressing-room – who is sitting where, of the team running onto the field and the roar of the crowd.

"We had problems with our rotations and I did not get back to camp for two weeks. In that time I was in agony wondering what the result was. I had had a number of contacts with the officers at the base during that fortnight, but unfortunately I was never lucky enough to speak to an Irish man. I spoke only to Finns and Austrians and the result of the Connacht final was unlikely to feature in our discussions. On my way back to the camp I accidentally bumped into Colonel Pierce Barry, a Kerry man who was the senior Irish officer in the Middle East at the time. I knew him very well and he told me the result. It would have been well worth the wait if Roscommon had won but it was a bitter disappointment to hear they had lost."

Wish You Were Here

Both terms on the Golan and in Sinai provided ample opportunities for sight-seeing.

On the Golan Heights there was a system which provided observers with three days leave in the first half of the month and three days in the second. Occasionally the six days fell together which opened up the possibility of a serious sight-seeing expedition.

"I was fortunate enough to be able to visit the majority of places I had read about in the Bible. I always considered Galilee the home of Christianity and I felt it was such a privilege to walk in the footsteps of Jesus. Then we went to Nazareth and on to Cana, where the famous wedding feast took place. The most striking thing was the peace and tranquillity of the place. To think that less than a two hours drive away you could be in a situation of great tension."

"Without any doubt the most beautiful place I visited was the site of the 'Sermon on the Mount'. Although tourists flocked there in droves and there were hundreds of people around, it had an incredible aura of quietness and peacefulness. Birds sang and flew around the orange and lemon bushes in the area. People walked reverently around the basilica. Each of the beatitudes was cut in stone. The Franciscans who are the custodians of the holy places are in evidence everywhere.

"Among the other memories I will treasure is travelling to Jerusalem from Jericho and visiting the Church of All Nations which was set up on the site of the Garden of Getsehemane. That Church was built by contributions from all the nations and each nationality has something to signify its participation. Ireland has a magnificent mosaic inside one of the entrances.

"Of course no visit would be complete without an expedition to Bethlehem. The tour begins with an examination of the field in which the shepherds heard about the birth of Our Lord and the place where Jesus was born.

"Initially I was very disappointed to see Calvary. It was in the street and when you got to the sixth or seventh station there was a butcher's shop where people haggled fiercely over the price of meat. This seemed to shatter the atmosphere of reverence but then as you get to understand the Middle East and how the people operate, it becomes less objectionable.

"In subsequent years I saw the towns of Tyre and Sidon in Lebanon. Almost everywhere you went you had the opportunity to see famous places in early Christianity and every opportunity we got, we went to see as many of those places as possible."

A Tale of Two Cities

Apart from the biblical places of interest, Israel is a fascinating contrast between the old and new. This is particularly true in Jerusalem where the modern and the ancient enjoy a strangely peaceful co-existence.

On the one hand there is the 'old' Jerusalem. To someone from the western world to visit this part of the city is like journeying through a time warp. People in traditional dress haggle in the markets. At one level the city is a hive of activity. Away from the hustle and bustle some people sip a leisurely cup of coffee in the shade of the cafes. The smells of a proliferation of spices are almost hypnotic.

On the other hand there is the 'new' Jerusalem which has much more in common with for instance, O'Connell Street in Dublin or Fifth Avenue in New York than many of the streets in its own city. This is a young and vibrant city which owes more to the culture of the West than the culture of the Middle East. Young people wear jeans and drink coca-cola. Pop music is very much in vogue.

It is as if there are two cities in one. Even more extraordinary is the fact that although they are poles apart socially, culturally and economically the do not seem to conflict with each other.

The phenomenon of two cities in one is also repeated in Damascus and Syria.

Service in the Golan also presented the opportunity to see an uniquely Israeli institution, the kibbutz. A kibbutz is almost like a little village or community where a group of people come together and everything is shared in common.

A wide range of economic activities are pursued, fruit farming, dairy farming, fish farming, hotels, restaurants and even one which specialised in the making of silver. In many cases the members through tenacity, ingenuity and hard work transformed the most inhospitable of surfaces into an area which was comparable to the finest land in Ireland. Barren basalt rock was almost miraculously converted into lush green grass.

"One of the most interesting things about a kibbutz which I visited in the Golan Heights was that the oldest person there was just twenty-three years of age. Here you had a huge number of people dedicated, committed and well organised living together in a very tight space. Each had their own living quarters which were very small and sparsely furnished. Profits are ploughed back into the kibbutz and a certain amount is allocated to each individual to allow for holidays and some personal spending from time to time. The kibbutz system has worked magnificently all over Israel because everybody puts their shoulder to the wheel."

Living in Cairo while serving with the UN in the Sinai desert furnished the chance of a lifetime to see the Pyramids.

"They were breath-taking. The huge rock and stone structures defy description especially during the sound and light shows which are put on at night. A camel ride around the area was an integral part of the experience.

"The size of the pyramids alone would leave you lost for words. Likewise, the precision of the architecture was without blemish. To get such stones so high must have required millions of people. It amazed me."

Our Man in the Lebanon

The experience of serving on the Golan Heights and in the Sinai desert was to prove invaluable when Earley took up a second peace-keeping mission in the Lebanon in 1982. However the situation there was radically different to his two previous areas of observation, both from a geographic and a military perspective.

His area of operation was a very mountainous area in the south-central region. The UN delegation had an enormous area to patrol, a problem exacerbated by the dreadful state of those parts of ground which were loosely and generously called roads.

Climatically too there were marked differences. As was the case in the Middle East, the climate was extremely hot. In spring and early summer the grass was very green but exposure to the extreme summer heat turned it into a sickly shade of brown. In winter though, there were showers of rain which were stormlike in their intensity. Snow and thunderstorms were regular occurrences causing flooding.

In peace-keeping terms the UN delegation were required to provide much more humanitarian aid. The Lebanese had suffered the trauma of invasions in 1979 and 1982.

Dermot Earley was to take the position of Staff Officer with responsibility for administration, morale and discipline. He had no reason to expect any particular difficulty in this area. Within hours that illusion was to be abruptly shattered.

He arrived in his new camp on 27 October, 1982. The first battalion of that particular group of peace-keeping soldiers had travelled out the previous week. He travelled with the second group. They flew on two Aer Lingus aircraft to Beruit, stopping only to refuel in Rome. Israeli forces, having invaded Beruit earlier that year, were very much in evidence as his contingent travelled down to their work base. Having travelled continuously for twenty-four hours, the entire group were exhausted and after a light meal they went to bed.

Dermot fell asleep almost before his head hit the pillow. He dreamt of playing a Connacht final against Galway. It was a close match with Roscommon making a valiant attempt to recapture the lead. He was just facing up to a fourteen yards free when he received a gentle waking up.

The former Tipperary hurling great Tony Wall, whom Dermot was to replace as Adjutant in the next twenty-four hours, stood by his bedside. Tragedy had struck. Three Irish soldiers had been killed during the night as they manned an observation post. Two of the victims were due to return home a few days later, while one had only arrived the previous week.

The incident was reported internationally. Initially the consensus was the the soldiers had been killed by one of the parties in the conflict but there was uncertainty as to which side was responsible. As the events of the previous night were unravelled a more sinister scenario presented itself.

"I remember walking out with Tony Wall the following evening to the place where the incident took place and looking at the type of night. It was a very clear bright night. The moon was high in the sky. Suspicions were aroused by reports of the type of gunfire that had been heard that night. The possibility none of us had envisaged had to be confronted. Perhaps one of our own group was responsible for the killings."

In the ensuing investigation Earley had a peripheral role. Essentially he facilitated those responsible for the investigation. Three disparate groups were responsible for wading through the evidence. Initially the investigation was conducted by UN military police. Their work was then complemented by a group of forensic experts from Sweden. Although the Irish battalion were serving overseas they remained under the jurisdiction of Irish military law. So the gardaí then took charge of the inquiry and eventually cracked the case.

The evidence was painstakingly collated over the next six months by which time the contingent had completed their term. The person who was eventually court martialled for the three deaths remained a member of the battalion.

"The court martial lasted about a month. I had to attend every day and sometimes I was called to give evidence. The whole experience was very traumatic because the families of the three dead soldiers were there. Of course your heart bled for them. I also felt sorry for the man who was on trial and his family. One of the widows was expecting a baby that her husband would never see. It was an enormous human tragedy."

Before any investigation was carried out the immediate priority was to arrange for the return of the three corpses. A ceremony was held in Beirut before the bodies were flown home. All the different nationalities involved in peace-keeping missions in the area were represented.

Troops took up a square formation around the coffins. A representative of each country carried their national flag. A UN flag was draped around each coffin and a UN beret lay on top. Everything was going to plan. Then the unexpected happened.

A delegation from the Lebanese army marched in unannounced to participate in the ceremony. Moreover, they brought their own band. They were intent on running the show. Such a situation was not covered by any protocol because it had never happened before. As Adjutant, Earley was in charge of ceremonies and the task of resolving this delicate diplomatic situation lay on his shoulders.

"In the middle of all this I learned a magnificent lesson in peace-keeping. Strictly speaking the ceremony was our prerogative. I had everything in place and I was about to hand over control to the Commanding Officer of my battalion, Colonel Tony McCarthy, when the Lebanese officer informed me of his intention to take over from us. I explained what I wanted to do. He explained his plans. There was a significant divergence between the two ceremonies.

"I wasn't completely sure how flexible I should be. I explained that the officer in charge of the UNIFIL forces, General Wiliam Callaghan, would be arriving in the next few minutes and that I would consult with him. Just as he arrived, his counterpart on the Lebanese side unexpectedly showed up. Both of them went into the VIP lounge at the airport.

"After a few moments I went in and explained the situation to General Callaghan. I knew him quite well. He simply said to me: 'Dermot do whatever the General wants'. That immediately indicated to me that no matter what preparations we had made ceremonial wise, the Lebanese were to call the shots. If they wanted to take over the ceremony it was their home ground and it was only fitting that they should take charge. They wanted to have pride of place in the ceremony and it was important that they should be allowed to do so.

"It was a very moving and appropriate ceremony. At the end the Lebanese government awarded a medal of honour to the three deceased. A medal was placed on each coffin. This was an unprecedent gesture and was deeply appreciated by the families involved, the UN, and by Ireland."

Returning to the camp was a difficult experience. A kaleidoscope of emotions was evident from the faces of the soldiers. Sadness for colleagues lost, fear for personal safety, (who knew who would be struck down next) depression and suspicion. As much normality as possible had to be returned to this abnormal situation.

A complicating factor was the importance of allaying fears back home. The news of a death of one individual or individuals has a domino effect on all the families. Special efforts have to be made to ensure that morale is kept a the highest possible level in exceptionally difficult circumstances.

Despite the grief for the three men who had been willing to put their lives on the line for the cause, there was an important job to be done. Peace-keepers cannot afford the luxury of allowing their personal feelings or problems to jeopardise the task they are entrusted to carry out. Nonetheless it was important to be particularly sensitive to the needs of the troops, both individually and collectively.

"I had outright administrative responsibility for six hundred and fifty soldiers, women and men. I was in constant communication with our sub-commanders. We discussed what had happened openly and how we could improve things. The suggestions came more from them than me.

"My main priority was to take practical steps to sustain and improve morale, for example, to ensure that soldiers got mail quickly and that letters were sent home quickly. If a soldier felt badly and came to me requesting a personal call home, I would arrange that immediately, or at the first available opportunity. There could have been many reasons for this, such as a family bereavement. Indeed my own father died while I was there. The priority was to keep both soldiers and family happy."

The three deaths were a great trauma for everybody in the unit and very draining in emotional and psychological terms. This type of situation is very conducive to severe depression. In extreme cases this can lead to suicide. It is important that any warning signs of suicidal intentions are acted upon.

"Loneliness can be one of the biggest problems when you are away from home, particularly when you are away from home on a constant basis. If you are occupied, time passes quickly, but when you are on observation, alone with your thoughts at night-time, in a curfew situation a lot of negative and destructive thoughts can enter your head.

"For individual soldiers events like birthdays, First Holy Communions, and anniversaries can be particularly tough. A trying time for everybody is when mail goes astray. A week goes by and the regular letter or letters from home fail to arrive. People on the ground and those at home can get very lonely.

"The worst time of all is Christmas. People become very conscious of missing their families at that time. The army makes every possible effort to recreate the type of Christmas atmosphere you would experience at home but this is very difficult in a hot climate.

"I have heard it said so many times in these situations that there was a build-up to a suicide. Someone would say: 'Be God now he was not himself last week. He was very in, on himself'. Bad news from home such as the dissolution of a relationship can provoke loneliness and depression. It is important that every action out of the norm is noted and acted upon so that any suicidal tendencies are detected in time.

"I don't think you ever get used to it. The tension, the loneliness and the abnormality have an unsettling effect. The first time you go on a peace-keeping mission has a novelty value, but it gets harder as you go back. It can become very boring. Some people get very depressed.

"The one positive development that has improved our quality of life has been the advent of video. We can now see sports programmes, football matches and current affairs shortly after they have been transmitted. This helps to boost morale."

From a Distance

Although an adjutant has to ensure that no stone is left unturned in the effort to keep morale at the optimum level, there are times when he, himself, is like a bird in a cage. In the Lebanon one way to counteract the loneliness was to make an international phone call from the UN military operations camp in Niquora. Such an opportunity presented itself to me four or five times during the battalion's stay there in 1982-83.

In recent years communication systems between Ireland and the Lebanon have improved immeasurably. Back in 1982 to ring home required booking in advance, joining a long queue and paying twenty dollars a minute. A call home was an expensive luxury but everybody felt it was worth it. However, there was one occasion when Dermot Earley was less than pleased with the value he got for his phone call.

"I can remember the operator telling me that my call was through. The phone rang just once and was answered by my daughter Paula, who was just 3 years old at the time. I asked her did she know who this was and after prompting her a few times she said: 'Daddy'. I asked her was she well and how was everybody at home. She said everybody was okay. Then I asked her was Mammy there and she said yes. I asked her to go and get her for me. She said she would but she didn't. I said: 'Go on and do it now'. This went on and on until I realised that Paula had no intention of calling her Mammy.

"There was a great sense of frustration as I hung up. Although it was lovely to hear Paula's voice it was very annoying not to be able to talk to

Mary. I couldn't afford to hold on any longer, because the call would have cost me a few hundred dollars.

"The whole thing was clarified in an exchange of letters. Paula had told Mary that she had been talking to Daddy, but Mary hadn't believed her. Paula had a phone call with me and she wasn't going to share it with anybody else."

Paula's enduring memory of that time is not that particular incident but involves her younger sister Anne-Marie. She relates how Anne-Marie, who was not even 2 years old at that stage, was afraid of her Daddy when he returned from his time in the Lebanon. She treated him like a stranger for weeks afterwards. Anne-Marie turns pink with embarrassment as Paula describes in vivid detail the lengths she went to, to avoid contact with her father.

For his part, her Daddy was finding it difficult enough without this burden. He had returned home following his father's death.

"It was a very traumatic experience, but at least there was a lot of family and friends around. It was great to see the children again. David, Conor and Dermot Jnr looked at me with great expectancy, wanting to hear about Lebanon. Paula was skipping with excitement. Little Anne-Marie didn't want to know me at all and every time I turned my attention towards her she just ignored me and turned away. There was fear in her eyes and she had no idea who this stranger was. It is a pretty humbling and wounding experience to be treated like a stranger by your own daughter. These are the problems anybody who is away for a long time has to cope with. To make the adjustment back to your family is difficult.

Brothers in Arms

Although the downside of peace-keeping was being away from home for long periods, the great advantage was meeting peace-keepers from other nationalities. Living with people with different customs, languages and cultures is a very enriching experience. Despite their differences, peace-keepers share, broadly speaking, the same training and interest in peace-keeping, which provides a 'professional' bond in the group. This bond is intensified when everybody picks up a rudimentary grasp of each other's language. When words fail imaginative use of hand signals, mime and gesture get the message across.

If in Ireland the 'family that prays together stays together' in peace-keeping the 'pair that work together stay together'. The atmosphere during long observation sessions lends itself to long conversations. Talking acts as a therapy in very tense situations when people are stretched to their limits in psychological and emotional terms.

Earley developed a lasting relationship with an officer from Austria. The story of their friendship embodies the close relationships which develop between peace-keepers.

"We were both based in Tiberius at the time and we worked closely together. He had a great sense of humour and we got on very well together. His wife was an exceptionally beautiful blonde lady who became good friends with Mary. Mary was expecting our first child at the time and would sit in the park outside headquarters. His wife would talk to Mary and they got on famously. Their two children would play in the park as the two women talked. Their little boy and girl had inherited her good looks. They weren't twins but you would think so.

"One night the Austrian and I were in total darkness in our observation point. We had to disconnect all our equipment because there was a horrendous thunderstorm and we were afraid that if lightning struck our masts we could lose our radio. There was no communication with base until the raging storm had subsided.

"We discussed our families, our hobbies and our upbringing, the Austria that he grew up in and the west of Ireland; finally the discussion moved on to meeting our wives. He asked me if I ever met my wife's father. I explained that unfortunately he had died sometime before I met her, God rest him.

"I repeated his question and he said no. Then he paused and I detected hesitancy as he deliberated whether he should elaborate further or not. I didn't prompt or say anything. After a while he said: 'My wife's father was a Russian soldier who came to Berlin during World War II and raped my wife's mother. As a result of that rape my wife was born'.

"I often reflect that as a result of such an horrendous crime that this beautiful woman and two enchanting children were born. The fact that he had shared such an intimate secret testifies to the close bond that develops between people in a tense close situation."

Did You Ever Kill a Man?

One of the questions that army personnel who have served abroad in a conflict situation are sometimes asked, is 'Did you ever kill a man?' Fortunately Dermot Earley has never been subjected to such an horrific experience.

To spare himself having to relate the most horrific things he has seen he sometimes tells an apocryphal story about a Roscommon soldier who did kill a man.

"He was an officer in the British army during World War II. At one stage he captured a German officer. They began to talk to each other. It emerged that the German had lived in Ireland for a few years while his father worked on the dam in Ard na Cruishe. When he heard that his captor was from Roscommon he said: 'I visited all the counties in the west of Ireland but I really loved Roscommon. It is on the Shannon and a beautiful place'.

"After much pleading the Roscommon man agreed to let his captive free. He explained though, that if anybody saw him releasing the German he would be court-martialled and shot. He said he would turn his back and count to ten and if the German was out of his sight he wouldn't bother pursuing him. The count completed he turned around. The 'enemy soldier' stood on a hill and waved down to him. The Roscommon man waved back up. Then without any warning the German shouted: 'Up Mayo'. The Roscommon man shot him on the spot.

"As he stood there holding his smoking rifle in his hand he said aloud: 'After he said that, sure I had to kill him'."

11. If My Father Could See Me Now

If I had the power I would try to change the attitude of the super powers towards one another and towards the areas of the world where violence, hunger and strife are to the fore. I would promote peace, and harmony among peoples and nations.
(Dermot Earley, 1980).

When Dermot Earley was asked for a profile piece concerning what changes he would like to see in the world in 1980 he identified peace as the number one priority. At that time he thought that he could play a modest, though significant contribution to this cause through his peace-keeping activities with the United Nations (UN). He could never have foreseen that just seven years later he would be close to the very centre of power with the opportunity to influence decisions about peace on a global scale, when he took up his appointment as Assistant Military Advisor to the Secretary General of the UN in UN Headquarters in New York.

In 1987, Ireland was asked to supply an Assistant Military Advisor to the Secretary-General of the UN, Mr Javier Perez de Cuellar. The name of Earley came up because of his two previous tours of peace-keeping duty. In particular, he had been in the thick of the action when he went out with the 52nd Infantry Battalion, as part of the UNIFIL peace-keeping force in the Lebanon, after the Israeli invasion of southern Lebanon. This was a very difficult assignment since the Irish lines were fired on, usually by the proliferation of militia factions operating in southern Lebanon. Following his return from the Lebanon he was Staff Officer in the Directorate of Operations with responsibility for overseas service. The office he worked in was known as the 'overseas room'.

He became the fifth Irish officer to hold the appointment following Comdt Jimmy Flynn, Comdt Con Creen, Comdt Brian O'Sullivan and Comdt John Ryan.

Like many others he had applied for the prestigious position at the nerve centre of the UN's world-wide peace-keeping effort. When he was informed in February 1987 that he would be taking up his appointment in June he could not have imagined that he would have first hand experience of the independence of Namibia from South Africa, a cease-fire in Angola, dealings with the Iraqi government following the Gulf War, and the awarding in 1988 of a Nobel Peace Prize to the UN organisation.

"I had mixed feelings when I heard the news of my appointment on the corridors of power in defence forces headquarters, from the Director of Operations, Col Steve Murphy, later Brigadier General Murphy. I volunteered not thinking that I might be selected. I had not given it much thought because I was very happy in the job I was in.

"Of course there was the positive and negative to be considered. On the positive side it was great to get the job in New York, my family would come with me, the opportunity was good, and it was exciting.

"The negative aspects were leaving home, football in Ireland was finished, selling the house, getting organised, getting a house over there, finding proper schools for the children and all the practical problems of moving a large family from one country to another.

"I had to ask myself was it worth it. However, I got a very positive feeling about the whole thing and looked forward to it immensely.

"I had been selected to go to the Middle East in 1985 as the Operations Officer with a battalion going to Lebanon. Just before playing Galway in the Connacht Championship that year I got a bad bout of hepatitis and had to spend a week in hospital. This made me ineligible for overseas work for a year.

"I had told Mary in 1985 that I had been selected to go to the Lebanon and I remember her being disappointed to some extent. I was going off again for six months.

"Thinking of that disappointment on her face I decided to play a trick on her. When I went home that evening, I managed to keep the news to myself until after dinner. When everything had been cleared away I called all the children together and said: 'I have news'. There was intense curiosity. I said: 'I am going overseas in June'. Nobody spoke. Then I said: 'And you are all coming with me'. There was great excitement. I said: 'We are going to New York'. David shouted out immediately: 'The Giants'. I will never forget it. He had been watching the American football and superbowl. In that split second I could see his mind working overtime, how he would be watching the Giants in the flesh. Then there were hundreds of questions about the practical aspects."

Not surprisingly the story of the appointment of such a high profile GAA personality to a top-ranking position in the UN was covered widely in the sports section of the Irish media. However, the *Evening Herald's* social column also took up the story. In a feature entitled 'Bronx Blues for Earley' it related the problems of finding accommodation for a family of eight in New York.

Although he had been informed of his new appointment, protocol dictated that he should also get formal confirmation from the UN headquarters in New York. However, there was a hiccup in the proceedings and the official telex did not go through normal channels but ended up in the international telex centre in Dublin.

"I was in my office one day when I got a call from a young lady in the telex centre. She asked me where could she relay the telex that she had for me. I asked her to read it out to me. She said: 'I don't know if I should or not'. After some gentle persuasion she agreed to do so. As she read out the conditions of service she got excited about it. Here was a fellow going off to New York for a year, the salary was mentioned as well as the conditions for my family,.

"In a voice that was almost breathless with excitement she asked me if I was going to take the job. When I said yes, she said: 'Oh good luck. I am delighted'. That was nice. I liked that."

Although the contract was initially for a year, he had the option of renewing it for another year should the Department of Defence agree to release him.

Look Up It's Not Aer Lingus

The arrangements for the sojourn away went very satisfactorily, with one notable exception.

"I really wanted to fly Aer Lingus but for UN bureaucratic reasons I was not allowed to do so. They had contracts with other airlines so I had to fly to London with Aer Lingus and then take a flight with British Airways.

"This was something I took up later with the UN because on other occasions when I wanted to travel I was also channelled to airlines other than Aer Lingus. Eventually I won. During my time with the UN it was important to me to use my national airline."

Three days of house hunting in April had established the temporary New York home of the Earley clan.

"I had been invited a long time before to speak at the annual dinner of one of the clubs in Chicago in April. They wanted me to go for seven days because it was much cheaper that way. Then when I heard I was going to live in New York I decided I would take Mary with me. I asked the people in Chicago if I could stay a bit longer than seven days in order to give me the opportunity to do some house hunting.

"The UN gave no assistance with finding accommodation. I wanted a house close to the railway so I could commute into work. The other important consideration was schools for the children.

Having arranged the accommodation, there were six weeks to make all the final arrangements for departure. Friday 19 June was the day the family's odyssey was to begin.

"The thing I remember about arriving in New York was the heat, which hits you as soon as you get off the plane. We were lucky insofar as Mary's brother, who works for Aer Lingus, lives in New York, and he was there with his father-in-law to meet us and bring us to our new home.

"One of the cars had a stack of baseball caps in the back. When we pulled up to the house as the three lads got out of the car they were wearing the baseball caps. To this day they still wear baseball caps. I remember thinking that we were only in the country twenty minutes and we were Americanised already.

"I could not remember what the house was like. Mary was happy with it and that was okay with me. It had four bedrooms, a dining-room, a sitting-room, a kitchen, a little garden and basement, though it was full of junk. It was semi-detached which was unusual for an American house. It looked nice, quiet, and residential."

Neighbours

As the Earleys began the task of taking their luggage out of the car, a little red-haired boy came along and made an instant friend.

"Before we had the luggage in from the car Dermot Jnr introduced us to his new friend Danny McCarthy from around the corner. His family were to become very dear friends and came to Ireland for a holiday with us in 1992."

As the Earley children surveyed their new home with undisguised delight the landlord was on hand to ensure there were no difficulties. He brought the entire family out to meet the neighbours. The first person they saw was a woman working in the garden who was introduced as Mrs Donnelly.

"I said: 'With a name like that you must be from Ireland'. She said: 'Sure I am from Roscommon'. I could not believe it. She turned out to be Roscommon goalie, Gay Sheerin's aunt. When Gay came out to visit me and play football with the Roscommon club in New York, I introduced him to his cousins next door. They had been home in Ireland for a wedding earlier that year. It was an unbelievable coincidence. Here was this lady from Ballyfarnan and was related to Gay Sheerin.

"Next door to Mrs Donnelly was the O'Donnell family, a marriage of Donegal and Clare. So in one block there were three Irish families. We had selected that place at random from the newspapers.

"Just across the road an old house was renovated and a few weeks later a new owner moved in. I met him shortly after, at Mass one morning. His name was Tony Johnson from Meath and his wife was from outside Swinford in Mayo.

"Within shouting distance of our garden, four Irish families were all getting news from home, and getting the local provincial papers. We would all be able to have chats about what was going on in the long hot evenings and after Mass on Sundays. We would have the same conversations as you would have outside any church in Ireland. Who will win on Sunday? Tony wanted to know about Meath, the O'Donnells about Clare and Donegal, and the Roscommon pair of Donnellys and Earleys wanted to know about the primrose and blue. The McCarthys who were second generation Irish were in awe at all of this. It was nearly just like being at home."

The new Earley home nestled comfortably in the fashionable Long Island suburb in which it was located. The actual place was known as New Hyde Park. The significance of the name did not go unnoticed.

"When I came back from New York a few weeks later to play for Sarsfields in the semi-final of the Kildare County Championship against Athy, which we lost, one of the lads who knew the area asked me where I lived in New York. When I told him he said: 'God you did not go far from home. Hyde Park Roscommon and New Hyde Park, New York."

Are They Yours?

The first day at work was spent familiarising the new UN recruit with the job. His primary function was to advise the UN Secretary General on situations monitored by the organisation that involved military conflict. To accomplish this goal, it would be necessary to participate in technical missions abroad as well as to monitor existing peace-keeping on a day-to-day basis. Another vital role was to plan for future peace and determine what kind and level of peace-keeping resources might be needed.

The UN does not manage its own spy network. Intelligence is collated from other UN agencies and published material. In such circumstances analysis rather than new information is the primary task. After a major war such as the Iran-Iraq war, the military advisor's task was to indicate which measures needed to be taken to ensure that hostilities did not resume.

Dermot's Irish predecessor, John Ryan, was on hand for the first ten days to help make the transition as smooth as possible.

"I had good experiences with my family on the trains. I did not have a car in my first days there, so at the weekends, when I was off, we did the tourist things and visited Manhattan, Madison Square Garden, etc. on the public transport. The sight of a family of eight was a novel experience for American commuters. People would look at us and then ask 'Are they all yours?' and I would say 'Yes'. Then there would be 'Ohs' and 'Ahs' and 'Aren't they lovely'.

"In the end I got a bit cheesed off with the whole thing and when people said: 'Can I ask you a question?', I would simply reply 'Yes, they are all mine'. That brought laughter.

"All the times I travelled I was never sure who was entitled to half fare. I had a monthly ticket which allowed me to travel at any time. I needed one adult ticket for Mary and perhaps one for David. The conductor would look in amazement almost at the eight of us and say 'Okay we will strike a deal, one adult and two kids, the rest free'. This was a very friendly approach and always impressed me."

On one of his first mornings on the train the new Irish representative in the UN shortened the journey by jotting down the following impressions of New York and working in the UN.

New York, New York

"Entering the New York subway each morning at about 08:00 hours I am reminded of the final scene from the movie *Crocodile Dundee*. with the platform crowded and everyone silent. On attempting to enter the train, which is already crowded, I am reminded of the 'Elephant Jokes' of some years back. Question: How do you get four elephants into a Volkswagen? Answer: two in the front and two in the back. How do you get four giraffes in? Same answer. No, you must take the elephants out first.

"The public address on the platform blares 'Let them in, let them in'. The intercom on the train crackles 'Let them off, let them off'. The elephants and the giraffes meet head-on.

"There is a steady stream of all nationalities into the UN at 08:40 hours. I get a smart salute from the UN Security guard at the gate 'Top o' the morning Commandant'. He is an ex-US marine who has served everywhere but Dublin. I remind him that he was not up to the standard of Dublin, but not to take it to heart. The elevators are crowded and the people mostly silent. When recognition takes place there is 'Good morning, how are you today?' The reply is "Busy, busy'. Everyone at the UN headquarters is always 'Busy, busy'. On the thirty-sixth floor, I encounter my friend from Trinity College who works in Human Rights. He is appalled at the latest news from the 'the old sod' and indicates that the pending closure of Brown Thomas is the final act in the collapse of the fabric of our society. I head for my office. It could be a good day.

"The cables from all the peace-keeping operations arrived at about 09:00 hours and included the summary of incidents from each, as well as news summaries, press reports and political comment. There were clear (not secret), code (disguised information) and eyes (top secret) only. The letter terminology always amused me. How many other ways were there to read? The cables were read, and marked and then maps and stats were brought up-to-date. The UN Irish Battalion has taken another pasting last night and the war of the cities continues with exchanges of missile attacks to Tehran and Baghdad."

Climbing the Stairway to Heaven

Although working in one of the greatest political, and diplomatic centres of the world was an exhilarating experience, the first working week at the UN brought mixed emotions. The excitement was curtailed as a frightening possibility loomed ominously on the horizon.

Within three days Dermot began experiencing dizzy spells. These spells became more frequent and more intense with each passing day. Coming out of the elevator he would feel unbalanced. To the outside world he was walking like a drunkard. While working in his office he would suddenly have to cling to the desk, to stop himself from keeling over.

The prospect of having to foresake his new appointment due to illness became increasingly probable. At first he put it down to nervous tension and rejected the idea of seeking medical advice. After seven days he could put it off no longer. After a particularly bad bout of dizziness in which his office started to spin around faster than the speed of light for a few minutes he decided he would have to visit a doctor.

Shortly after the dizziness subsided he had one of his many introductory briefings with John Ryan. As the meeting concluded, John Ryan casually remarked as he walking out of the door: 'Oh, by the way, one of the things that happened to me when I came here first was that I got unbalanced from travelling so often in the elevators. I thought I would have to be sent home'.

Two days later Dermot Earley had the last of his dizzy spells. His office was on the thirty-sixth floor of the giant building. As part of his work in liaising closely with other departments and officials such as the cartographer, it was necessary to be constantly on the move within the building. Frequent travel on the elevator was an essential component of the working day. The Secretary-General was on the thirty-eighth floor, the top floor.

Out of Africa

The top Military Advisor in the UN was Major General Timothy Diboama, a Ghanian. He had been a full-time staff member of the UN since 1976 and had acquired extensive experience of peace-keeping throughout the world.

"Immediately we got off to a good start and struck up a good relationship. When I arrived in the US in 1987 peace-keeping was stagnant. But that was to change and change quickly."

In 1988 because of the cease-fire between Iran and Iraq, and the UN's participation, and also because of the change in the status of the relationship between the US and the Soviet Union, there was a window of opportunity for the resolution of conflict in many places.

"With the co-operation of the Soviet Union and the US, the UN had the opportunity to use its diplomatic skills to bring about peace. Since

1988, we have had eight to ten operations established, whereas in the previous fifteen years we had very few."

Dermot Earley's new job would take him to such countries as Angola, Iran, Iraq, Kuwait and Nambia.

In 1988 he was active in the UN's role that brought an end to the Iran-Iraq war that had lasted the previous eight years. In 1990, he worked with the UN forces that helped Namibia gain its independence from South Africa. Members of the Garda Siochana were also involved in this operation.

"Being Irish is a help. We are not aligned and consequently we are accepted as being impartial."

In his dealings with the Polisario in Western Sahara his Irish roots also proved to be an invaluable tool in the peace-keeping mission. An all-party Irish parliamentary delegation had visited the area and had made a big impression on the Polisario which the Roscommon man was able to use to the advantage of the UN. Not alone was there an Irish connection with the delegation but there was a Roscommon connection. One of its members was John O'Connor, Fine Gael T.D. for Roscommon.

To be English speaking was an additional advantage: "English is the working language of international negotiations and peace-keeping." His reasonable competence in French and Spanish also helped.

In 1991 he took part in negotiations between the government of Angola and UNITA - an organisation which sought to overthrow the government. These talks produced a cease-fire, which came into effect on May 31, 1991.

"The civil war in Angola had been going on for sixteen years. The UN had been involved for three years, monitoring the withdrawal of Cuban forces, but that was not going to bring about peace".

"In negotiations at Lisbon, which I attended on behalf of the UN, the two sides finally reached an agreement, and, as a result, elections were scheduled for 1992 to let the people of Angola decide their future. To me that was a great achievement and to be involved in it was terrific."

The UN's trojan work for the promotion of peace on a regional and global basis was well recognised in 1988 when the UN was awarded the Nobel Peace Prize for its peace-keeping accomplishments. After the award ceremony, Earley accepted a presentation from the United Nations Association of the USA on behalf of Secretary-General, Javier Perez de Cuellar.

My Man

Dermot's arrival at the UN in 1987 coincided with the renewal of the UN mandate for their peace-keeping mission in south Lebanon for a further six months. A meeting to ratify this extension provided an early chance to meet the Secretary-General face- to-face.

"Prior to that meeting I was introduced to all the Military Attachés who attended as support for their Ambassadors. The meeting did not really give me any great insight into the mind of the Secretary-General. It was only much later, having been involved in many meetings with him, particularly in regard to his task-force in Namibia and other problems such as Iran-Iraq and reporting to him on visits to Western Sahara, that he got to know me.

"In all meetings Perez de Cuellar conducted himself in a very formal manner. He went around the table and shook hands with everybody, regardless of whether he had met them three times already that day or never met them before. As he got to know me he departed from normal procedure at meetings. For some reason whenever we met he would always take me by my elbow, give it a squeeze and say: 'My man'.

"I do not know why, or how it began but it was something that went on all the time at meetings.

"Towards the end of my time in the UN he invited me to go with him to Lisbon for the meeting of the cease-fire in Angola, in recognition of the work I had done to help bring the cease-fire about.

"He was a very quiet man, very shy, very respected but I would say very alone. Everything was done in a formal manner. Even in the most intimate meetings, everybody addressed him as Secretary-General. Prior to my arrival in the UN he had had either triple or quadruple by-pass surgery but he was a much better man health-wise for it.

"He worked very long days and was constantly in meetings, either in Council meetings or one-to-one with Ambassadors or visiting Heads-of-State. He was constantly in demand. It was a most demanding job. His evenings were generally taken up with social events. There was a sort of matter-of-factness about all meetings with him. You could meet him on the corridor and you would be asked for an input from your work. No pleasantries were exchanged. Everything moved so fast, which allowed him no opportunity for small talk. Every second counted.

Although ultimately Earley was answerable to Mr Perez de Cuellar, the man he normally reported to was Marrack Goulding, Under Secretary-General for Special Political Affairs with responsibility for peace-keeping. Goulding had been a career diplomat in the British service since the 1950s, having served in Lebanon, Libya, Angola, and Kuwait, before taking up his appointment with the UN in 1986.

"He had a great knowledge of the Middle East. We exchanged stories and struck up a good relationship. We worked closely together for four years. A lot of the time when he travelled on peace-keeping missions I travelled with him."

A frequent topic of conversation during their quiet moments on trips abroad was Ireland. Although he was British, Marrack Goulding was married to an lady with Blessington connections. He knew Ireland well and visited the country in an official capacity in November 1991 to give lectures at the Royal Irish Academy and the Military College, in recognition of Ireland's involvement in peace-keeping.

Marrack Goulding became a familiar figure on Irish television screens in the spring of 1992 because of his efforts to secure a cease-fire for the war torn remnants of the old Yugoslavia. Most Irish viewers will remember the dramatic television picture of RTE's Eastern European correspondent, Orla Guerin, hunched down in a flimsy shelter as the guns of battle boomed all around her. As the catalogue of human misery unfolded, Marrack Goulding struggled to maintain the voice of reason and peace over the din of the gunfire and slaughter.

In this task he had one important ally, Commandant Colm Doyle, an Irish officer, who was the special representative of Lord Carrington in Sarajevo for the EC.

"Colm Doyle was in my senior class in the cadet school. I know him well. He has a great understanding of what conflict is about. He is a very personable man, ideally suited to conduct negotiations to achieve a cease-fire. He made great efforts to negotiate a cessation of hostilities and also to see if the ingredients were in place for a peace-keeping mission.

"One of the things that Colm Doyle's position in Sarajevo reflects is the quality of our education system in the army. Our senior Irish officers have the ability to go into any peace-keeping job and do it well."

Working with Marrack Goulding at close quarters taught Dermot the fickleness of diplomatic life. Diplomacy is like sport. You can be at the top of the mountain one moment and crashing into the abyss the next.

"One day Mr Goulding and I were negotiating with the Iranians. After a lengthy session in which we seemed to be going nowhere, almost unbelievably the Iranian deputy Foreign Minister left an opening. I remember that when the opening came, it was like going for a goal. I was ready to pounce in and so was Goulding. We could sense it in each other. Goulding took the opening and gained a great point. In our discussion afterwards he used a cricket metaphor to describe the situation. He said: 'I hit him for six'.

"Later that night we were negotiating with a different group on a similar issue. There was an interval for tea and Mr Goulding casually asked the head of the Iranian delegation if he had ever been to England. 'Oh yes, I was there in 1972' came the instant reply. 'How long did you stay?' 'Oh I was deported after two hours'. Mr Goulding went purple with embarrassment. He looked over at me and whispered another cricket metaphor: 'I have just been clean bowled'."

Although there were a number of trips abroad, the ordinary, routine, daily office work was as important to the cause of peace as the travel to distant lands.

"I would arrive in my office at 08:30 a.m. After reading all the cables and plotting maps, I was able to brief anybody by nine o'clock, Mr Goulding in particular. The office of the Secretary-General would also require clarification if there had been serious incidents. As soon as I had read the cables, I was on the telephone to Jerusalem or Cyprus or wherever to find out more details if something was not clear.

"The other thing I had to be able to do was to brief the Secretary-General's press team, who needed to be ready when they briefed the world's press every day at twelve, midday. Usually after their meeting they would contact me to get answers to further questions.

"We would usually meet Mr Goulding at 09:45 a.m. We would have an input into everything because the military dimension impacted on the political.

"It was also vitally important for me to maintain the closest relationship possible with the countries who supplied troops for our peace-keeping missions. They had to be kept constantly up-to-date.

"Before you knew it, it was lunch-time and as you became known you got invitations to lunch. Generally it was to pick your brains. You had to be very careful with every word you said. There is no such thing as a free lunch."

High Society

Another consequence of his growing reputation in the diplomatic world was regular invitations to visit and speak at various military institutions and functions on peace-keeping. He was also in great demand with research students who sought interviews for the purposes of gaining greater insights into peace-keeping.

"On one occasion I briefed the general officer body of the Military Aircraft Command of the US forces. As I got a tour of the base, which was the headquarters of the search and rescue centre of the entire US, I asked a number of questions. At one stage I was told that the guest speaker for lunch had asked the exact same question. I was a little chuffed when I discovered their speaker at lunch was Mrs Dan Quayle. I was to be their guest speaker for dinner.

"Mary had been invited to attend as well and had planned to travel with me but at the last minute we had a baby-sitting problem and she had to stay at home.

"Before the dinner I spoke with the conductor of the band of the Military Airlift Command who were playing that evening. He asked me if my wife was here and I explained the circumstances. He whistled an Irish tune to me and asked me if I knew it. I was not too sure of its title. I knew it as 'The girl I left behind me'.

"In the middle of the dinner the conductor stopped the music and turned around and told the audience that he would like to dedicate the next piece to the guest speaker, Lieutenant Colonel Earley from Ireland. Unfortunately his wife could not be here tonight as she had to stay at home and mind their six children. There were 'Oohs' and 'Ahs' all around the room. The name of this Irish tune is 'The girl I left behind me'. "

In 1991 he featured as guest speaker at the Sheridan Circle luncheon in Washington D.C. The Sheridan Circle is an organisation of Irish and Irish Americans involved in, or connected with public service. It provides a forum to address the membership on various topics of interest to both countries.

In speaking at the lunch Lt Col Earley followed a distinguished line of speakers from Roscommon including Rooskey born Albert Reynolds, Mr Eddie O'Connor, Chief Executive Officer of Bord na Mona and former US Supreme Court Justice William Brennan, Jnr, whose parents were born in Roscommon.

Introduced to the audience as the 'Joe Montana of Irish football, who like Montana, allowed his skills to do the talking on Irish football fields, Earley provided the audience with useful insights into the inner workings of the UN at a time when the Gulf Crisis was a critical issue.

In responding to the address, Sheridan Circle President, James Power, observed: "Colonel Earley is a credit to himself, the armed forces of Ireland and to the young people of Ireland whom he represents so magnificently."

In his formal UN capacity Earley was frequently sought after by visiting dignitaries for briefings. One briefing was with a man who was to go on to achieve world-wide recognition during the Gulf War, Colin Powell. Two weeks after that briefing Colin Powell became Chairman of the Joint Chiefs of Staff.

"Two weeks after that again, another senior US officer came for a briefing and I opened the discussion by saying he had come four weeks too late. I told him Colin Powell had been with me and now he was Joint Chief of Staff.

"I was very impressed by Colin Powell. He is the first black officer to become Chairman of the Joint Chief of Staffs. I was impressed by his confidence. He was a fine, tall, and fit looking man. For the Supreme Commander of the US forces, he did not expect special treatment. His questions were precise and to the point, and tidied up areas that I had not really clarified. He was easy to understand. I remember especially the firmness of his handshake."

Although Colin Powell attracted great media attention, his popularity was eclipsed by the man who spearheaded the Coalition forces in the Gulf, Norman Schwarskoff, known by the popular press as 'Storming Norman'. While his forces attacked the Iraqis, 'Storming Norman' fired a number of verbal scuds against the Iraqis which endeared him to the American public. His tough talking matched his massive physique.

"The Americans love a hero. They loved a man who told Saddam that America was going to kick his ass. There is no humility in the US. This is something that runs through all levels of American society."

How the Other Four-Fifths Live

Although there were many moments of quiet satisfaction as painstaking efforts for peace bore fruit, there were other moments when despair was the predominant emotion.

"The lowest points were when I would arrive in the morning and see a cable informing me that a UN peace-keeping soldier had been shot or blown up. Immediately you would think of a grieving family at home. Then you would have to brief the Ambassador of that country. Sometimes, the notification of casualty might indicate on the bottom that the next of kin were not informed. I had to ensure that the press did not get that information until the next of kin were informed.

"You would remember times when you were in Beirut airport and bodies were being flown home. You would also think of cold dark winter evenings in Dublin airport, meeting the corpses of heroic Irish soldiers who had shed their lives for the cause of peace."

Another big frustration was the unwillingness of some countries to co-operate fully with the UN.

"The Iranians were very difficult to deal with. I think they distrusted the UN. It took a long time for them out see that we were there for their good. It was not helped by some incidents that took place with our observers.

"Alcohol is banned in Iran. A non-Irish observer acquired alcohol and in a drunken state pulled down a lot of placards of the Ayatalloh. He was arrested but because of his semi-diplomatic status he was released. This caused a lot of resentment.

"The slowness of the negotiations was very irritating. It seemed so simple, for example to allow vehicles to travel from A to B, but the Iranian answer was always 'No'. There was never any reason given for this, other than an apparent desire to be obstructionist. Perhaps there were valid reasons for their refusal but we could not see them. It would make you tear your hair out.

"It was also very frustrating to hear countries praising the peace-keeping operation to the fullest but who would not pay the cost. It left everybody on the ground in a bad condition. That would really annoy me."

In his travels in Africa and the Middle East, Earley witnessed the scenes of real-life horror stories with his own eyes and heard the deafening, terrifying and deadly guns of battle.

There were many corpses, far too many. Faces were bruised and swollen. He saw young people who looked old. Passive people, totally and absolutely innocent, now dead. Some would have tiny bullet holes on their fronts. Others had their backs blown off. The final result was the same.

Mothers or fathers were left to rear children on their own. Hearts were broken by grief and racked by bitterness. Love affairs were abruptly shattered. People had only memories to hang on to. Families were in turmoil. Regions in chaos.

People who had joked and laughed and who were full of the joys of life were suddenly transformed into creatures of fear. Nobody knew what was going on. The people were existing rather than living, their hearts and spirits painfully and tragically exorcised. Despair and loneliness were their only companions. Above all, people were hungry. Many were simply walking, or more correctly stumbling, they were human skeletons.

"The thing I saw most of all was poverty. You could go into any of the magnificent palaces, such as that of the King of Morocco but when you came out and saw the Bedouins, shepherds roaming with their camels, you often wondered 'what they were living for'. Were they existing just for food? What did they do when they sold a camel? Was there a junior championship out there? Did they know what was happening in Iran and Iraq?"

There were also people who were working against the odds. In Angola people worked naked in the fields, digging with spades and using oxen. It was back-breaking work, working against the elements to eke out a subsistence. They toiled long hours but were lucky if they did not go to bed hungry.

In some countries incredible wealth and total poverty went side-by-side.

"In South Africa I visited Capetown where I saw the southern tip of the Cape of Good Hope. The line where the Indian and the Atlantic Oceans meet was pointed out to you. What was not pointed out were the shanty towns, tin shacks where people clung on to life by a thread.

"Immediately, my mind flashed back to visiting the local supermarket the day before, to buy some toothpaste. Outside, there were three black girls, half-naked, begging. We really have no idea in Ireland about absolute poverty."

One of the biggest impediments to eradicating poverty is nature, or more precisely lack of rain. It is a big cultural shock for an Irish person to see so many people praying so earnestly for rain, when we complain about the rain so much.

"The other thing you saw was fear. That was particularly evident from the children. You might see them running with a tyre and steering it with a stick. Your attention would be drawn to their laughter. Any of us who had children ourselves might make a friendly, playful gesture in their direction. But they would flee immediately and there would be terror in their faces.

"In war when you move, you have to move quickly. You are running all the time. People become programmed to run. When the war ends and the UN moves in, people continue to run. Women and children catch hands and run at the sight of strangers. It is hard for the people to learn to trust again.

However, poverty was a reality of Earley's everyday working life, even in New York. The huge inequalities in South Africa were mirrored in New York. The contrast between the 'haves' and 'have-nots' was just as stark in the Big Apple.

"I remember a family friend, Paddy Clarke and his wife, coming out to visit us one Christmas. We went into Manhattan on Stephen's Day. There was freezing snow and the wind-chill factor was very apparent. We walked up to see the UN headquarters. A man was lying over a manhole-cover, which channels the hot air up from the underground, trying vainly to keep warm. Paddy's wife was horrified and wanted to do something but what can you do? I had seen him there many times before."

We Are the Champions

Although twelve hour days, six and sometimes seven days a week were a regular part of life in the UN as Deputy Military Advisor, for a footballing legend some time had to be found for Gaelic football.

"When I was going over to America in Spring 1981 I had received a phone call from John Lyons, President of the Roscommon GAA Club in New York, inviting me to be the guest of honour at their annual dinner in September. I said I would be delighted. He asked me where he should sent the ticket. I knew by the tone of his voice that he expected me to be in New York. After I had said that I would indeed be living there, he said: 'Don't forget to bring the gear'."

Dermot had only been in New York a few days when the Roscommon club there made contact with him, to inform him about the training schedule. The Roscommon club were making a determined assault on the junior championship and for the latter stages of the competition had assembled a talented team which included three players who were regulars on the Roscommon inter-county team, Donal Brady, Pat Doorey and Gay Sheerin. However, despite his long career at the top with Roscommon back at home, Dermot Earley had some relearning to do when he began playing in New York.

"In my first game I caught the ball, cut up the middle and gave a perfect hand-pass to a team-mate. The referee blew his whistle. I turned around and said there was nothing wrong with that. He said: (in more colourful language): 'Learn the bleeping rules before you come out to this bleeping country'. A playing colleague informed me that no hand-passes were allowed in New York.

"The other thing that amused me in the same match was that before I played I was photographed and got an ID card in Gaelic Park. For every game the manager turned up with a book of photographs of his players and their signatures. At the start of the second-half there was a twenty minute delay. The manager of the opposing team had questioned the registration of one of the Roscommon players, so our manager had to produce his photograph and signature. Then as a counter-measure we questioned the validity of one of their players. This happened quite often, usually at half-time."

Another bureaucratic wrangle which was less amusing was a long battle with the minor board to have the three Earley boys cleared to play under-age club football in New York.

"I had to bring my passport and UN visa and the boys' passports to a meeting and show that they too had UN visas and that it was our intention to stay in New York for two years. Although the lads were allowed to play in the end, I felt the decision was taken with reluctance."

The Roscommon team qualified for the junior championship semi-final where they came up against Donegal. The match was scheduled for the Sunday after the All-Ireland final in which Meath beat Cork. As

Earley took up his position at centre-half forward in a downpour of rain he saw a figure wearing a Donegal jersey and Cork sockings approaching him. He was to do battle with Anthony Davis, who had played for Cork in the All-Ireland final the previous Sunday. Things had started badly for Roscommon.

"We went on the attack at the start. The ball went up between myself and Anthony Davis and all I can remember is a blur of red socks going away with the ball at ninety miles per hour. He went straight up the field and crashed the ball over the bar.

"I thought to myself: 'Oh my God, how can I cope with this'? He was like a young leopard, so sleek and fit. Thankfully he was switched to midfield after ten minutes and I had a field day after that."

Roscommon went on to beat Donegal and had a six point winning margin in the final. Armagh missed two penalties. This match was recalled in Roscommon GAA circles in New York in May 1992 when Cork missed two penalties in the Munster championship against Kerry.

Interest in the GAA in New York fluctuates. There was a big interest when Cork travelled over to play the League Final against the local side in 1989. The initial New York panel for training for the match featured the forty-one year old Dermot Earley. However, overseas peace-keeping duties with the UN caused him to miss the training. He returned in time for both games and was Mick Dunne's co-commentator for the match on RTE radio.

"I would love to have played but I had to miss the training. New York gave a spirited performance in the second game. Unfortunately my memory of the game is an incident in which Cork's Colman Corrigan was seriously injured. It should not have happened."

Gaelic games are an important part of the social fabric of the Irish community in New York. They provide a unifying force and an invaluable link with the 'Auld sod'.

"I think the GAA at home should give more help to the Association in New York because of all the good work it does for our emigrants. They sometimes find it very difficult to raise the money to have teams travel out to them from Ireland. It's good for our teams to travel out there but we should not necessarily expect them to pay for everything."

An important development in recent years for Irish emigrants has been the good work done on their behalf by the emigration reform movement.

As a sports fan one of the most galling things for Dermot about his four year exile in America was missing the tidal wave of excitement that swept through Ireland during the European soccer championships in Germany in 1988, in particular the hysteria which followed Ireland's historic victory over England.

The desire to be back home in Ireland was never more acute than during the magic days of Ireland's great World Cup adventure in Italy in 1990. He made elaborate plans to see Ireland's opening match against England on a big screen but he got stuck in the mother of all traffic jams and missed the first sixty-three minutes of the match! However, he was just in time to savour Ireland's equalising goal.

As he drove home after the match he found himself humming the Irish World Cup anthem 'Que Sera Sera'. That in turn brought back a childhood memory.

"Vera Morley was my cousin. She lived four or five miles away from us and came to stay with us every summer. She was the same age as me. Every night she would sing 'Que Sera Sera' for us. She had a beautiful voice. It was her song. We all identified that song with her.

"One lovely summer's evening Vera was playing in our garden. Our next door neighbour had been working with his horse all day in the fields. The day's work completed he got up on the horse's back to give him a drink down at the pump. Just as he passed our gate Vera ran out the gate and the horse hit her. She died some moments later. Every time I hear that song I remember that incident. I can see it still. I was fifteen yards away.

"I was only nine years old at the time but I always remember Versa's mother. We were all devastated, especially my mother. I can still remember the family who owned the horse. They were distraught. Vera was laid out in our house. Her mother was a fantastic, practical woman. She said: 'Listen, I have eight more children'. I can remember her words so well. She accepted death so peacefully."

The pressures of work meant that Dermot was unable to see the other World Cup matches including the crucial match against Romania. He was, however, able to take some time off to journey down to the bowels of the UN building and see the penalty shoot-out to determine if Ireland would qualify for the quarter-finals or not. He prayed silently that the hand of God would intervene. He was not disappointed.

"When Packie Bonner saved that penalty I knew we were through. I had no fear of David O'Leary missing. All we needed was one save. When it came I was so excited that I banged my hand extremely hard on the table. It was sore for days afterwards."

Long before Packie earned himself an international reputation as one of the world's great goalkeepers, he played Gaelic football at all levels for Donegal, not as a goalie but as a midfielder. One of his role models was Dermot Earley.

"Dermot Earley was a great player, possibly one of the greatest ever. Those of us growing up who had our hearts set on becoming great footballers looked up to him. He was a great source of inspiration to us all, not just because he was a great player, but also because he was a great sportsman. I can only say that if I had continued my career as a Gaelic footballer, I would have been very honoured if someone had ever spoken of me in the same terms as Dermot Earley. He set such high standards for so long. I think he was one of the great ambassadors for the game."

A Sort of Homecoming

When it emerged in 1987 that the Earley family's projected two year stay in New York was to be extended for a further year, a three week holiday for the entire family in Ireland was decided on. The sense of being home was apparent long before their plane touched down on the Emerald Isle.

"As soon as we got on the flight at Kennedy airport, I felt I was home already. I knew the pilot because he was an ex-Air Corps, the Irish papers were there for all of us to read and all the people around us were Irish."

The temporary return provided a welcome opportunity to meet neighbours, visit relatives in Tipperary and Roscommon, to sleep at home, and to do the gardening.

Trips to Croke Park were almost mandatory. The All-Ireland football semi-final between Mayo and Tyrone was taken in, as was the All-Ireland hurling final in which Tipperary beat Antrim. Tipp's victory made the holiday especially memorable for Mary Earley, but the more dispassionate family members were enthralled by the artistry, scoring power, and magic of Nicholas English. The day after the hurling final was the day of the flight back to America.

It had been great to be home but the Earley children in particular were looking forward to going back to the States and meeting their friends again. An important consideration was that September is the month when the soccer season starts, the under-age Gaelic football championships begin and the baseball play-offs are staged.

As the family planned to return permanently to Ireland the following year nobody was too upset at the prospect of leaving again. However, there was one poignant moment as their plane took off from Shannon when the thought of leaving home became almost too much for Dermot Earley.

"I put on the earphones to listen to some music as we took off. The very first song that came on was Mary Black singing 'As I leave behind Neidin...won't you remember, won't you remember me'. I told Mary to put on her earphones. As we looked down we could see the Cliffs of Moher. It was early September at about 2.30 in the afternoon. The green grass and the cornfields looked lovely. I can still hear Mary Black singing that song. I loved it before then but it was so appropriate for that day. I remember getting emotional as we listened to it."

A few weeks later, on Sunday 17 September, Dermot's thoughts turned to home again as it was the day of the All-Ireland final between Mayo and Cork. From a helicopter in southern Iraq he scribbled down in shaky handwriting the following reflections on the match and his work situation.

Sunday 17 September 1989 – Thinking of Sam

"It's just 17:00 hours (5 p.m.) in Basra, southern Iraq. (14:00 – 2 p.m. in Dublin). The Mayo and Cork teams are about to enter the dressing-rooms in Croke Park for the All-Ireland final. The Bell twin-engined helicopter has just taken off from the new airport at Basra as we prepare for a reconnaissance of the Shat-al-Arab on our visit to the UNIIMOG peace-keeping operation. It's 40°C or 104°F here. It's probably the same temperature in the dressing-rooms.

"The helicopter flies steadily along the river – we circle to take a second look at certain Iraqi defences. Down below, doing a ground patrol is Comdt Noel Langan, a cadet school class-mate, brother of former Mayo midfielder Joe Langan and having more than a passing interest in Dublin today. I was home for the semi-final against Tyrone and as I came out of the stand after the game I met Noel. He was delighted at Mayo's performance but the sadness in his voice told me how he felt about missing the final, 'I'll be in Iraq with UNIMOG by then', he said. I told him that I'd miss it too, as I would be back at UN headquarters in New York by then, 'but never mind I'll watch it live in a pub in the Bronx and I'll think about you, Noel'. On my return to New York, a short discussion with the Under Secretary General responsible for peace-keeping told me that I would be nearer Noel for the All-Ireland Final than I had originally thought.

"The distance between the Iranian and Iraqi forces on the 'Shat' is the width of the river, so their defences are strong. Will the Mayo defence hold the Cork attack? The dressing-rooms must be full of activity now. At 14.15 (2.15 p.m.) the players are in various stages of preparation. The boots aren't on yet – too early. Wonder what sort of a day it is? The weather will decide the boots! It's hot in the chopper as we fly away from a river full of the wreckage of partially sunken ships. The wind below blows sand across the bombed out villages. How strong is the wind in 'Croker'? There is always a wind there. Will Larry or Fitz be on target first?

"The flags of the respective countries are evident on many of the bunkers. Red is common to both countries as it is common to both counties in the final. Mayo on the hill and Cork on the canal end. I close my eyes and remember another day. Although we lost, there are great memories – the colour visible during the parade is a vivid one.

"Soldiers in their defences below wave up at the chopper but there is tension here. There is tension and friendliness in Croke Park too. I visualise the crowds heading into the stadium. Maybe 70,000? Friendly banter among opposing supporters and tension, wondering – will we win?"

A Metamorphosis

A year after his four year term with the UN, in a very challenging and fulfilling job at a momentous time for peace-keeping, Dermot evaluates the effects of the experience on him personally. There were positive and negative consequences.

"I am a more confident person now. I am more understanding of the slowness of change and I see the reasons why things do not happen as quickly as we would like them to. Every country has a separate agenda. We may strive to be a 'United Nations' but the reality is that countries are willing to make concessions only if they can gain a long-term advantage. I think I am now more tolerant of slowness.

"I also understand the problems of rapid change. It is great that the Berlin Wall has come down and to see all the new democracies springing up from the ashes of the old Soviet Union. But are we ready to accommodate them if the powers that control the wealth are not ready to finance this transition?

"On balance the American experience was good for the children. It was good for them to see another part of the world. I saw them become much more confident in themselves, particularly the girls.

"On the downside, I think that they were left behind a bit educationally. There were tremendous material distractions. Consumer goods were cheap. Every young person seemed to have their own fishing rod, bike, television, and radio. I think that children get too much too quickly over there. I think you should have to work before you get everything handed on a plate to you."

Conor Earley smiles broadly when asked about his American adventure.

"I loved it. School is much easier over there. They don't put nearly as much pressure on you as we have here."

Exposure to American values challenged Dermot Earley to reflect on his own principles.

"My views were consolidated. If I had had any doubts about my basic principles, all that doubt is gone. You have to be an honest person, a hard worker and know what you are about. I would think that my beliefs are solidified now."

In Roscommon Earley's name is a byword for courtesy and 'niceness'. Small boys follow him like lambs. Older people nod approvingly when he is held up as a role model for young people. Yet this image was threatened by some aspects of his American experience

"I became a more aggressive person. For instance, there is no doubt that when living in New York, if you hold the door open for people you are just walked on. After much frustration over holding doors open and being pushed to the back of the queue, I decided that was enough. I became more aggressive and fought my way to the front, skipping the queue and so on.

"Mary would say the same thing about her experiences in the supermarket queue. Someone would say: 'I was there before you'. Mary would reply: 'I beg your pardon' and then step back. After a while she would see that she had been in the right place all along.

"Gradually you became a bit like that yourself. Thinking of educating our family, it was good to recognise these traits in ourselves, to see how we were being conditioned by our environment.

"This was really brought home to me when Mary's sister and brother-in-law came to New York for a funeral. There were a number of people working on the trolleys and in greeting our visitors we did not see them. Maybe one of them said: 'Excuse me' or 'Sorry Mam, would you get out the way'. But when I saw him I thought he was about to knock Mary down with a trolley. She jumped out of the way just in time. I just roared at him: 'What about excuse me?' He simply ignored me. Liam O'Brien who came over for the funeral said: 'Listen it is time you came home'. I remember that distinctly. I remember the aggressiveness and I did not like one it bit."

If Only

While his UN sojourn was worthwhile and gave him a sense of achievement there were two major regrets, one professional, one personal.

When he left the job in 1991 he was not succeeded by an Irish officer but by a Finn. When Dermot was promoted to the rank of Deputy Military Advisor, it would not have been appropriate to have another Irish officer as Military Advisor because the UN wanted to share the posts around. From 1978 to 1991 an Irish officer had held the post of Assistant Military Advisor continuously.

"I have no doubt that an Irish officer will hold a similar post in the near future. There was some resentment in the army that I was not replaced by an Irish officer. Some people said: 'Earley lost us the job'."

On a personal level there was only one significant disappointment about the four years.

"I was always very proud about being in the UN. The first time I had ever heard about it was from my father. He explained it to me when I was young. I often thought about him when I was there. When my mother came over I thought about how proud he would have been to see his son as the Deputy Military Advisor to the Secretary-General of the UN.

"There were other occasions when I thought of him. I got a call late one night at home to return to the UN building for a crisis meeting about the Gulf War. When the meeting was over we sat waiting for the next development. I started thinking of him. I thought it would be wonderful if he was here and had the opportunity to see me. When I came home I was involved as trainer of the Connacht football team for the 1992 Railway Cup competition. In that capacity I had a lot of dealing with P J. McGrath from Mayo. We talked about all the things that had happened while I was away. As he walked away he said: 'If only your father had been there'. This was something that reinforced all the thoughts I had had about him earlier. He knew my father well and understood what it would have meant for him to have seen me there. He would have boasted about it I know but it would have been out of pride rather than arrogance.

"There were many times in those four years there that I said to myself: 'If my father could see me now'."

12. The Mother of All Battles

The contrast between the start of 1990 and 1991 could not have been greater. In 1990 the physical and mental baggage of a bankrupt ideology were collapsing. The world seemed captivated by the music of promise. In 1991 danger and destruction lurked ominously in the air.

In the first month of 1990 the world's second superpower was apparently directing its attention towards internal reform and external co-operation. Eastern Europe had been released from the shackles of oppression. This transformation had been achieved with unprecedented victories for non-violent methods of remedying injustice. In Czechoslovakia the change-over was so smooth it was described as 'the velvet revolution'; in Poland the champions of 'Solidarnose' never even broke a window; at one stage in East Germany a massacre of the scale of Tiananmen Square was threatened, but eventually the authorities crumbled passively to the weight of popular opinion; in Romania alone was there loss of life.

The partisans of peace, equality and liberty had solid reasons to hope that finally things were heading in the right direction. If a week is a long time in politics, twelve months is a lifetime in world affairs. A year later the mood was palpably different. A war of incalculable dimensions loomed on the horizon, in the world's most vicious cockpit. The year began against a backdrop of crisis.

The Final Countdown

The seeds of this explosive situation had been sown five months earlier when Saddam Hussein invaded Kuwait on 2 August 1990.

Saddam's intention did not come as a huge shock to the UN.

"We were very much on the scene in Iraq particularly because we were there to supervise the cease-fire between Iran and Iraq. We saw the changes which took place in Iraq and although we had great difficulty in bringing about these changes through negotiation, all of a sudden the Iraqis, gave ground and agreed to all of the terms we had been negotiating. Almost overnight the problems we had in finalising the border between Iran and Iraq were agreed to.

"During the time that led up to the final agreements between Iran and Iraq, Saddam Hussein did take actions that suggested he was diverting his attention to another theatre. This knowledge was available to us. We could see the movement of forces to the Kuwait border from the Iranian border. In the days prior to his invasion of Kuwait it was obvious that he was building up quite a sizeable force in that theatre.

"However, from a UN point of view this was something we were not mandated to discuss or bring to anyone's attention. The world knew of this situation from press reports. They may not have expected a full scale invasion, but they knew Saddam had diverted his attention to Kuwait."

Although the conventional wisdom is that Saddam invaded for oil, another interpretation can be argued for.

"I think that he had thought out his position far more cleverly and clearly. Apparently, the Kuwaitis were not too honest with him about the amount of oil they were taking from the disputed oil field along their border. That was one theory but I think there was a much greater reason behind it.

"Saddam was looking at the whole question of the Middle East and in particular the situation in Israel and the problems which Israel creates for the Arabs, or those that the Arabs create for the Israelis, depending on how you look at it. I was of the opinion all along that more time should have been given to allow the sanctions to take more effect and to create more difficulties for the Iraqi regime and to have him withdraw his forces from the area."

From his office in New York Dermot Earley greeted the invasion with dismay but at that stage he did not foresee a major war breaking out in the Middle East. Diplomatic initiatives were initiated to prevent such a contingency.

However, as the New Year approached, niggling doubts about such a doomsday scenario entered his mind as diplomatic efforts were increasingly complemented by military action to prepare for war.

In the middle of January 1991 he found himself in the Middle East as the Coalition forces came together to drive the Iraqis out of Kuwait.

"It was our intention at that time, knowing that there was a serious possibility of war, to ensure that all the peace-keepers in the area would have maximum security and protection from whatever hostilities broke out. Of course there was a huge threat of chemical weapons and perhaps nuclear weapons by Saddam. He had indicated that Israel would be a target. From the information that was available world-wide, particularly to the US, scud missiles were pointed in the direction of Israel. Clearly our personnel would be under threat in such a situation. It was our intention that we would have families out of the danger area. The threat of nuclear, chemical, or biological attack put our personnel in serious jeopardy."

The world sat back and watched in fascination, thanks to the on the spot coverage of CNN, as the first missiles thudded into Baghdad and technology introduced a new dimension to war. The UN personnel watched in a state of numbed disbelief.

"I was absolutely devastated. I never thought that it would come to a war and that the Coalition forces would have to invade. I thought that the negotiations that were taking place right up to the last moment would turn up something. I felt Saddam Hussein would pull something out of the hat and make a small gesture that would indicate his willingness to withdraw. It might have taken three months, it might have taken a year, but an indication of intent to withdraw would have diffused the volatile situation and prevented the war from taking place.

"In all the negotiations that had taken place with him prior to the war breaking out there was always an element of brinkmanship. I always thought he was holding his cards to the very end. I thought that he would be satisfied that his negotiations would leave the possibility of him withdrawing with honour. Although the situation appeared closed there was always the possibility of a little opening. Even when the Secretary General went to Baghdad and spoke with Saddam Hussein at the eleventh hour and came back without any success, I still believed that the war would not take place.

"Even Saddam must have foreseen the potential catastrophic consequences, massive loss of life, and the huge destruction of a war. I was convinced that he would step back from the brink. When the war began I was shocked to the very core."

Despite his UN position, Earley was also dependent, to a large extent on the media for news of the war until he returned to his UN base. However, this was not a satisfactory position to be in from his point of view.

Professional journalists and broadcasters like to speak with certainty, to tell the public they know what is what, and that they can discern the truth from falsehood. They are confronted with the problem of putting a shape onto the war when there is little information to go on. Military briefings, understandably at least to some extent, leave a lot out; much of what is given to journalists is therefore less than the truth, the whole truth, and nothing but the truth.

War reporting has changed enormously down through history. The first war reporters may have furtively tip-toed their way through the battlefields of Balaclava or Gettysburg getting their shoes red from treading in the blood of the corpses. Today most reporters are insulated from the effects of bombardment. Certainly in the Gulf War situation most reporters were unable to see with their own eyes anything more concrete than the airy trails of missiles in the sky.

If a little knowledge is a dangerous thing, the same can surely be said for ignorance, particularly in a war situation. In the absence of facts some tabloid newspapers reported the war like a sporting event. The morning after the war broke out the *Sun* newspaper's front page was simply a Union Jack, the face of a soldier and the call to 'put this flag in your window'. A few days later their headlines were: 'Bastards of Baghdad' and 'Hang Saddam long and slow'.

However, even serious journalists were presented with major difficulties. A high-tech war nestles too comfortably with our bloodless high-tech versions of violence on the computer screen. Many of the 'quality' newspaper used video-game analogies to describe the war. In the US, the *New York Times* and the *Washington Post* were more specific, using the tag of 'Nintendo war', after the biggest make of computer games, because of its extra-neat raids, the bombs and missiles guided by micro-processors into the very doors and air-shafts of buildings. Some reports spoke of 'military precision'.

On 24 January the *Daily Mail's* headline was:. 'The Score so Far'. The BBC's *Nine O'Clock News* featured nightly the number of scuds shot down and Tornados lost, and they were read in much the same calculated dispassionate tones as the score of a match between Queens Park Rangers and Nottingham Forest.

News reporters on the scene were victims of the pooled system of reporting employed by all the Coalition forces in the Gulf. It gave the military control not only of what was written, but also who would write it. Thus access and accreditation could be withdrawn from critical voices or worse still, from those who refused to obey the rules.

The noted journalist Robert Fisk who won a Jacobs award for his coverage of the war observed that some journalists: "Behaved as if they were soldiers and not journalists." This problem was exacerbated by the fact that the British military insisted on the addition of uniforms on reporters staying with troops. Although the Gulf War was the most covered war of all time, it was also one of the most censored.

When the war was over and the censorship was lifted some of the real stories began to emerge. Anybody who saw RTE reporter Charlie Bird's harrowing reports on the problems of the Kurdish refugees is never likely to forget the sheer scale of human suffering and misery.

In the print media, another Irish journalist Maggie O'Kane painted pictures of the human tragedies and the misery of the death camps. In her report from Sulaymaniyah, a town in north-eastern Iraq, she uncovered horrific evidence of Hussein's campaign of terror against the Kurds. Her story of a boy named Abbas Mossin scribbling in faint pencil on the wall of his death cell encapsulates the terror of it all. He wrote: "I am 15 years old. But they said to me 'you are 18, so we can hang you'. But God will receive me, death is my release. It's better to say Allah arbar (God is great)."

In her research for the BBC's *Everyman* programme, a British journalist, Gwynne Roberts, uncovered frightening evidence of the immensity of the slaughter. She managed to get a recording of Hussein's cousin and Defence Minister, Mr Ali Hassam Majid, who was in charge of the area, dismissing with contempt the pleas by a senior Iraqi army officer for the Kurds, with the chilling words: "They way I look after them is to bury them with shovels."

Although such journalists considerably enhanced the reputation of their profession with their sterling work, Earley watched the initial television reports of the war from his quarters in Israel with considerable discomfort. The war was frequently portrayed as a soap-opera, which served only to trivialise the war.

"I was watching the television myself all the time when the war was going on. CNN were bringing us 'up to the second' actual live footage of the conflict. Even some of the briefings that were given by the US forces were drawn from CNN reports. I remember General Kelly, the Operations Officer for the Joint Chiefs of Staff, answering questions to reporters with the words: 'I am telling you what I am seeing on CNN'.

"Although we saw real up-close shots of what was happening, from a technical point of view, I don't think we saw the real story of the war. The fact that technology has advanced so much in terms of aircraft, artillery, rockets and all the machinery that is involved in war, allowed us to have cameras in the cockpits of aircraft, for example. You had cameras in the trapdoors as the bombs went away to the ground and cameras on the bombs. You had another camera somewhere else to show you the massive destruction, the bridge falling into the river, and the bunker scattering all over the place. All of that brought everything very close to us and that technology was fascinating and rivetting. However, we didn't see the outcome of the explosion, what was underneath, how many people were killed or what sort of destruction existed.

"I think only two occasions that I am aware of described events in which there was massive loss of life. One was a bunker that was hit by a bomb, inside the bunker were women, children and families. The Coalition forces reported that this was a command centre but the Iraqis said there were families sheltering there and apparently that was the case. The second was alleged to be a nuclear chemical factory but the Iraqis indicated that it was a baby food factory. Naturally there was a lot of controversy as to which version was the correct one.

"We never saw the real destruction, or the fear in the eyes of children or the fear in the eyes of civilians and soldiers. We never saw how many people were actually killed. While we had an up to the minute view of what was happening from a technical point of view, we never saw the human side, the maiming and the killing. None of that came home to us as it probably could have."

Does this mean that the real truth about the war has not emerged yet?

"I think the real truth has not emerged but as time goes by we will hear more of the truth. We will discover the real number of casualties. Certainly on the Coalition side we have an accurate breakdown of the loss, but we need figures for both sides.

"We will hear more stories about the difficulties of those who have been displaced, particularly of the problems of the Kurdish people in both northern and southern Iraq.

"There is also the question of some of the accusations levelled against the Iraqi troops. There were many stories of atrocities being carried out by the Iraqi troops when they went into Kuwait but then you heard little snippets which suggested that some of these did not take place. There is the question of whether the babies in incubators in the hospitals had the machinery unplugged or not. It is now reported that this didn't happen, or it certainly didn't happen to the scale that it was reported to have happened. You have problems with the truth of the horror, problems with the truth of whether the horrific things happened or not. You must balance both sides of the story.

"There are therefore question marks, at least in my mind, about the accusations and the real truth but I think that the massive destruction and loss of life that took place will never be known. Of course, what we say about war, is that the first casualty of war, is truth.

For the UN peace-keeping staff the outbreak of the war was very frustrating. Their raison d'etre is to keep the peace. When war breaks out they feel almost redundant. It is also very soul-destroying to see that all one's efforts have come to nought.

"There is a tremendous feeling of emptiness because all your efforts have been fruitless. You also know that after all this destruction, no matter how long the war goes on, that eventually there will be a cease-fire. When it is all over both sides will get together and there will be an agreement and then they will shake hands and build bridges. To have to sit back passively and watch all the destruction that takes place, the amount of money expended which could be used for many worthy causes, and to see the loss of life, whether it is massive or just one individual, is very distressing.

"I think particularly in relation to the role of UN sanctions, enough time was not given for sanctions to be allowed to tighten the screw on Iraq to ensure that they would be in some sort of crisis. I felt greater efforts could have been made by the bigger powers to play a greater role in sanctions. If economic might had been used to greater effect the war might not have been necessary. Certainly more time could have been taken to see would the sanctions work."

Basic Instinct

In recent years a number of films such as *'Platoon'* and *'Born on the Fourth of July'* have highlighted the long-term psychological damage caused to soldiers by war. Only someone who has actually been in the heat of the battle can understand what soldiers go through. The instinct for self-preservation takes over.

"When you go into battle, in a situation that is very tense, where there might be loss of life, you think of your loved ones, your family and your friends.

"You are also very concerned about your own personal security and being under fire brings that home immediately. Of course you also worry about the group you are in. You are concerned that you will be supported by them and that you will provide them with support and that you will work together as a team rather than as individuals.

"From my experiences with the Irish troops in the Lebanon in particular, I notice that in very tense situations where there is a very real threat of loss of life, people tend to turn to religion very quickly. Those who believe in God tend to think about the prospects of facing their God. There is a marked increase in religious devotion.

"It may appear to be a contradiction in terms but this increased level of religious sentiment is frequently complemented by a marked increase in aggressiveness. One of the things which provokes this aggressiveness is injury to colleagues, and especially the loss of life of colleagues. This prompts a strong desire to extract revenge. Sometimes soldiers become more destructive in taking ground."

Dermot has a specific incident in mind as he speaks about this aspect of the psychological war.

"I can remember before the Gulf War watching television footage of a helicopter on a medical evacuation. This was a female US Major piloting a large helicopter across the Sinai picking up the wounded and ferrying them back to aid posts. That same footage was shown after that young lady had been killed while executing another mission.

"This brought home to me and I am sure to everyone else watching, the whole vibrancy of life of that young woman. Then we saw that this highly skilled, motivated, excellent lady, who was doing a very worthy job of flying helicopters to evacuate people, was blown out of the sky by a rocket. Such a horrific tragedy would concentrate the mind of all her colleagues around her and soldiers would become more aggressive and want to extract revenge.

"Soldiers are trained in a very aggressive manner and one of the problems you can have is trying to rehabilitate soldiers after defence operational activities. They return to normality, but after being used to abnormality, some people cannot cope with real life."

A major contributory factor to the psychological pressure on soldiers is the difference between the training ground and the battlefield. An important feature of a soldier's training is 'battle inoculation' which attempts to simulate actual war conditions in military exercises.

"I suppose it is like being on a football field. You can train hard, run great races in training, and kick great free kicks in training but in the tension of a big match you might not reproduce your form in training. While the analogy might help clarify the situation, comparing war and sport might seem facetious."

"On the training ground, all you are really practising are the skills. In the battle it is a life and death situation. Every move you can make can be threatening, either to you or your company. As you move forward at night, for example, with your next step you might walk on an anti-personnel mine and you could get wounded or killed. You can create noises that are picked up in the stillness of the night. In the tension of the situation, people can make slight mistakes, which can turn out to be fatal."

Another problem which can arise is the curiously titled problem of 'friendly fire', where soldiers can mistake colleagues for the enemy and fire on them. 1992 has seen a major controversy in Britain about the death of some British soldiers due to an attack by American soldiers during the Gulf War

Although there are many negative aspects of this situation, the cut and thrust of war can also bring out a greatly enhanced performance.

"I remember being in Western Sahara on a long trip in 1987, and being with the commander of the Moroccan forces at a place called Dakhla, on the Atlantic Ocean in the southern most part of western Sahara. We were having dinner with the commander, a tank commander who was a veteran of three major wars. He explained to me that in the drilling exercises his soldiers would conduct in training when a tank was hit, the minimum time for a soldier to evacuate was fifty-eight seconds.

"However on the Golan heights in 1973, in the raging battle the crew evacuated in less than thirty seconds. That is one difference between the training ground and the real thing.

"General Bill Callaghan, former head of UNIFIL was a young officer in the Congo in the early 1960s leading Irish troops in various engagements with the opposition. In training he had found it very difficult to get his recruits to keep their head down when they were under fire. Many of them were sitting ducks for an accurate marksman. When they were involved in their first battle he had a very different problem. After the troops came under fire he could not find anybody because everybody had their heads down and they were incredibly well concealed.

"In a different battle situation, as his troops came under fire and as he exhorted his troops to move forward, he had great difficult in getting them to advance because they were up to their necks in drains and bushes. Suddenly two heavy mortars went off nearby. After the fog was clear General Callaghan, found that he was up to his neck in water also. That is the difference between practice and doing it for real."

Earley shivers as he recalls with animation an experience of his own. The memory of the incident elicits a tremor in his voice.

"One day in the village of Bara-Shiit in South Lebanon I was in a very tense situation. Our position had been attacked. Grenades had been thrown at the position. The position was now secure but a threat existed of the firing of a rocket propelled grenade (RPG) at the location. I was watching the situation with another officer from a mile away through binoculars. As we watched, we knew the situation was very tense. Although we were removed from the flash-point, we felt the tension.

"As I was looking through the binoculars, two Israeli aircraft flew high overhead. I did not see them or hear them fly over because they were flying faster than the speed of sound. Of course that created a sonic boom. When I heard it I was sure that our position had been hit. There was definitely a cold sweat down my back and I can feel it now down my backbone. Then I realised what had happened. Relief was great but it is impossible to describe the tension, the fear, the concern for my colleagues."

Sleeping with the Enemy

It is one of the many paradoxes of war that soldiers on opposing sides can feel intense hatred for each other, but that extreme contempt can dissolve almost immediately when peace breaks out.

In January 1984, Paul McCartney went to number one in the charts with a song called 'The Pipes of Peace'. The award-winning video which accompanied the song elicited more attention than the song itself. It recreated a real life story from a Christmas Day during World War One when the Germans and the Allies ceased hostilities and left their trenches and came into 'No Man's Land'. There they played a soccer match and shared drinks and celebrated the season together before returning to their trenches and resuming the war with vengeance the following day. The comraderie of the previous day had given way and was replaced by the normal 'them and us' mentality.

Through his involvement with the negotiations to end the Iran-Iraq war, Earley observed a similar situation at first hand.

"The morning after the cease-fire between Iran and Iraq was announced the soldiers from both sides came together. They drank tea and they celebrated and danced for joy. Shots were fired in the air to mark the cessation of hostilities. However, when it was time for them to go back they would not. This created a situation where they had to be separated from one another again.

"There was an accusation that one side had captured soldiers. Then there was a counter-accusation that the other side had used the celebrations to sneak up and claim extra territory. So out of the celebration another major incident almost sprung up."

The normal 'this is my ball and you can't play with it' syndrome of a major war was also breached in the Iran-Iraq war in a bizzare occurrence.

"There was a situation where a soldier from both countries lived happily together in the one trench because both sides felt that it was their trench. They lived together as friends and they were fed by both sides on alternate days. Their trench was in the middle and twenty or thirty yards on either side was the Iranian and Iraqi trenches."

Operation Desert Storm

Although the UN was a hive of activity before Operation Desert Storm in the forefront of efforts to prevent war, the peace-keepers had to take second stage once the war broke out.

"When the Gulf War broke out nothing really happened in headquarters in terms of monitoring, receiving reports and having debates or discussion. All of this was because everything was controlled from Washington. The US played the leader in everything connected with the war.

"The Security Council had passed various resolutions allowing a coalition of forces to come together and do a particular job but it was that coalition of forces alone that executed all the actions in relation to the preparations for the war itself and their aftermath. Nobody reported to the Secretary General or would ask for clarification.

"I think the general consensus in the UN was that things should have been handled differently. People began to get worried that the UN had indeed been hijacked and were being controlled from Washington. The Secretary General was briefed by the US on a number of occasions during the war. He had been informed by President Bush when the war was about to begin. In my opinion this was merely a courtesy extended, rather than a suggestion that the UN had a major role to play.

"For me in the UN at that time, the contact in the area was to our existing personnel in the Middle East, namely the Golan Heights, in Israel, and with our mission in Cyprus. We had of course a mission in Iran and Iraq and they all evacuated out of Baghdad just prior to the war starting. In fact our operation there ceased because of the agreements between Iran and Iraq.

"There were no reports coming into us daily about the war but we did follow closely the military operations through CNN reports".

"We were always ready, of course, to respond to a message from Saddam Hussein that he would withdraw. As the war went on this became less likely. Our main task was to prepare plans for some kind of buffer zone between Iraq and Kuwait.

"In fact as soon as the war ended a demilitarised zone was established. Almost from day one we were able to put military observers into place to oversee a peace-keeping operation.

"However, quite a number of scud missiles fell on Israel and there was a possibility, because the weapon is so inaccurate, of Syria being attacked. Nobody was sure what Saddam Hussein would do. As the missiles fell we had to ensure that our people were safe. When sirens sounded to indicate raids we had to ensure that our personnel took precautions to safeguard themselves. All of this was ongoing."

Although the UN peace-keeping forces had a peripheral role during the Gulf War itself, other UN agencies were very involved in efforts to alleviate the suffering of people in the Gulf.

Initially the world was spared the human tragedies of the Gulf War. Selected and censored coverage had anaesthetised public opinion against much of the reality of war, producing a buffer between armchair followers and those out in the field.

The world got a satirised picture of the effects of 'Operation Desert Storm'. Some reporters watched artillery fire illuminating the night skies of Baghdad like firework displays on '4th of July' celebrations. Others waxed lyrical about the moon in the desert sky. Commentators accompanied allied forces wearing desert scarves wrapped around military uniforms à la Peter O'Toole, in *Lawrence of Arabia*. Pilots were interviewed and clinically described their pin-point precision in locating distant targets through long-distance lenses.

While these images were being projected at home, UN personnel were seeing very disturbing images: the hideous outlines of charred human beings, empty eye-sockets, teeth gritted with unbearable pain and flesh disintegrated into mud-like form.

One of the most vivid artistic portraits of the horrors of war is Goya's 'Disasters of War'. This nightmarish scenario was mechanised and updated at Mutla on the Kuwait-Basra road. A vast morass of military machinery lay intertwined with countless strewn and incinerated bodies of Iraqi soldiers trapped in headlong flights in the dying days of the war.

A Bird's Eye View

After the war ended Earley had to go back to the Gulf to supervise the introduction of peace-keeping forces and to deal with the problem of the Kurdish refugees. The memory of a flight over the battlefield when the fighting was over will remain forever entrenched on his brain. A landscape once virgin pure, lay shattered like a broken bottle. The desert was covered in an ugly blanket of Iraqi tanks.

"It was an awesome sight to look down on the battlefield. It was frightening and alarming to see that all of this could happen and to see that it did happen; it was very sad, almost unreal."

Having grown up in the lush, green fields of Roscommon, Earley was particularly sensitive to the ecological consequences of the war.

"The first thing that struck me was the pollution from the massive oil wells. There were seven hundred burning oil wells and they clouded the skies with their fumes, spewing massive thick clouds of pollution into the air. At the time I was there, the wind was taking it in one huge cloud, covering hundreds of miles and carrying it eastward. Just before that it had gone southwards and had engulfed the city of Kuwait and had turned midday almost into midnight."

"On occasions bodies still lay on the ground. Helmets had obviously fallen from the head as the face was buried in the sand. A boot stood standing on its own. You wondered who owned it and where was that person now.

"Further up the desert and you came to a crossroads just north of Kuwait city, just leading into Iraq where at some stage in the last few days of the war there was a massive withdrawal of the Iraqi forces. They had been caught by a coalition forces air-strike. I have never seen such destruction. The vehicles seemed to be piled on top of one another. There were hundreds, perhaps thousands of vehicles piled up on that junction. They lay in a monstrous mess of twisted metal, shattered tanks and burned out cabs. In all the chaos perhaps there was a tank in the middle which had not been touched at all, that had escaped the destruction. When you saw all this you wondered what the loss of life in this area must have been.

"Then as you moved further north you saw the sand blowing below. You saw minefields appearing as the sand blew away. In the distance you could see shepherds coming out with their flocks, trying to get their lives going again, trying to rehabilitate their flocks and carry on as they had for hundreds of years before the battle took place. You wondered how they were going to survive with all the war debris and all the unexploded mines. All of that would bring home to you the futility of it all. The war only lasted a few weeks but the long term consequences were frightening.

"I had been to Kuwait before the war had broken out. I had flown from Tehran to Kuwait, having been involved in the negotiations to end the Iran-Iraq war, in order to get an aircraft back from New York. I had come into Kuwait with Marrack Goulding, the Under Secretary General for Special Political Affairs. He had been a junior diplomat in Kuwait in the late 1950s and early 1960s.

"Here was a magnificent city. The wealth that was there could not be described. This was a city that had been built out of the desert. I saw beautiful lawns in front of peoples' houses that would put any lawn in this wonderful country of ours, which has rain every day, to shame. In the desert you had the massive wealth available to create magnificent lawns, grass, beauty and wonderful buildings.

"I walked with Marrack Goulding through the city of Kuwait. He gave me a little history lesson of what Kuwait was like when he was there and it surely was a magnificent city.

"Then to return after the war and see the city. The walls were covered with a horrible blackness. The hotel where I had stayed during my first visit was now totally burned out. It was just a shell. All the windows were gone. The area that I had walked around the first time was now almost impassable because of the rubble.

"I looked in places that I had been in on that particular night with Marrack Goulding. All that was left was graffiti in Arabic scribbled on the charred walls. The magnificent lights on the side of the streets were gone. The airport had no air traffic control. Their lights were gone. All of this happened in such a short time. It was impossible to comprehend."

There Are More Questions Than Answers

According to conventional wisdom it is easy to be wise with the benefit of hindsight. The experience of the 'Mother of All Battles' throws that theory into question. The question: 'Was it all worth it?' demands an answer. Although the din of battle subsided relatively quickly, the fog of war remained much longer. The burning oil wells served as a potent reminder of problems yet unresolved, of vision still distorted.

The war itself exposed the flawed logic of much of the debate that preceded it. The dire consequences, predicted by those who opposed any military response to the invasion of Kuwait, did not materialise. In fact there never seemed to be a serious threat of a nuclear war. The fighting did not engulf the entire Middle East region. Despite considerable provocation, even Israel was not sucked into the war, because she chose to take a predictably shrewd and calculated view of her longer term advantages. Relations between Muslims and Christians have not been fatally wounded. While there has been considerable environmental damage it has not assumed the dimensions of a global catastrophe.

On the other hand, those who championed a military response anticipated that a crushed Saddam Hussein would certainly be removed from power. Although it was not their espoused aim, that hope was apparently a significant factor in the calculations of the Allies. Tragically the Kurds and Shiites were to fall victim to the same error after the fighting stopped. The Coalition forces were proved correct in their projection that war could be contained, but they failed to appreciate the full enormity of the job required to restore peace and prosperity to Kuwait, not to mention Iraq, in spite of the fact that their tactics during the war made such difficulties almost inevitable.

Casualty figures, still not known with any degree of certainty were wildly bloated by opponents of the conflict. Technological achievements were gloated over in a deeply disturbing and dehumanising way by its supporters. Stories of atrocities were narrated in some cases with only the flimsiest of evidence to substantiate them. On one extreme there was alarmist propaganda, on the other there was wanted over-optimism.

Peace did not exist in the Middle East before the invasion of Kuwait, nor did it exist there after the war. There was not in fact a stark choice between war and peace, despite the rhetoric which presented the matter as if those were the alternatives.

The Gulf War triggered a variety of emotions to the surface, but for many people the sheer insensitivity of the financial markets were hard to take. The outbreak of war, precipitated a sharp surge in the world's stock markets, as if to signal that this was the best news financial pundits had heard in years.

Every loss of human life is a price paid by humankind for war. Every item of human energy and expenditure devoted to war is an item diverted from other uses.

It is a curious fact that the world's leading powers could gather billions of dollars and assemble thousands of soldiers in defence of a semi-feudal desert kingdom such as Kuwait, but they cannot or will not exert themselves to provide less than a billion dollars to save millions of starving people in Africa.

Although the Gulf War poses many difficult moral questions, the most urgent questions were raised by the problems of the Kurdish refugees.

A Living Hell

The Kurdish problem predated the war. The Iraqi defence minister, Ali Hassan al Majid, spearheaded a campaign of genocide against the Kurds. He was known to the Kurdish people as 'Ali of the Chemicals'. An example of his campaigns occurred on 16 March 1988 when he ordered the dropping of chemical bombs on the town of Halabja. More than 5,500 people lost their lives in that one incident. The bombs were 'supplemented' by dynamite and death squads. People were tortured in groups so that when one broke down and confessed, others would follow suit.

Listening to Earley talking about the problems of the Kurdish refugees chills one to the bone. Hannibal Lecter in *The Silence of the Lambs* would not inspire the same naked horror and terror.

"In the days after I had flown over Kuwait I was involved in the attempt to negotiate a settlement of the Kurdish problem. Of course you had the problem of the Kurds in northern Iraq and you had the problem of other parties in southern Iraq. We were involved in negotiating a solution to the problem in the north. The Coalition forces had sent troops up there to the refugee camps to protect the Kurdish people and set up camps for them and then hopefully to bring about a final solution to their problem.

"Of course the problem of the Kurds had been identified long before the war. During the Iran-Iraq war they had suffered terribly at the hands of Saddam Hussein. I had flown over northern Iraq to look at the ceasefire line between Iran and Iraq and saw the villages that had been destroyed by the Iraqi forces and the purge against the Kurds. The villages were absolutely flattened. The houses were lying like scattered stones on the ground. Then you saw how isolated the Kurds were. They were so vulnerable.

"I had seen pictures of Saddam Hussein's assaults on the Kurds. One picture stands out in my mind. It appeared in *Time* magazine shortly after that particular assault on the Kurds. A father and his child lay dead on the ground having been gassed. It appeared as if he was carrying the baby and as he breathed in the air he died and the baby fell from his hands and rolled along the ground. The baby lay beside his head. Both of them looked in perfect condition but were victims of chemical weapons. This gave me an insight into the scale of the Kurdish problem.

"The Kurds themselves were involved in separate negotiations with Saddam Hussein as we were trying to get him involved with the UN. Unfortunately we were unable to solve the problem. Tragically the refugee problem and the Kurdish problem still exists."

When asked if the cruelty and suffering he describes means that the Kurds are living in a modern day version of hell, Earley does not disagree.

"Remember all their difficulties. They lost their homes. They often had nowhere to lay their weary heads at night. The belongings that you have are all in a bag over your shoulder, a plastic bag with a few bits and pieces tied with a string. As they went along they probably lost some of these possessions. They were not sure if they would have food that night or the next morning. The babies or very young children might not be able to walk and would have to be carried long distances in difficult situations. Some of those who could walk might not have shoes. Some might have slippers walking through the mud. Others might have sandals, like Irish children might wear on hot summer days, during the torrential rains that were falling in the winter time.

"In the southern part of Iraq you would see the sand blowing in small little tornadoes swirling around. Women tried to protect their children by putting cloaks around their faces to prevent the sand from blowing against them. They had no homes to go to. Perhaps half of the family was missing. The absence of a father or mother's care would be clearly visible in the eyes of the children as they looked with bulging eyes in wonder. They were wondering what all the foreigners were doing around them. Were they there to help them or not? The confusion was obvious to everybody.

"To describe the situation as a modern day vision of hell is probably a very accurate analogy. I am sure that when any of these people meet their maker that none of them will experience what hell is like.

Dire Straits

Now that the ghastly nightmare is over it is the memories of the human tragedies that linger with him, the tears, the heavily lined faces, the letters home that can never be written, the aching hearts for loved ones missing, the assembly lines of dead bodies and the stench of carnage everywhere. Three enduring images of the war remain for Earley.

"Firstly, the crushing disappointment that the war broke out in the first instance. The image that I have is that of the Secretary General Perez de Cuellar, coming back from his negotiations with Saddam Hussein without having reached a peace agreement. I watched him on the television as I was in the Middle East and he was gone back to New York. I saw him go through the entrance to the building as he had done on so many occasions before. Normally he could deal with the press so well and give clear precise answers to their questions. On that particular day he was almost lost for words. I could see the tiredness in his face and the sighs that he expressed as he tried to respond with answers to the press. He was so disappointed that his efforts to prevent war had come to nought that he was distraught. That sense of complete loss was shared right across the board by UN personnel.

"Secondly, that flight over the Kuwaiti battlefield and seeing the massive destruction, the pollution and the loss of life. I suppose that even though I didn't actually see that many dead bodies, the number of casualties must be horrendous, particularly at the crossroads north of Kuwait.

"Thirdly, I recall my visit to the beautiful city of Kuwait. I had visited the city in its finery and splendour but to see the incredible destruction was extraordinarily depressing.

"The other thing about it was the lines on peoples' faces. They had been through so much and that was reflected in their faces. The laughter was gone from their eyes.

"I had seen this once before in Iran, in a small village right on the battlefield, when I went there at the end of the Iran-Iraq war. There was an emptiness in the back of peoples' eyes. They had a total loss of belief in society and in all institutions. I went back there many times over the years in negotiations about the end of the war. Gradually people would realise that peace had arrived and the laughter would slowly come back. Their attitude towards you would change. On the third time, you went, you might get a smile. On the fourth or fifth time you might get a word of greeting and finally you saw children running like children should. Then that memory of Kuwait came back to me. That's probably my single enduring image of the war."

Although that unhappy chapter in the world's history is not entirely closed it has had an educational value. Humankind can learn an invaluable lesson from the 'Mother of all Battles'.

"I think I learned something that could be described as a very simple thing. There is violence all over the world, we experience violence in our own country, we had violence in this case on a massive scale and I ask the question: what does it achieve? Is it worth it? The lesson we must all learn is the futility of violence."

13. A Military Union

The GPO has a central place in Irish history because of its association with the 1916 rising. In the life story of Dermot Earley the GPO has a similar importance because it was outside this building that he laid eyes on his wife-to-be for the first time.

Appropriately enough there was a sporting context for the story. Earley had been to see the All-Ireland hurling final and was going into the GPO to make a phone call when three doleful looking girls caught his attention. They were wearing 'Up Tipp' rosettes and were obviously extremely deflated because their native county had lost the final. His eyes focused on one of the trio and the look was returned but no words were exchanged.

Eight weeks passed. Then to Earley's astonishment, he was walking in the Curragh camp when he saw the same girl again. At first he did not believe it was the same girl again but a second look confirmed it. He had the impression that she recognised him also but they passed each other by without as much as a nod.

Love Story

A few weeks later they were introduced while playing badminton in the Curragh. It emerged that the girl's name was Mary and that she was a military nurse based in the camp. A conversation developed when Dermot asked her if she was the girl he had seen outside the GPO and Mary said: 'Yes'. As chat up lines go it was not the stuff of which great romantic stories in the best tradition of Mills and Boone are written but it was to lead on to greater things.

"One thing led to another. She had a great understanding of sport and was probably the best supporter of hurling in Munster. We started to go out with one another and enjoyed one another's company. Gradually a permanent union looked right."

In explaining his attraction for Mary two qualities in particular are singled out.

"I would think that one of her greatest attributes is that I have never seen her flustered. I don't know if her training as a nurse has anything to do with it, but her calmness in dealing with any situation is extraordinary. It could be anything as serious as a possible crisis with one of the children, to driving the car in a tight situation. Everybody else might react and put their foot hard on the brakes and wonder when the bang was going to come but the coolness of Mary would take us through every situation. The rest of us in the car might be numb with panic but she would want to know what the problem was. All her family would say she was always a cool customer.

"The other thing about her is that she has an immense honesty which is not always favourable to hear. Her honesty can sometimes be interpreted as criticism. When she asks for an opinion she expects the truth and when she is asked for her opinion she replies with total honesty."

Mary's recollection of making eye contact with her future husband is equally vivid.

"I first saw him in O'Connell Street after an All-Ireland hurling final. I won't say what year! We looked at each other and when I met him sometime later in the Curragh I remembered the exchange of glances in O'Connell Street. How can I put my impressions into words? He was certainly athletic looking and handsome too. I enjoyed his company, he had a good sense of humour and was fun to be with. All my family took an instant liking to him. He got on real well with my brother Tom. Dermot liked farming and Tom liked the help. All my family were interested in sport and because of this they already knew of him.

"Our courtship was not all disrupted by football. I was always interested in sport particularly hurling and football. As soon as I was old enough my father always took me to Munster hurling Championship games in Thurles, Cork and Limerick. Going to games with Dermot was just an extension of that."

After a three year courtship they were married in September 1971. The date for the wedding was decided late, to allow for the possibility of Roscommon playing in the All-Ireland final that year. However, Galway ensured that such a complication would not arise by beating Roscommon in the Connacht final.

The Trip To Tipp

The Earley family travelled en masse to Thurles the day before the wedding to stay in a local hotel. That night there was a bit of a rumpus outside the hotel. As Dermot Earley wondered if the country was being invaded his mother informed him that a number of his army colleagues were outside shouting for their fellow officer to join them on: "His last night of freedom."

When this gracious invitation was not accepted they congregated in a local pub. One report was that the hostelry had run out of drink the next morning.

The next morning as Dermot got ready to leave the hotel in his dress uniform with accompanying sword (which was to be used to cut the cake), a number of Americans arrived. There was a chorus of 'Oohs' and 'Aahs' when the circumstances were explained. When one of the Americans asked what regiment Earley belonged to, a colleague shouted up: "The First Nigerian Rifles" to the amusement of the army personnel. The joke was lost on the American who replied in a totally genuine voice: "Oh. Isn't that wonderful."

The reception was not without incident. The country was in the middle of an ESB strike and a power cut occurred half way through the evening. As he got ready to leave the hotel, Earley got a little bit of disconcerting advice from the Roscommon county secretary, Phil Gannon, who told him not to worry if he heard any strange noises coming from the car, someone had placed a number of stones in it and he should not be worried that the engine of his car might explode.

The plan was for the newly weds to fly out on their honeymoon the following night which meant that they had a free Sunday in Dublin beforehand. By mutual agreement they decided to check the paper to see if there was a match in Croke Park. There were two matches on. The second featured Roscommon in a junior hurling game. They decided that the Roscommon contingent would most likely be in the Hogan stand so they slipped quietly into the Cusack stand. They were completely taken aback to discover that they were actually sitting behind the Roscommon team who were watching some of the first game before they togged out. One of the Roscommon players had been at the wedding the previous day and a collection of smart comments and advice for their honeymoon was freely given to the newly weds.

Rock-bottom

Having bought a house in Newbridge they began their married life with a wish for a large family as both had come from large families themselves. However, it was not until 1975 that they got news that they were parents to be. Although it was a very joyous occasion, particularly as they had waited a few years, the news came at a strange time.

After the winter break Roscommon played Dublin in a league match. In the course of the game Earley was fouled and fell heavily as the sizable frame of Jimmy Keaveney came tumbling down on top of him. As Earley rose to his feet a scuffle broke out in which there were four minor altercations with Dublin's Bobby Doyle. After the fourth incident Earley's patience snapped and he punched Doyle on the nose. The referee had no option but to send him off. As he made the lonely journey to the dug-out Earley's brain was spinning and his spirits were absolutely crushed.

"It was the most devastating thing that ever happened to me playing football – much worse than losing the All-Ireland. As I walked back to the line the realisation of all the things that were going to happen came to me. First of all it meant that there was a blot on my career. I always tried to be as fair as I could. Even if I fouled I always felt it was wrong afterwards. I would be concerned if I fouled in the course of the game on a number of occasions. To be warned by a referee is a blot on your copybook but to be sent off is incredible."

Although he was just a young boy at the time Paul Earley remembers that day well.

"I have to confess I remember being delighted he did what he did that day. I always felt that he took too much punishment on the pitch without ever taking any action. When the game was over our eyes met through the crowd. He came over to me with his head down in a state of total dejection. He was unable to look me in the eye as he said: 'I'm sorry I let you down'."

The sending off was extensively reported the next day in the newspapers. The incident was the major talking point as his colleagues gathered for their coffee break the next morning.

"There was a sort of an 'Oh' and an 'Ah' when I entered. Someone said: 'What have you to say?' There was silence. I said: 'I have only one thing to say. I shouldn't have done it'. There was no more discussion."

The situation was complicated by the fact that Earley was due to travel with the All-Stars the following month. Would he be eligible to play? A new twist was added to the saga the following Sunday when the captain of the All-Stars, Galway's Johnny Hughes was sent off following a tangle with Bobby Doyle.

It all boiled down to the referee's report. Earley was suspended for two months whereas Johnny Hughes got the minimum two weeks suspension. The Roscommon county board appealed Earley's suspension to the GAA's mercy committee. Although Earley appreciated their motivation he felt it was an inappropriate gesture. In his column in the *Sunday Independent* the late John D. Hickey reported on the rejection of the appeal under the heading: 'There is no mercy Earley'.

Long before this suspension and appeal had been rejected Earley had decided that he would not travel on the trip. The only regret he had was that all the arrangements had been made for Mary to travel with him and he was worried that she would be disappointed.

Over the next few weeks a number of events happened which provoked a change of heart. A lot of his friends and colleagues pressed him to go for Mary's sake as much as his own. He also received a telegram from John Kerry O'Donnell in New York who offered to pay his expenses for the trip because:

"Red-blooded men are welcome in Gaelic Park"

A meeting with Dr Donal Keenan and the PRO of Carrolls, Pat Heneghan, at the Railway Cup final swung the balance back in favour of travelling. A discussion with Mary confirmed the decision.

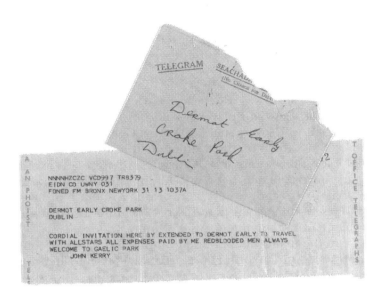

After communicating his decision to the organisers of the tour Earley acceded to a request to assist the tour manager, Sean Purcell, with the coaching of the team. There was no going back now.

Within days a further dimension was added to the saga when Mary announced that she was pregnant. A visit to her gynaecologist brought the news that it would be unwise for her to travel to America at this stage of the pregnancy.

Mary Earley was not distressed by all Dermot's travelling.

"On the plus side I liked travelling to the many games all over the country. I also had the opportunity to travel to the States on All-Star tours. I also saw him play in Wembley. There are no minuses in this story! I never felt that I was a football widow. I accompanied him as much as possible. I understood training was necessary and I never minded being at home.

"1980 was different because they were in an All-Ireland final. He usually left home at five-thirty every evening and we didn't see him again until next morning as it would be 1 a.m. when he returned. Closer to the final he stayed in Roscommon for a full week as they trained twice a day. Holidays were not affected as there were none."

Out in the Cold

The decision to travel was a decision Earley regretted although the travelling GAA officials and players could not have been more friendly to him. A number of players such as Down's Colm McAlarney were very appreciative of his efforts on the training field.

Another high point came in Los Angeles when he was asked to do a commentary on the match between Dublin and the All-Stars. He was promised that an assistant would be provided to help him take note of the scores. He got quite a shock to discover that his assistant was no less a person than RTE commentator, Mick Dunne.

Apart from the major disappointment that Mary was not joining him on the trip a serious problem was that Earley had been given to understand that he would be part of the touring side, the same as everybody else but that was not to be the case. This was brought home to him almost immediately. A welcoming committee greeted the team at the airport. Each player was called forward individually and presented with an envelope which included details of accommodation, itinerary and the allowance provided for the tour. Although Earley was called forward there was no envelope to be found for him. He wished the ground would open up and swallow him, he was so embarrassed. Similar incidents were to occur three more times on the tour.

However, the most galling part came at the end of the tour when a non-GAA travelling official reminded him that John Kerry O'Donnell had paid his expenses on the tour and accordingly he should thank John Kerry before he left. Earley felt like the most junior pupil in school receiving a lecture from the headmaster. Such a reminder was totally unnecessary.

The City of David

In July of that year Earley began his peace-keeping duties in the Middle East. Six weeks later Mary joined him. On 9 November 1975 Mary and

Dermot Earley became first time parents. The birth took place in the Arab quarter of Jerusalem. Arabic protocol dictated that the father should not be present at the birth.

As Earley paced anxiously up and down in the front garden he heard his name being shouted from the window. The call came from Bernie Stapleton, a Roscommon girl married to a Tipperary army officer Mick Stapleton, based in Athlone. She had given birth to a baby girl two days earlier and now she was relaying the news of the birth of a baby boy to a Tipperary girl married to a Roscommon officer.

Cultural differences and prohibitions were temporarily put to one side as Earley went chasing up the stairs in time to see his new son being wheeled out of the delivery room on a trolley. A score of attendants shouted: 'Not allowed. Not allowed,' but Earley turned a deaf ear.

The health care personnel shared the great joy of the Earley family particularly because the baby was a boy. The whole experience proved a fascinating insight into the Arabic culture which is very patriarchal. An Arabic woman who had her fourth daughter left the hospital in floods of tears because she had not given birth to a son.

In the light of the location with all its Biblical associations the most appropriate name for the baby was David. There was a number of legal niceties to be observed. The most important thing to be done was to ensure that David had an Irish birth cert. Under a provision of the 1954 Defence Act, the offspring of an Irish soldier born abroad during an overseas mission can be registered in Ireland. Consequently David has two birth certs.

The good news had to be communicated immediately to the families at home in Roscommon and Tipperary. This required the assistance of Barney Mullin who worked in the non-military side of the UN field operations. In the course of this activity Earley met Barney's young son Brendan who would go on to play International rugby for Ireland and the Lions, and become Ireland's record try-scorer.

While in the Middle East Earley took the opportunity to play rugby with a side called 'The Wild Geese' who were comprised of Irish army exiles in the Middle East. In matches against the top club sides Earley made such a big impression that he was invited to become an Israeli International! Israel were facing a big match against a touring South African university side and felt they needed additional presence on the field. Hence the invitation to Earley and a few other Irish players to become full International players. Politically this was out of the question. From a sporting perspective it probably would not have been a good idea either, as the Israelis lost by 70 points to 3.

Heartbreak

Having returned home to Ireland in January 1977 it was straight down to Gorthaganny to bring David to see his grandparents for the first time. The warmth of the welcome was enough to dispel the bitter chill of the black winter's night. There was never a prouder grandfather than Peadar Earley.

For Dermot Earley memories of his oldest son and his father are entwined forever because of a tape they made for him during his second peace-keeping mission abroad in 1983. Mary was to join him for a two week holiday in Cyprus. His father and mother would look after the kids in Newbridge for the fortnight. Mary brought over a tape with the recorded messages. It was to be the last time he would hear his father's thoughts because he died a few days later. The tape was carefully stored away and played for only the second time in May 1992.

David comes on first and with all the excitement and vigour of youth gives a wildly enthusiastic report on Roscommon's victory over Kildare the previous Sunday. Even though it was February he also gives an in-depth account of what everyone got from Santa Claus and gives a rousing rendition of 'Jingle Bells' to finish off.

The contrast between boy and grandfather could not have been greater. It is emotionally draining to listen to this part of the tape. We are unable to look each other in the eye. The words are not spoken but gasped. I was unsure if Dermot would be able to endure the pain. His father's obvious struggle to breathe cut like a knife. Although the chest is clearly failing the brain is as sharp as ever. He gives an up-to-date account of local and national news and gives an informed opinion about events in the Lebanon. Clearly every media report during the previous months on the troubled area has been assimilated. He gives assurances that his health is on the mend. The words say one thing. The breathing gives a very different message. There is a long silence between us when the tape is over.

On 24 February 1983 Earley took his wife out to dinner to celebrate his 35th birthday. There was a note waiting for him when he got back, telling him to report urgently to HQ. Despite the high temperatures he felt chilled to the bone. He knew intuitively that it was bad news about his father. The previous night following a bad turn, his father was admitted to Naas hospital.

When Dermot returned to Ireland the first place he visited was the morgue.

"I never saw my father looking so good. You never understand what death is like until it comes that close to you. You hear about the coldness of death but it only struck me when I touched him on the forehead.

"I will never forget the burial. The funeral Mass had to be held in the parish church because the local church would not be big enough to hold the crowds. The funeral had to pass the house and school. The hearse stopped outside the school and the coffin was taken out and carried the mile to the graveyard. I was calm and in control of the sorrow within me until we stopped outside the school. This was the hardest moment of all. Mary understood what was happening and told me: 'You have been very good up to now. Keep control'. The moment passed and that is the single moment I remember clearly.

"His final resting place is a bit special. The graveyard in Gorthaganny is on a hill overlooking a lake. My father had been involved in the campaign to get a graveyard for the area. I remember seeing Frank Hall read out a headline from the *Roscommon Champion*: 'People in Gorthaganny are dying for a graveyard'.

"The coffin was draped in the Michael Glaveys colours. The local people had taken care of all the arrangements. Their support eased the trauma. I remember the magnificent response of the people of Roscommon, Kildare and Connacht on the day. It was a great gesture by a great people to a great man."

Baby Boom

After David came Conor two years later, then Dermot Jr, Paula, Anne-Marie and on 19 December 1984, Noelle. Earley jokes: "At the time when I was asked how many kids I had I used say five and one for centenary year."

Although there are disadvantages in having a large family Earley feels that they are outweighed by the advantages. However, as the children get older the problems magnify. Earley subscribes to his father's dictum: 'Mól an oige agus tiocfaidh siad.' (Praise the children and they will come to you). He feels that the two most important things in parenting are to give credit and to develop a sense of responsibility.

"One of my failings is that I find it very hard to tolerate what I consider 'stupidity' from those that are close to me. I am so anxious that they will not suffer from their mistakes that I usually rush in too quickly, before they have a chance to make them, depriving them of valuable learning experiences.

"It is important to train them that they cannot have everything they like. Choices need to be made. In the summer of 1992 I was snowed under with requests. Everybody wanted to see Guns and Roses in Slane, Whacko Jacko in Landsdowne Road, the Trip to Tipp and numerous local events. You would want a bank of your own to pay for all the these things. The hardest thing to do is to say no and see the hurt in the children's eyes. It is crucial to always explain why you are saying no. I always remind them that I was their age once. Again I got great advice from my father. He always said: 'Think Young'.

"The other important thing you have to do is realise that all of your children are different. They all have their own personality, their own priorities, their own outlook, and their own way of organising their lives. The second in any family can be different from the rest and in our family Conor certainly is no exception. He is the most relaxed person you could imagine. He has the most wonderful quality of being able to relax in any company. I always describe him as somebody who could sleep on a harrow. David on the other hand is very organised and committed while Dermot Jr is very outgoing.

"When I was young I played a lot of matches. As long as I impressed my father I didn't care who else thought I was playing good or bad. That was the most important thing for me. Now as a parent I realise just how vital it is to show interest in one's own family and be supportive of them in whichever sport or pastime they decide to pursue."

I'm No Hero

A regular feature of Earley's life are invitations to speak at GAA functions to give advice to up and coming players. It is a task which he finds very enjoyable but one which he takes very seriously. He is frequently asked to widen his comments to include his philosophy of life.

"There are three pillars in my life – family, religion and work. If you have a strong family unit, little can go wrong. The way I was brought up thought me that a strong belief in God was necessary. That does not mean that you have to have your hands joined all the time. Work is important because it helps you to develop as a person. It allows you to see that you are making a contribution to something worthwhile. "

Earley's philosophy of life is derived from his childhood influences. Although he has been to many places in all parts of the globe a piece of his heart will always be tilted to West Roscommon. The publicity-shy people who never made the headlines with him, left notions of decency, honour and courtesy which have remained firmly entrenched in his soul since the day he left home to become a boarder in St Nathy's.

Although Earley is very reticent about 'preaching' or setting himself up as a some kind of authority, hero, or saint, he sometimes gives lectures on temperance. One of these talks had an unexpected ending. He was talking to a group in Clonown (a small town on the Roscommon side of Athlone). At the time Brendan Shine had a very popular record out called 'Carrots from Clonown'. As the talk drew to a conclusion a man came in weighed down with a big sack on his back. He promptly deposited it on the stage saying: "Here's a few carrots from Clonown." The Earley family did not need to buy any carrots for the next two months.

In 1992 Earley became involved in the 'faith friends' programme in Newbridge. The programme is designed to help children who are preparing for their confirmation to develop their faith. It was a very enjoyable experience which allowed for great creativity. The only thing which disappointed him was one session which involved the question: "What would you do if someone stole your bike?" The group he was working with all responded with very aggressive remarks. He wondered if it was a sign of changing times.

Working in the army Earley himself is provided with plenty of opportunities for spiritual direction, although the army is reviewing its policy on attendance at religious services at the moment. Traditionally the army has a mission every Lent. In 1979 the mission was given by Fr Michael Cleary. In one of his talks he spoke about determination and compared determination with Dermot Earley going through with the ball for a goal, much to the amusement of the rest of the congregation. On that Ash Wednesday Earley was going up to receive the ashes when Fr Cleary revised his blessing somewhat. Instead of: "Remember man thou art but dust and into dust thou shalt return," – his blessing was: "Up the Dubs."

Preacher Man

Earley himself got the opportunity to preach from the pulpit in 1989 when he was asked by the local curate to preach the homily at Paul's wedding.

"The priest said that he knew nothing about marriage and would not be able to preach the sermon and asked me to give it. I was very surprised but said yes."

In making his 'sermon' Earley drew heavily on the example provided by his own father and mother.

"The quality I admired most in my father was his patience. He rarely got cross and allowed the situation to cool down before dealing with a problem. Himself and my mother had great communication. They talked about everything. He always told us if he was going anywhere. I can remember one night when no one had seen him for an hour or knew where he was. There was panic because this was so unusual. He returned a short while later. He had gone 300 yards down the road to the neighbour's house with some books.

"When I spoke at Paul and Mairead's wedding I said there were three things which were essential for a good marriage. Firstly, unselfishness – my mother always talked about sharing, and everything in our house had to be shared. Secondly, communication – a problem shared is a problem halved. As I travelled home from the States for the wedding I read a report in the paper about a prominent Russian dissident who had been released from prison after many years in jail. When asked about what kept him going he said: 'We all need God in our lives'. I quoted this story for my third point."

Paul Earley is ideally equipped to comment on Dermot's family life.

"Dermot really enjoys the simple things in life. He gets a great kick out of his family. He might play a football match with his sons in the back garden and still be talking about it two weeks later as if he had played in an All-Ireland final. He can great pleasure from drinking a cup of tea and having a slice of homemade appletart when he goes home to see our mother.

"My wife Mairead says that when you hear that Dermot is coming down for the weekend you look forward to it. He has an aura about him. He radiates enthusiasm and even when he has grounds for complaint he is always positive. Even more importantly he inspires these qualities in those around him. He is a great motivator because people feel good about themselves when he is around them."

A Woman's Heart

Dermot's footballing exploits gave Mary a whole new insight into the: 'Monday morning wash'.

"Thank God for the washing machine but grass stains on white togs were always a problem."

She has very strong views on all aspects of the game. Are players' wives treated adequately by the GAA?

"Generally no, although I must say Roscommon County Board were always very good in recognising players' wives. In the GAA I would like to see the players recognised as the number one asset. The administrator should take second place. Without players there would be no GAA."

Mary laughs heartily when questioned if she ever regretted not marrying a farmer from Tipperary.

"Only if the Tipp farmer was a county hurler! Dermot is the perfect husband and father, very unassuming, modest and tolerant. He is very conscientious in everything he does and is extremely loyal. I would not change him – not even for the farming county hurler from Tipp!"

Happiness is ....

For a long time the great ambition in Earley's life was to win an All-Ireland medal. The dream was never fulfilled. With each passing year the disappointment melts away. Although there is a gap in his trophy cabinet Earley realises that his real treasure is greater than any collection of All-Ireland medals – it is his family.

It is said that a man's home is his castle. To visit Dermot Earley in his home one understands what Seamus Heaney had in mind when he wrote in a different context: 'He is steeped in luck'.

14. The Silent Revolution

Time is a thief. The passage of time can rob of us of our objectivity. The human mind is a curious phenomenon on many levels. Looking back on our childhood can induce such nostalgia, that we see our early lives through rose-tinted glasses.

The Ireland of the 1950's faced a number of problems. The memories of the hardships of the emergency were still fresh in peoples minds. Rationing of fuel and food had ended but consumer goods were scarce. Transport was problematic. Ponies and traps, bicycles and the occasional 'crock' of a car remained the most common ways of commuting. The priest and the doctor were the only ones who had a 'real' car and more crucially, they were the only ones who had the money to buy petrol. The Irish 'solution' to economic problems – emigration, was churning out an assembly line of bodies for the boat to England and America. Agriculture was depressed. The only silver-lining was that the murderous grip TB or 'the decline' had on Ireland in the 1940s was loosening.

For all that, Earley recalls the 1950s with undisguised affection.

"When I look back to when I grew up and see the alleged shortcomings we had, and notice the absence in our lives of things that would have made us 'better', I can only think that the world I grew up in was the perfect world. I never thought that I needed anything extra."

A Helping Hand

Economic life in west Roscommon was dominated by agriculture. Only once did the quiet village of Gorthaganny experience an injection of economic activity. The initial proposal provoked controversy.

"The only time I can remember something of benefit coming to our area was when the sand pit at the back of our house was used to supply the stones, chips and sand for the tarring of the road from Castlerea to Gorthaganny. There were some obstacles to be overcome.

"Roscommon County Council had arranged to have the road tarred but the materials for the road were to come from outside the area. Local opinion was that the stone should come from the local quarry pit owned by Tom Hart.

"There were meetings in the protest about it. The guiding force in all of this was Mick Hand, a bachelor. He was a man of great stature. He had been to England many times and knew a lot about everything. He was great friends with my father even though they were on opposite sides politically. He was very popular because he would always listen to other peoples' point of view.

"The thing I remember most about Mick was his ability to whistle. You knew he was coming out from his house when on a clear summer's evening in the stillness of the air the next thing you heard was a whistle. He whistled all sorts of tunes as he walked or cycled from his house for a pint in the local pub. Our one pub had two names 'Coney Island' or 'Molly the Bogs'. I remember trying to be as loud as Mick in my whistle but I never came anywhere near it.

"Mick was a great leader in the community. He was very opposed to the material coming in from the outside because he felt it should be from our own area.

"A meeting was arranged to resolve the issue once and for all. The meeting was held in the school. Councillors came down to tell us what their plans were. Their comments were not well received and the meeting broke up when the locals all marched out together.

"Frantic efforts were made outside to achieve a settlement. I can remember Mick asking out loud: 'Is the material going to come from this area here?' One of the councillors said: 'No'. Mick replied: 'Well in that case material from nowhere else will be used either. Lets go down to the head of the road and make our stand. We will not let any lorry bring down somebody else's stones when we have the finest of stones in our own backyard.'

"They made an effort to walk down when they were called back by the councillors. Their demands were acceded to. The quarry opened. The crusher came in. Employment was provided. The hard surface was placed on the road.

"I would climb up on the hill, and stand over the sandpit and watch with awe all the activities that were going to separate the sand and feed the crusher which crushed the stones.

"I remember this activity stopped the young men leaving the area for a short while. All of the other people, male and female, who did the Primary Cert in my year, 1960, left and went to England. They did not all leave immediately but by the time they were eighteen they had all left.

"Some of them have returned and are married with children and living in their home area. Those who have not a trade are working in one of the local meat factories."

However, in his travels abroad Dermot meets more of his old school friends than when he returns to Roscommon.

"I have often gone to cities like Manchester, Liverpool and Birmingham, having been invited over by clubs to speak at their annual dinners and been reunited with old friends. They would come specially to hear me. I had sat beside them in the class-room but had not seen them since."

"Emigration was accepted as an inevitable feature of life. Other members of the family had gone before. Most young people expected that they would have to do the same.

"In the summer the Church would be much fuller, especially in the month of August. There were others who went just for the winter months, to Scotland to pick potatoes. From time to time people would acquire slightly different accents. This of course would attract the comment: 'That fella is only gone a wet week and he is back with an accent'."

Although times were hard people did not go hungry. They had their own food. The most reliable index of poverty was the standard of housing. Many families, particularly large families, lived in difficult conditions. For a lot of people, life was a perpetual struggle.

God Bless The Work

Although Earley was fortunate in the sense that he came from a family where there was one regular income, his father's salary, he nonetheless regretted that he was not brought up on a farm. This desire was not prompted by financial considerations but by a spirit of adventure.

"Often one of my classmates would tell me that they would not be in school the following day. When I would ask why they would tell me that they were going to the fair, or making hay, or having the thresher. There were so many reasons which would keep these lads at home and there was so much excitement which I was deprived of.

"I remember walking in to school and hearing the drone of the thresher and knowing exactly where it was and who would be absent from school that day.

"I was lucky, I lived beside great neighbours, in particular Michael McNulty, God rest him, the farmer next door. I don't know why Mike was so tolerant of me. His son Haulie was three or four years older than me but he was my best friend. We did everything together until he went to England to find work as a young man. His father was in his fifties. He was most understanding of me. I often wondered why he was so patient with me. He would explain farming methods to me. It was important to teach the skills in a particular way. He had been taught them by his father before him and was anxious to pass them on to the next generation."

A note of sadness enters Earley's voice as he contrasts that situation with the present day.

"Nowadays we do not tend to pass on skills as we did before. It is too time consuming. The pace of life is much too fast. Instead of explaining everything and teaching a child to do it for himself we just do it for them. We are not willing to take time to explain things the way the old people used to. "

At a time when boys of his age were playing 'cowboys and indians' the young Earley was enthralled by the magic of the land. His mind is a theatre of happy memories of his childhood.

"I remember that as soon as I could walk, I was following Mike McNulty with the horse and plough as he made drills for the spuds. There must have been three or four acres in the field. It took the best part of a day to complete the task. I had walked the field as a three or four year old and had to be carried in by my mother that evening because I was too tired to walk home my own.

"Farming gave me such satisfaction. As a young lad all I wanted to do was to be involved in as many aspects of farming as I possibly could. I tried to milk cows with my bare hands and later with a milking machine.

"Michael McNulty was understanding enough to let me do that. He let me harrow and drill when I was a ten year old, even though I was hardly able to hold the plough. I felt on top of the world. Once Mike let me harrow the whole field. I was still going to national school and I remember as I was going into the field, the horse stood on my foot and even though I was in great pain I said nothing because if I had I would not have been allowed do the harrowing."

Land Of Milk and Honey

Any indication that hay-making was going to take place and Earley was off like a shot. He wanted to be involved in all aspects, from the raking to the more skillful and physical aspects like making cocks and putting hay into the shed.

"One day when we were making hay I pulled the rake across the grass and disturbed a bees nest on the ground. The bees shot out and maybe twenty or thirty started to buzz in the air. Mike told me to just stand still, that the bees would go back to the ground, and then the disturbance would be over. Mike very slowly moved the hay back around the hive, I was confident that no harm would come to me. Mick got the edge of the rake and took a cone of honey from the hive and we ate it. It was delicious. Then he got a second one and a third. All of this time there were bees swarming all over the place but they did not bother us.

"You would know when things were happening from the sounds, particularly the sound of a mowing bar of a mowing machine. This would rattle across the countryside in a particular way. There was one man who specialised in this and he had a mowing machine which was pulled by two horses. You would hear it on the gravel first because it had iron wheels. It would crunch along with a particular ring from the metal and then there would be a particular clack clack from the machine as the hay was being cut. This signified not only that hay was being cut but that summer was here and that meant football and fishing."

Although Earley's agricultural activities brought him great pleasure they were a nightmare for his mother who saw her washing load increase to alarming proportions.

"One of the things I wanted to do was to spray potatoes. We used a mixture of bluestone and washing soda as the spray. Mixing them was a messy activity. A big barrel was filled in the middle of the headland from the pump. The mixture was then loaded into the spraying can. Mike was so patient he would let me walk beside him and use the handle of the sprayer letting me feel like I was spraying, because I was not strong enough to carry three gallons of water on my back. I thought it was a great achievement but I would go home to my mother drowned in sweat and my clothes would be destroyed. She would tell me that I was only a nuisance to Mike because I was only in his way."

One Boy Without His Dog

Although he never graduated to the guild of sheepshearers 'young Earley' did leave an indelible impression on a group of farmers who were carrying out this task. He also left his mark on one of the sheep!

"I can remember the sheep being rounded up for shearing. There is a particular skill in shearing with a manual shears. I got a chance to shear a few times though I never sheared a sheep fully.

"I was very involved in gathering the sheep. One day there was a ewe that we could not get into the pen. Through stealth I got near her and then made an unmerciful charge after her. Unfortunately I was unsuccessful and as she got away I dived full length and grabbed her by the wool. I was dragged for thirty yards down the field. Eventually the weight of me got too much for her and she fell down. I thought I had done a magnificent job. Nobody else had done it. Everybody had a great laugh at the sight of me being dragged all over the field."

The Earley household did benefit from Dermot's farming activities especially when it came to killing the pigs. This event was not so much a farming task as a communal event with everyone sharing the final product.

"There were a lot of different experts involved, people to kill the pig, one to shave the pig, one to carve up the meat and so on. I saw how the white and black pudding was made and resolved never to eat any myself having seen how it was done.

"When we lived near Cruck in Mayo I saw the whole process for the first time on the Kennedy's farm. The pig was laid out on the horse's cart and the sides were taken off. There was a lot of blood and I can still see the red pools of water when it rained that evening. I remember Bridgie Kennedy coming into our house that evening with bundles of bacon.

"I was in Cruck last winter and called to the Kennedy's. There had been two spinster sisters and two bachelor brothers in the family when we lived in the area. I knew that all but one had passed away. It was pitch dark when I knocked on the door. I knew immediately I was not recognised so I gave her a little clue, I said: 'Hello Bridgie you do not know who I am but you often gave me slices of brown bread with country butter and a sprinkle of sugar on it'. Immediately she said: 'Dermot'. We talked about the killing of the pigs and another day when a cockerel flew at me and nearly knocked me down. "

Number One Dev

Another great social occasion was elections. The 1959 presidential election of Eamon DeValera as third president of Ireland is vividly recollected by the lad from Gorthaganny.

"Everybody was either Fianna Fail or Fine Gael, the majority were Fianna Fail. There was never any bitterness from the civil war. Everyone listened courteously to their opponents.

"The elections were held in the school and that meant that we got a day off. I can remember one occasion sneaking in to see what was going on. A man who was blind came in. My father was presiding officer and the rules stipulated that he had to cast a vote for anyone who was unable to do so for themself. My father discreetly asked the blind man how he wanted to vote. In a strong clear voice he said: 'Number One Dev.'

"The election provoked great excitement. I saw people I had never seen before, and old people who were normally confined to their homes. The majority travelled by car. The odd time people would arrive in an ass and cart or horse and cart or pony and trap. The thing that now stands out in my mind and I can see it now, was the respect given to the old people. People would tip their hats to the senior person. There was a genuine respect for old people. "

The Old Bog Road

Self-sufficiency in fuel was as important to people as self-sufficiency in food. Hence everybody had their own turf. Although Earley was deprived of his wish to own land, a small measure of compensation was derived from the fact that his family had their own bank of turf.

"Going to the bog was a great adventure though there were one or two parts to the job that I didn't like such as footing the turf when it was all on the flat. The bog was so close to us that we could go for a little while and come back and do something else. We could see our house easily from the bank of turf and one of the things that used to happen in the evenings was that my mother would put a big white sheet on the tree to signify that our dinner was ready. There were many evenings when we wondered if the sheet was ever going to go up.

"We had cousins in Ballyhaunis, the Morleys, who would come and stay with us during the holidays and join us in the bog. We used to make up our own games. We used to have great turf fights and competitions to see who could jump the highest clamp of turf. We also had competitions to see who could stack the most turf and I can remember time and time again footing turf like a demon only to see that the Morley girls had knocked it all down. We would come home covered in turf mud, tired and satisfied after a great days work.

"Bringing home the turf was a big event. Most of the time you would bring home the turf in a tractor and trailer and get the job done in one day. I remember one summer saying I would bring it home myself in the ass and cart. I borrowed them from a neighbour. I would bring home six or eight loads a day. If I had gone at it every day it would have taken twenty or thirty days back to back. However, the donkey was not available every day so the job was spread over the whole summer. My biggest worry was waking and finding that the donkey had broken out from the garden while he was under my care."

Days spent in the bog have taken on an entirely new meaning for the Earley family following Paul's sojourn in Australia in 1983-84.

"Paul was staying with a family of Irish extraction. He was there a day and a half when his landlady said he should call his mother and let her know that he was okay. There was not an automatic exchange in Gorthaganny at that stage so Paul had to go through the switch but there was no answer at home. The family in Melbourne inquired if he had got through. Paul said that his mother was probably in the bog. An hour later Paul was watching television when the landlady asked him if he would like to try again: 'Ah I won't' said Paul 'she is probably still in the bog'. After another hour came the same question and the same answer. This provoked titters from the landlady's family. The landlady posed the question: 'How long would she spend in the bog?' 'Maybe an hour maybe half the day' said Paul. There were frantic efforts by the family to conceal their laughter. The next question was how far the bog was from the house: 'About a mile and a half' responded Paul. This brought howls of laughter. Then the penny dropped with Paul that bog was obviously Australian slang for toilet!

"I have told that story, three or four times in Paul's presence at functions, much to Paul's embarrassment and to the delight of the audience."

The Ballroom Of Romance

In 1956 a new addition to the Gorthaganny landscape was a new dancehall built entirely by voluntary labour. The main driving force behind this venture was the parish administrator, Fr Edward Higgins.

"He was a real ball of fire. My father and him got on extremely well. When either of them came up with an idea, the other would be in like a shot. They were a great team."

This dancehall was one of the harbingers of the ballroom blitz which exploded in the 1960s. At the forefront of this development was an enterprising young man from Rooskey who was destined for greater things. His name was Albert Reynolds. He ran one of the most successful chains of ballrooms in Ireland. A link in all his ballrooms was the word 'land' with the result that there was 'Fairyland' in Roscommon and 'Roseland' in Moate and many others.

Another enterprising figure who would later make a spectacular impression on the west of Ireland was Fr James Horan, who was responsible for the location of an international airport at Knock. He established the dancehall in Toreen in Mayo. This new outlet of social activity caused ripples of excitement in the surrounding area. This ballroom acquired an aura of mystique, a trend fuelled by stories that no less a person than the devil had become a patron! The dancehall put Toreen on the map as it quickly attracted national media attention.

A curious success story was the ballroom in Pontoon, between Ballina and Castlebar. Pontoon's prosperity was strange because its location was so remote. It seemed a more likely venue for a high security jail than a dancehall.

The dance every Friday night in Gorthaganny did not quite reach such dizzy heights but it did introduce Earley to the world of ballrooms. He helped his father with the less glamourous aspects of running the dancehall, notably, cleaning out the toilets.

The desire to get to other dances brought the best out of Earley's imagination because his parents did not believe that attending dances would be in the best interests of a fourteen or fifteen year old. On the pretence of going to Ballyhaunis to the cinema with Haulie McNulty, Earley cycled to the Toreen dancehall one summer night. However, the subterfuge backfired. The film was due to end at 10.30 p.m. which meant that he would be expected home that night at 11.15 p.m. The dance did not really begin until after eleven which meant that they saw nothing except the band. Through a series of covert operations they were able to sneak a look inside without paying and survey the scene. This meant that Earley was able to salvage something from the evening because when the school holidays were over he was able to boast to his school friends that he had been at a dance in Tooreen.

From helping his father at the Friday night dances at home Earley learned the rituals of the dances which were portrayed so evocatively in William Trevor's film *'The Ballroom Of Romance'*. The men stood on one side, the women the other. The first sign that romance was in the air was when the lady agreed to stay with her new partner for the second dance. A really promising sign was when the lady agreed to be taken to the mineral bar and allowed a bottle of orange to be bought for her.

To be allowed to go to a dance for the first time without parental supervision represented a 'coming of age' ceremony. At sixteen, when Dermot went to stay with his bachelor cousin, Pat Flanagan, for part of his summer holidays, he went to a dance as an adult for the first time. His attendance provided a good luck charm because that night Pat met the lady who would become his wife.

Crocodile Earley

Traditional Irish music was very much in vogue in Gorthaganny and the Earley family made their contribution to Ireland's musical heritage when Dermot's sister Denise became a 'radio star'. Ciaran MacMathuna travelled down from Radio Eireann to record her singing in 1958.

Touring groups regularly visited towns and villages in rural Ireland in the 1950s. In May 1992 Shane Connaughton's film *The Playboys* described this phenomenon.

"We had a diesel generator which was started manually. From time to time the generator broke down. At one stage in the middle of the play the lights went out. People had walked to the hall with their torches and they turned them on and nobody complained. I can remember distinctly one of the girls on stage saying: 'We can't go on without the lights' and a man shouted up from the back: 'Ye are doing fine. Its only mighty, keep going'. "

Although Gorthaganny did not have its own cinema, a touring company also came with films which were shown in the hall. The films were invariably in black and white and tended to be westerns.

"The first colour film I saw was *The African Queen*. I was eleven years old and saw it with my mother. I cannot remember much of the plot, but the 'African Queen' was a boat and I can see the crocodiles slithering into the water. At one stage a guy had to get into the water and fix the boat and they emerged covered in leeches."

Local talent was also nurtured through the organisation of concerts.

"All of these concerts were organised by my father. I remember treading the boards once myself. I was in a group of ten who sang 'The Harp that once through Tara's halls'. My father taught us the songs and got us to practice them. The hall would be packed.

"One night a concert of Irish music was arranged. A crate of Guinness mysteriously found its way into the back of the hall. Some of the musicians had imbibed and arrived on stage in a more intoxicated state than was desirable. There were two accordionists, two violinists and one tin whistle player. They started playing and they went on and on, playing the same tune over and over again. It was obvious to everyone what was going on. After twenty minutes over their allotted time there were frantic efforts to get them off the stage. Eventually one of them realised that they had outstayed their welcome and stumbled on to his feet. The sound of this activity woke up the rest of them and they all staggered off the stage."

Fire and Brimstone

Dances ceased everywhere during Lent. This was a small indication of the predominance of the Catholic religion in the Ireland of the 1950s. No meat was consumed during Lent on Wednesday or Friday. Fish was the main food for the 'Friday fast'. Lent was also the time for the parish mission, when the wrath of God was invoked on wayward souls with extraordinary fervour.

"I remember one mission which was conducted by the Redemptorists. It was the ferocity of his preaching which sticks in my memory. He scared us out of our wits when he told us we were all going to hell."

Lent was also the time when the 'Stations of the Cross' were said every Friday evening: "In light of his pastoral activities at the other end of the parish, Fr Higgins was sometimes unable to make it back to the Church on time for the stations. He asked my father to stand in for him when he was late. Daddy would wait a few minutes and when there was still no sign of him, he would begin. I was normally one of the two altar boys he had on either side of him. There was one time, when we were at the sixth or seventh station, when the door opened at the back of the church and Fr Higgins came in. He simply sat down in the back seat and said: 'Carry on Peadar'."

The closeness of the relationship between Peadar Earley and Fr Higgins was dramatically underlined one evening in the sanctuary of the confessional box! "My father went in to the confessional and solemnly confessed his sins. He was the second last person for the sacrament. As the priest was giving his final absolution his closing remark caught my father by surprise: 'By the way Peadar, I will be down to your house for a cup of tea when I am finished here'."

The younger Earleys were less than enthusiastic about being 'encouraged' to attend three Masses on Christmas morning.

Earley's first experience of performing in front of large crowds came not on the football fields but in discharging his duties as an altar boy. An initial problem to be overcome was to make the correct response to the 'De Profundis': "There were times when all the altar boys were simply mumbling whereupon the priest took us to task after that."

The big perk of being an altar boy was that it meant regular attendance at Station Masses in October and February: "From an altar boy's point of view the big thing was to be asked to serve at the stations. You missed a morning at school and you also had a massive 'Station Breakfast' with all kinds of food and cakes. One fly in the ointment had arisen years earlier when a householder had refused to have the Station Mass in his house. The parish priest refused to let any other householder have the Station Mass in their homes until the offending party repented. All the Station Masses were held in the Church for a few years. My father intervened and worked out a compromise."

The most noteworthy feature of Earley's time as an altar boy was that he never served at a wedding mass because not one wedding took place in those years. This curious fact serves as an invaluable social commentary on rural Ireland in the 1950s – a country haemorrhaging with emigration.

Advent was another time when religious adherence intensified, providing a mini-Lent. In Patrick Kavanagh's incisive line, Advent was the time of: 'dry black bread and sugarless tea'. The Earley household's additional religious practice was the '4000 Hail Marys'. The first three days of Advent saw heaven bombarded with Hail Mary's. The family were stunned on the fourth day when Denise announced that she had completed the 4000 prayers. Even her mother who had been very assiduous in her praying duties had only managed 150 Hail Mary's. It then emerged that Denise had simply repeated the two words 'Hail Mary' 4000 times!

'Tis The Season To Be Jolly

Christmas brought a merciful release from the abstinence of Advent. However, the memory of one particular Christmas has a unique power to thrill and chill both Dermot and his mother.

"On one Christmas morning it was snowing heavily outside as I left our house to serve Mass. My mother insisted I wore wellingtons and made me carry my shoes to change inside. I did so with great reluctance. When I got to the Church I put on my uniform but forgot to change my wellingtons and I went to the altar wearing them. My mother was mortified but I never realised I had my wellies on. I was not allowed to forget that incident for a long time."

There were many times when childhood memories of Christmasses in Roscommon came flooding back to Earley during Christmasses spent abroad.

"Christmas has always been the most magical time of the year for me. What is special about Christmas is that it is such a family event and the sense of love you get no matter where you spend it. However, the material side of Christmas varies enormously from country to country.

"Christmas in the States was much more material. Although the ceremonies and religious events are the same, the extravagance is hard to absorb. At one house near us the lights remained up the whole year and were simply shut off because they were so intricate it would have taken too much time and energy to put them up and down every year. "

The main difference in the celebration of Christmas in the Middle East was the radically different climatic conditions: "I had the opportunity of going to Bethlehem for Christmas in 1976 and it was wonderful to be there. Although it was actually very difficult to get there because of the security checks, it was a very special experience."

Christmas on the Golan Heights was a much more forgettable experience because of the volatile military situation in which war could break out again at the drop of a hat. In such circumstances it was vital that nobody relaxed, vigilance had to be maintained at all times. The risk prohibited any alternative.

Although Christmas in the Lebanon was celebrated in a very tense environment, there was sufficient flexibility to allow the troops in the battalion to attend Midnight Mass in the local Marianite Church: "Our lads made great efforts to get everything right in terms of a choir and so on. It was a good opportunity for locals to attend religious services. The villagers were very impressed that we took it so seriously. It was a very moving experience."

The Pepsi Culture

The increasing homogenisation in the celebration of Christmas worldwide is a disappointment to Earley and is a symptom of a bigger problem, the emergence of the 'Pepsi Culture'.

We are living in a pluralistic world. Although pluralism is not new, the scale of it is. The world has become evidently smaller and so other 'world-views' confront us daily. Pluralism leads to changes in social relationships, economic patterns and cultural groups, and many people start to question their traditional values. Paradoxically, although this situation might be expected to lead to greater cultural diversity it has actually had the opposite effect. Increasingly, Western culture, particularly American culture, is colonising the world.

There is growing unease at the scale of American cultural imperialism. A French commentator typified this disquiet when he described the opening of EuroDisney outside Paris in the spring of 1992 as: 'cultural Chernobyl'.

"I noticed a big change when I came back to Ireland in 1991. We, as a nation, seem to be slavishly following the American culture to the detriment of our own culture. One of the things that always impressed me about Austria and the Scandinavian countries was their pride in their native dress. The Scandanavians will always begin a meal by welcoming everyone to the table in their native language. It is a very small thing but it is a tradition they retain."

In cultural terms little things mean a lot and little rituals are a powerful statement of the identity of a people. However, other countries seem more than willing to submit themselves to the yoke of American cultural bondage.

"In the remains of the old Soviet Union, to have a pair of jeans is more important than to have food for the next meal. Communication is so good that young people world-wide are *au fait* with the music of Michael Jackson. They want to share the same type of culture that is prevalent in the West."

Another universal cultural problem is smoking: "Almost everybody smokes in the Third World. In Ireland not as many people smoke as before, though I am not convinced that the decline is on the scale reported.

"I honestly feel that we have a responsibility to contribute to the development of the Third World. They have the same difficulties that we had decades ago. Our responsibility as citizens of the planet is to educate those who are now experiencing the problems we have been through ourselves. We need to share our knowledge and our resources."

The Swinging Sixties

In the last twenty years Earley's peace-keeping duties have enabled him to see rapid social, cultural, and political change on a global level at first hand. However, the excitement of witnessing this change does not match the excitement he felt living in Ireland in the 1960s, a decade of extraordinary change in Irish society.

In 1959 Sean Lemass had become Taoiseach for the first time. Modernising the Irish economy was Lemass' primary political objective. He set about this task with gusto, finding an invaluable ally in the senior officer in the Department of Finance, Dr T.K. Whittaker who had formulated a Programme for Economic Expansion in 1957. Ireland was to embark upon a planned course of industrial development, using grants and loans to attract companies to set up factories and businesses in Ireland. The country was to become an export driven economy. The prevailing political philosophy was encapsulated in Lemass' own phrase: 'A rising tide lifts all boats.'

The 1966 census provided encouraging evidence that these economic policies were bearing fruit when for the first time since the Great Famine, the Irish population recorded an increase. The cancer of emigration had abated. For the first time since the Middle Ages the vulnerable Irish economy was showing promising signs of being able to support all its people.

The figures from the 1971 census documented three revolutionary changes in Irish society during the 1960s. Firstly, Ireland had moved from being a predominantly agricultural society to being an industrial society. Secondly, Ireland became an urban society for the first time. In 1971, 52 per cent of the population lived in urban areas. Thirdly, because of the falling emigration and the baby boom of the 1960s the country had a young population for the first time in living memory.

Another pioneering figure was Donagh O'Malley who became Minister for Education in 1966. He made free post-primary education available to all. In addition, grants were made more widely available, to allow more young people to get third-level education. Curriculum change was introduced at secondary level with greater attention given to scientific and technical subjects.

Television brought Ireland into the global village and allowed people to see major world-wide events. Pressure of work meant that Earley was unable to see the most dramatic development of them all, when a man walked on the moon for the time.

"I was on the side of Croagh Patrick in 1969, doing an intensive army training course when I heard the immortal words: 'A small step for man and a giant step for mankind.' I heard these words on an army radio which I was carrying on my back. It was a miserable evening with a depressing drizzle but I will never forget the excitement I had, listening on a crackling radio to such an historic moment."

And Nobody Cried Stop

The promise of the 1960s was not fulfilled. The 'economic miracle' based on multi-national companies and EEC subsidies which was to take the west of Ireland to the 'promised land' did not materialise. The figures speak for themselves. In the past 55 years the population of Connacht has declined by 24 per cent whereas the population of Leinster has increased by 62 per cent.

In February 1992, the Archbishop of Tuam, Joseph Cassidy, warned of the danger of the west of Ireland being reduced to the: 'status of a native reservation where tourists come with cameras and tape recorders to capture the people in their native costumes and the curious rhythms of their speech'. He went on to comment that because of emigration, westerners find themselves: 'looking at a beef sandwich without the beef; at a cross section of society without its central strand or at a typical western face that's either ageing or very young'.

Falling farm incomes and escalating unemployment have also cast their own dark shadow. In the town of Tuam alone 1,817 people are on the live register, statistical reminders of a system that does not apparently care. The closure of the sugar factory and the failure to secure a replacement for it, serves as a microcosm for the problems of the West. The town needs action but to date all it has received is lip service.

Tuam's greatest success story in recent years has been the 'Sawdoctors'. The lyrics of their songs resonate deeply with all westerners. The anger, depression, irreverence and cynicism for institutions embody the feelings of the community. Their songs are anthems for a community in mourning.

Perhaps the greatest tragedy is human rather than economic. The masses have been divorced from their aspirations. When Earley returns to the place of his childhood the only thing that remains the same is the scourge of emigration. Like many, he had thought he had seen the back of emigration in the 1960s but now it has returned stronger than ever. The title of one of Paul Brady's first songs was 'Nothing But the Same Old Story'. It describes the trauma of a nineteen year old who is forced to emigrate to England. The title of that song has a particular relevance for the west of Ireland in the 1990s.

The West's Awake

One difference between the 1950s and the 1990s is that there is a greater determination now to fight back. The old deferential mentality of 'tipping the cap' is dead and buried. In the 1990s the Bishops in the west of Ireland have led from the front on this issue.

Ten years earlier, Dermot Earley had addressed himself to the need for the west of Ireland to take pride in its identity in a speech to the Connacht Men's Association in San Francisco. All the Connacht members of the touring football and hurling sides were invited to a dinner. As the senior member of the Connacht delegation Earley was asked to speak on behalf of the players. Among the hurlers in attendance was Galway great, Joe Connolly, no stranger himself to inspirational speeches. Connolly recalls that evening vividly.

"I will never forget Dermot's speech that evening. It was without doubt the finest speech I ever heard. He spoke about the problems of Connacht and of the mentality of 'To hell or to Connacht'. He went on to talk about our need to hold our heads high, that we had a lot to be proud of and a lot to contribute. He finished off by saying that we needed to take control of our future. The audience reaction was amazing. He had everybody eating out of the palm of his hand. He whipped us all up into a frenzy. The applause afterwards was incredible, wild with enthusiasm. We must have nearly raised the roof. "

In recent years there are signs that people are fighting back. Roscommon provided one of the big shocks of the 1989 general election when former minister, Sean Doherty, lost his Dail seat to independent Tom Foxe, 'the hospital candidate', who stood on a single issue ticket, opposition to the downgrading of Roscommon hospital. The result gave us the phrase "the Roscommon factor" which symbolised the importance of local issues in a national campaign. The election of four "pothole candidates" in the Cavan local elections was further evidence of this trend. However, the Roscommon result was more noteworthy because it was the first signal to those who thought that they could ignore the west of Ireland and get away with it. The era of platitudes alone, is dead and buried.

The importance of the local post office in rural Ireland was memorably portrayed in John Waters' evocative book *Jiving at the Crossroads*. In 1991 there was a lot of speculation that many of these post offices were to be shut down. Another signal that westerners were no longer prepared to passively tolerate government neglect was indicated when Castlerea postman, and former Roscommon selector Danny Burke was elected as independent County Councillor again on a single issue ticket: 'Save our post offices.'

The Village I Loved So Well

Returning to Gorthaganny today the biggest disappointment for Earley is the decline of neighbourliness.

"When I was small and helping or probably annoying Mike McNulty one of the things he said to me was that the most important thing anyone could have was good neighbours. It was no use in a crisis to have a lot of relatives five miles away. When the chips are down its your neighbours who help you out.

"That was one thing we always had when I was growing up. People called into one another's houses without invitation or any formality. I found that things were much different when I moved to a big community in urban areas. I found that it takes a long time to get to know the neighbours."

Paradoxically Earley feels that the decline in neighbourliness has been offset by a greater sense of community.

"When I was growing up in school there was no such thing as a community centre. People rowed in together with farming tasks like the threshing and machinery was shared. When a person got sick everybody helped out. If there was a bereavement everybody lent a hand.

"I feel though that now we have taken it a step further with the building of community centres. It brings everything on to a more professional footing, bonding people together in a different way and gives a great sense of belonging to a wider community rather than to just a village."

Nonetheless, while the greater sense of communal identity represents a major advance there is the problem that there is less 'rambling' which means that loneliness is a potential problem for older people living on their own. This is also a major worry for the children of these people.

"Sometimes I worry about my mother being at home on her own. There were a spate of burglaries in the West a few years ago when old people suffered greatly. People who were seen to be vulnerable were taken advantage of. This is part of a world-wide trend to a greater amount of violence. We used to have an open house. People came in casually and there was always a cup of tea. Now things are much more formal, people are more hesitant about calling.

Economically, socially and culturally Earley's birthplace is now almost unrecognizable from the same area forty years ago. Modern methods of farming have revolutionised agricultural practice and the ballrooms have gone; the people are not there any more to make them economically viable.

One casualty of all this has been the virtual disappearance of the sound of the corncrake from rural Ireland. Modern silage making has substantially destroyed their natural habitat. Traditionally, the sound of the corncrake provided irrefutable proof that summer had arrived, yet a new generation of Irish people is emerging who have never heard its cry.

It is tempting to apply Yeats' comment: 'All has changed, changed utterly' to the west of Ireland, but that would be too glib. It would also be untrue. Nonetheless it is an indisputable fact that profound changes have imperceptibly taken place in Irish society. Ironically the one aspect of Irish life which people would most want to change, emigration, continues to fester.

Dermot Earley realises that in his lifetime Irish society has been transformed at all levels by a silent revolution.

15. Where Do We Go From Here?

In August 1991 when the Earley family returned after their four year sojourn in the US a lot of readjustment was necessary, particularly as half their furniture languished in America! It was a minor price to pay for the joy of being home.

"I have always been a home person and I was looking forward to coming home all the time I was in the States. I knew I was going away for a period of time and at the end of that time I was coming home."

More practically it also afforded Earley the opportunity to engage in one of his 'passions' D.I.Y. Although he set about the task of redecorating his house with gusto there was a significant discrepancy between his enthusiasm for the task and his ability to perform it successfully: "Mary always says that if she had to pay me by the hour she would be broke long ago." One of his unfulfilled ambitions is to build his own house.

Trainer

Earley returned home just in time for Roscommon's All-Ireland semi-final against Meath. The Roscommon team manager, Marty McDermott had indicated that he would be stepping down from his position when his side made their exit from the championship.

Discreet soundings had been made to Earley about his interest in the position. Press reports suggested that former Offaly manager Eugene McGee was the frontrunner for the position. There was some discussion among Roscommon supporters that Earley was 'too nice' for the job. A wry smile emerges on Earley's face when this argument is put to him.

"It is said that if you are a nice guy you will always be second. I would rather be a nice guy and not a winner, than not be a nice guy and be a winner. But I believe you can be a winner and be a nice too. Some people would counter-argue: 'Now he is accepting defeat because he is not ruthless'. But I am ruthless and I was when the ball was near me and when I wanted to get the ball. The ball was all that counted. I did not want to hit anybody out of the way but I would go through him fairly to get the ball! As a trainer I think I can get the best out of my players without being ruthless.

"I favour positive coaching, i.e. play within the rules, and I work at all times for a raising of standards. In Sarsfields we have a reputation as a side that always plays clean and open football."

In the event Marty McDermott agreed to stay on and the job did not become available. Earley was pleased by McDermott's decision.

"The performances of the Roscommon team in recent times are a result of the great amount of work and thoroughness of preparation that Marty and his team have put into it. He has a good record. Every year since he took over, Roscommon have a qualified for the Connacht final. They have also got to two league semi-finals."

Almost immediately he became involved with training various grades at Sarsfields and at the end of the year was chosen as manager of their senior side. This was not a new role but the difference was that he was no longer playing. He still believes that with proper training he could play at the highest level, but only for one match, because he needs a much longer recovery time now.

He is unable to escape the fact that his playing days are over because his children delight in reminding him that he is 'ancient'. Another sobering reminder is when he is coaching kids and their fathers tell them to get his autograph, the kids have to ask who he is. Even more distressing is the number of times they ask who he was! The days when every schoolboy in Roscommon modelled himself on Dermot Earley are gone. Tony Mc, John Newton and increasingly Derek Duggan are the role models.

Another reminder is provided by the retirement of players who were just beginning their career as his was tapering off. A case in point was the retirement of Jack O'Shea in 1992 following Clare's victory over Kerry in the Munster final.

"When I got over the euphoria, excitement, and delight in Clare's victory I felt very sorry for Jacko. It was a pity he had to finish such a wonderful career on that note. That is not to take one bit from his career. He was one of the greatest, if not the greatest, midfielder of all time. He had tremendous fitness, great skill and, above all, he was as clean a player as you could ever hope to play on."

For his part Jacko's assessment of Dermot Earley is almost identical with that of Matt Connor, Paddy Cullen, Jimmy Deenihan, Tommy Doyle, Dermot Flanagan, Billy Joyce, Robbie Kelleher, Brian McEniff, Frank McGuigan, and Colm O'Rourke. When each of these players were asked for their opinion of Earley there were four elements common to all the interviews. Firstly, he was an exceptionally talented player maintaining the highest standards for an incredible length of time. Secondly, he was extremely unlucky not to have won a senior All-Ireland medal. Thirdly, he was always an excellent ambassador for the game because of his sportsmanship. Fourthly, he continues to have a major contribution to make to the game in a coaching capacity.

The Agony in the Garden

After Roscommon's defeat at the hands of Mayo in 1992 Connacht final, speculation was rife about the selection of a new manager to the Roscommon team. With the announcement of their most influential player, Tony McManus' retirement, and Marty McDermott's resignation as team manager, a new beginning was necessary for Roscommon football. Discreet soundings were made via Paul about Dermot Earley's possible interest in the manager's job. In the middle of August a definite offer was made. It was the most difficult decision of Earley's whole life. It was the age old dilemma of the battle between the head and the heart.

Deep down he ached for the job but he was very worried that the price for his family would be too high. The offer coincided with his summer vacation, which he spent working on his garden and painting his house. As he cruised through his tasks on automatic pilot, his mind was agonising over the pros and cons of the appointment. The balance ebbed and flowed like the sea on a calm evening. At times he was carried away making plans for training routines, team selection, his management team and targets to be achieved. Often he got caught on a flight of fantasy and visualised himself giving his team talk to the team before they went out to play in the All-Ireland final. Then the practicalities of accepting were teased out. It would require a huge sacrifice not just for himself but for his whole family. The harsh reality was that because of the geography he would have to spend a lot of time away from the bosom of his family. Every training session would require him to leave home at 5.30 p.m. and not return until 1a.m. In the height of the championship he would only get very limited access to his family. Equally, he was conscious of the respect and affection he had received from the Roscommon fans for years. He did not want to let them down particularly as he felt he could do a good job with the team.

Apart from these considerations two specific events happened which pulled him in opposite directions. Firstly, a number of the Roscommon minor team pleaded with him to take the job. After the Connacht final all the supporters he talked to urged him to accept the job even before it was available but it was the request of the minors which really touched his heart strings. He had been asked to give a talk to the team a few hours before the Connacht final against Mayo. He stressed the need never to give up on the field of play, no matter how bad things looked. In the match Roscommon rallied and pegged back a big Mayo lead to win the match. After the game Earley went back to the team hotel to congratulate them on their success. As soon as he entered the door one of the team shouted up: 'We did what you asked us.'

A week before the minor team's All-Ireland semi-final against Armagh Earley was invited to conduct a training session with the team. As I travelled down with him for the session there was no need to ask him if he was looking forward to working with the Roscommon stars of the future. He was like a child in a sweet shop. The evening was much cooler than expected, one of those times when you curse yourself for not bringing a coat or jacket. The mentors joined the team on the pitch. It was a strange experience watching the session from the stand as the sole spectator. The atmosphere was almost eerie, it was like visiting the place for the first time. Equally it was a novelty in terms of emotional involvement. So many times I watched Earley on the same pitch in a very agitated condition, Roscommon's fluctuating fortunes reducing my precarious mental state to nothing less than a shambles. It seemed extraordinary to be sitting in Hyde Park with my heart beating normally.

A number of things caught the eye and the ear about Earley's performance. Although he was not shouting I could hear everything he said distinctly. He never had to ask for attention. He commanded it. The training was all done with the ball. He talked a lot, offering words of encouragement as the players were performing. He was very affirming but noticed the main faults in each of the exercises. He exposed the errors but not in a way which would undermine the player's confidence.

He integrated physical, skill with psychological preparation. Points were never made in the abstract but to the extent they would apply to the Armagh game and the big match atmosphere in Croke Park. A recurring theme was the importance of concentration at all times. He drew on his own vast reservoir of playing experience to pass on tips. His enthusiasm was unabated after the session was concluded. On the journey back he was full of chat about the possibilities of the team as a unit and the potential of individual players.

Again he spoke with the team in their hotel before the game. In one of the best games of football in the 1992 season the physically more powerful Armagh team emerged victorious, despite a superlative performance from Roscommon star in the making Dermot Washington. There is a curious irony in this situation. Dermot Washington got his name from Dermot Earley. After the match Earley went to console the team and remind them that his own career in Croke Park had begun with losing a minor semi-final and his personal ignominy of missing the decisive penalty. A number of the team implored him to take the job with the senior side.

A few days later the Leaving Cert results came out. As the family talked about relatives who were planning their futures after getting their results, Earley was forcefully reminded about the pressures on teenagers today and the help and encouragement they need with their academic work and career choices. All going well, four of his children will be doing their Leaving Cert in consecutive years between 1994-98. He wanted to be absolutely sure that none of his commitments would interfere in any way with the time he could give to his family. After lengthy consultation with Mary he reluctantly turned down the offer. Accordingly the Roscommon County Board gave him a week to reconsider his position.

The very next evening Earley was driving his oldest daughter, Paula to a camogie match. Having answered the phone a number of times to officials from the County Board, Paula was aware of the situation in relation to his managerial opportunity. She inquired if her father would be accepting the position. The question was turned around and she was asked what her opinion was. She said: "Oh Daddy it would be great." Much taken aback by her enthusiasm for his acceptance of the job Earley consulted the rest of his children for their views. Although he dispassionately outlined the practical implications of accepting the job they were all extremely keen that he should accept. Both Mary and he were swayed by their excitement and unbridled insistence that he should take it. Not for the first time in his life, especially in relation to the Roscommon team, the heart ruled the head.

This was the turning point which caused him to reverse his original decision. A new chapter of his life is unfolding. There are no rash predictions, no inflated comments. He just wants to get on with the job. Part of the beauty of sport is its unpredictability. The only certainty is that Earley's commitment will be total. No effort will be spared to bring Roscommon to the top.

If You're Good Enough You are Young Enough

Earley lines out for Sarsfields whenever they are stuck for players due to a clash of fixtures with the junior side. He jokes: "I bring a new level of pace to the attack."

He was forcefully reminded of the passing years when he lined out at full-forward against Fingallians, the Dublin side managed by his former Roscommon colleague Harry Keegan, in a challenge match in June 1992. Playing alongside him at corner-forward was his son David. Such was David's performance that the game was an occasion for pride rather than sadness. With the other two Earley sons also showing promise the future of the Earley name on the playing fields looks assured. Their father could not imagine himself without some involvement on the coaching side of the game.

The one positive feature about his retirement from the game is that it has enabled him to become an analyst of big matches on television and radio. He enjoys this task immensely because it brings him closer to a game when he has to interpret it for others. He would like to continue and develop this strand of interest if the opportunities present themselves.

One of the nicest aspects about his retirement is that he often bumps into total strangers who greet him as if was an old friend. His happiest such memory came when he was attending a function in Tipperary. An elderly gentleman approached him and said: "You were a great footballer. I used to think you had dack on your hands." This image resonated deeply with Earley. In the 1950s dack was used extensively on farmyards to catch mice and rats because it was a very sticky substance. As a boy his mother had always warned him not to get dack on his hands. He regards this compliment as the nicest he ever got in his entire career.

Earley Changes

The four years away from the football scene has given Earley the opportunity to reflect more about the future of the game. His main concern is with the perceptible increase in intimidation and the physical approach to Gaelic football.

"A major concern would be the physical off-the-ball activities that have come into the game. You now have to, apparently, be prepared to hit your opponent when the ball is not near you to assert your superiority. I think that has to do with the coaching and possibly watching other physical contact sports. I am very disappointed by this trend. You should be able to beat your opponent through skill, timing and physical fitness and jostle him when he has the ball. You should not have to hit him with your fist. Tragically that is what is happening."

One factor which Earley believes could help reduce this problem is higher refereeing standards. He feels that the fact that some players get away with these fouls means that the victims end up by playing the game the same way with the result that the game suffers.

The normal affability of Earley's manner vanishes as he points to the aspect of the contemporary game which alarms him the most. His face grimaces and he clenches his fist.

"When I was playing football you had threats and so on but it was all in the heat of the moment. But no one ever came out to me and said anything about my family, about myself, about how I looked. It never happened with any other player I played on. Today though, there is verbal intimidation both on the field and from spectators. Threats were part of the competitive edge. But now there is that planned forethought on how to intimidate and how to slow down your opponent so that when the ball comes to you, you have the advantage."

The other major area where he feels change is necessary is in the fixture list. He keenly advocates the idea of three major competitions, all being run concurrently. Firstly, the League would start in late February and finish at the end of November. Secondly, the championship would continue as normal. Thirdly, an open draw competition which would replace many of the challenge and tournament games in the year. In 1984 he calculated that if Roscommon had played in three such competitions and won all three they would have played 25 games. In reality they played 29 games and won nothing. This may necessitate a break with tradition and playing matches on days apart from Sundays.

A smaller problem which he would like to see addressed is attention to detail seeping through all levels of the organisation. In many cases the attention to detail is superb but Earley has a plethora of plaques with his name mis-spelt which serve as an ongoing reminder of this problem.

A related problem is matches at club level which do not start on time. He would like to see better punctuality levels with more realistic start times so that all games may start on time.

The Field

Having been brought up in the country, though never actually owning any land, Earley often fantasises about owning a few acres of land and walking out to count his own cattle. Some of his children have a more romantic notion of what farm life involves.

"When we got back from America we all drove down to Tipperary to see Mary's family. The countryside looked fantastic in the August sun, especially the corn. We were talking about farming and I said to Noelle: 'Do you know that every morning before breakfast your Mammy milked 20 cows?' There was silence until Noelle said in a most genuine and envious voice: 'Oh Mammy weren't you lucky'. Those of us who knew what milking 20 cows involved had a good laugh."

"There is a great scene in the priest's sitting room in John B. Keane's film *The Field* when the Bull McCabe explained what the land meant and particularly the field. Bull talked with passion and fervour about making hay on a cloudy day in the field with his father and mother. He described how his mother had been taken ill and collapsed in the field as the rain was looming. His father shouted at him to get the doctor but he answered back: 'Lets get the hay in first'. That was what the land meant to the people of Ireland."

Mindful of the needs of six growing children Earley does not envisage a situation where that dream will ever become a reality. He smiles wistfully as he says: "But there is always the Lotto."

Should Lotto riches ever make their way into the Earley clan Noelle has plotted the way the money is to be spent. She has been trying to convince her father to buy the local chip shop so that the family will never run out of chips.

Action Speaks Louder

Earley is a great believer in the old adage: 'Strike while the iron is hot', when opportunities present themselves they should be seized enthusiastically. However, he is dismissive of the idea of plotting one's way to the top.

"A lot of people get carried away thinking about climbing the ladder but in plotting the climb they often forget to do the work. All I want to do is make a positive contribution in whatever role I am given. My hope for the army is that we ride the storm of transition that we are now in and do so in a mature fashion, examining all our priorities."

His brother Paul despairs of this attitude.

"There are times when I feel Dermot should take the initiative more. He is very reluctant to impose himself on any situation without being asked to do so. My worry about him is that he might end up waiting for things to happen only to discover too late that he has missed the boat. I feel he should work to a plan for his future."

Remember Me

Earley laughs heartily when asked about his epitaph. Whatever about his playing days he still feels that there is a lot of life left in him yet.

"I heard Fr Michael Cleary giving a sermon once. He recalled passing a Church once where a funeral was taking place. He asked who had died. A man told him the corpse's name and said: 'He was a good man'. Today a lot of flowery language is used with a lot of adjectives and adverbs. If you want to get down to the core you can dispense with all the adjectives. I would be delighted if my tombstone carried the epitaph: 'He was a good man'."